OPINIONS: "It is a superstition that it is always a good thing to speak your mind. It is nothing of the sort. If wc always spoke our minds, the situation would be entirely chaotic."

NIXON AND DETENTE: "Nixon's lack of ethical discrimination brought him down and is even now damaging the prospects of the free world."

GUN CONTROL: "In Switzerland, there are 60,000 loaded rifles kept in individual homes—pursuant to the tradition of the well-ordered militia. But the Swiss simply do not have a penchant for shooting each other."

WILLIAM F. BUCKLEY, Jr.

A HYMNAL:

The Controversial Arts

BERKLEY BOOKS, NEW YORK

This Berkley edition is an abridgement of the 502 page
Putnam's edition published in 1978.

This Berkley book has been completely reset in a
type face designed for easy reading, and was
printed from new film.

A HYMNAL: The Controversial Arts

A Berkley Book / published by arrangement with
G. P. Putnam's Sons

PRINTING HISTORY
G. P. Putnam's Sons edition / October 1978
Abridged Berkley edition / August 1981
Second printing / September 1981

For information address: G. P. Putnam's Sons,
200 Madison Avenue, New York, New York 10016.

ISBN: 0-425-04583-8

A BERKLEY BOOK ® TM 757,375
Berkley Books are published by Berkley Publishing Corporation,
200 Madison Avenue, New York, New York 10016.
PRINTED IN THE UNITED STATES OF AMERICA

Acknowledgments

My thanks to the proprietors of the following where this material originally appeared: *The American Spectator*, *Commentary*, the *Daily* and *Sunday Telegraph* (London), *Esquire*, *Flying*, Gateway Editions, *National Review*, the New York *Times*, *The New Yorker*, *Vogue*, and the Washington Star Syndicate. My thanks to Joseph Isola for his fine copyreading, and to Frances Bronson and Robin Wu for help of every kind.

For Pitts, with love

Contents

III. *Abroad*

IV. *Manners, Morals, Mannerists*

V. *Crime and Punishment*

VI. *At Home*

VII. *Education*

VIII. *Sport*

Introduction

THIS IS THE SIXTH volume in which I collect some of my writings on the assumption, so far happily justified by experience, that some of them weather at least the shorter seasons. To be sure, this is primarily an economic assumption, by which I mean that this book would not be published except on the expectation by the publisher that it will, manfully, shoulder its capital burden. That it will do so does not of course say anything about it beyond that exactly: that there is a market for it. What its prospects are in the long, critical term one cannot know. That statement is not merely a ritual gesture to modesty. After all, it is altogether possible that the future will welcome that which is inferior, rejecting that which is virtuous, witty, eloquent and wise. Who knows? All an author can say is what I have said before, namely that it follows that the views expressed herein are—in the author's judgment at least—illuminating, at best sublime: else why not present different views which *are* that? There is no reason to advance these positions except on the asumption that they are the very best in current circulation. That is why, in an age where even the most sacred objects permit themselves to be used as metaphor, I call this book: *A Hymnal*. And subtitle it, "The Controversial Arts." Controversial because for almost everything that is said here, there is an opposite, if intellectually unequal, reaction set down somewhere. This is of course a pity but on the other hand I have not expected to bring around the world by acclamation.

Correspondence provoked by previous volumes suggests that there are a few questions, some of them mechanical, concerning which there is considerable curiosity. Those that I can answer, I take this opportunity to do, adding a point or two of possible interest.

How much editing is done by an author bringing together a collection? I don't know about the generality of collections. In my own case very little, unless you count as editing the process of selection. In the course of a typical year, I compose 150 newspaper columns, a dozen longer articles or reviews, eight or ten speeches, fifty introductions for television, the editorial arrangements of twenty-five columns for *National Review*, and a book. Times three ends you up with a vast amount of material from which to pluck out a volume of this size. In that sense there is editing. Here and there I shorten a piece, and occasionally I run two columns as a single article, adjusting the transition. And—rarely—I substitute a different word, or phrase, for what was in the original.

I have discovered, in sixteen years of writing columns, that there is no observable difference in the quality of that which is written at very great speed (twenty minutes, say), and that which takes three or four times as long. Perversely, it is sometimes otherwise, which is to say that pieces that take longer to write sometimes, on revisiting them, move along grumpily. This could mean that they had been interrupted, from paragraph to paragraph, to introduce intricate figures or analysis. Or it could mean nothing at all. I make the point only because a number of correspondents express curiosity about it.

While on the general subject, I note that the preparation of these volumes requires, for me, more time than the writing of a brand new book. Between assembling my previous collection and this one, I wrote two novels and a book about sailing, each one of which I completed in fewer working hours than were consumed by this hymnal. That is in part because I read very slowly, and the sheer bulk of the material I need to go through consumes a great deal of time. Subsequent parings, and groupings, also take time, with the added disadvantage that when you put aside such a book as this to resume work on it the next day, only after doing your routine work, having lunch, and skiing (this always precedes work on my books), it is harder to pick up the story line. In assembling collections, I find it difficult at first to remember where I had put all the straws on which I had concentrated so heavily the night before and, inevitably, work is repeated.

A note or two about items in *Hymnal*. It contains two pieces commissioned by the New York *Times* but never published there. The first is called "A Tory's Tribute to Hubert Horatio Humphrey." It was known in October 1977 that the senator would not live for many more weeks and the editor of the New York *Times Magazine* thought it would be arresting to publish an essay on the senator by a member of the political opposition. I thought the whole notion risky, but I was dealing with an editor of great and communicable personal conviction who persuaded me to take on the assignment. I did, composing the piece while flying to Tokyo and telephoning it in from there to meet a deadline. A few days later, reaching Honolulu, I got word that the piece was deemed "too savage" to run about a dying man. So I published it in *National Review*, and then sent it to Senator Humphrey. I cherish a note from his assistant, written shortly after the senator's death, that Mr. Humphrey had enjoyed the piece and would have acknowledged it save for his diminished energy. None of this is to reproach the editors of the *Times*, who by the way instantly and uncomplainingly paid over the proffered fee. It is difficult exactly to recapture the emotions of a transient national mood, and conceivably such a piece as this, critical of the senator's positions and of his intellectual habits, would have outraged the *Times*'s readers appearing at a time when the senator was terminally ill. Still, it will be interesting to know how it is received at this point.

It was I who proposed to the editor of the New York *Times Book Review* that I review a volume by John Greenway. The idea approved, I did so: and the months went by. Pressuring an editor to publish a review which editor holds life and death power over your own books is a temptation authors even brasher than I know how to modulate. I expressed my pique by declining several proffered reviews over a period of a year, but managed a reconciliation in plenty of time to cure relations before the appearance of my novel, *Stained Glass*. I mention this because it is the only piece in this book that has not previously appeared in print, and readers may wish to speculate why. The easiest explanation, of course, is that it contains an obscenity; but I tend to think this insufficient.

A word or two, finally, about the two final selections. The first is an introduction, written in the fall of 1977, to the reissuance of my first book, *God and Man at Yale*. This appeared, in drastic truncation, in *Harper's* Magazine, and although it was skillfully edited, it did not, in that form, communicate what I wished to communicate. The essay is long but I think spicy and in its way convincing. It gave me a sense of consummation twenty-five years of silence had, I discovered, denied me. As is so often the case, a controversy that reaches rabid proportions (I think of all that whirled about the head of Senator Joseph McCarthy) is sometimes more interesting as experience than as disagreement. It is hard to believe, in the uproar over *God and Man at Yale*, how some people behaved as recently as twenty-five years ago; but they did, they did, and now that activity is preserved in amber. I did not edit out the page numbers appearing in the essay because I found them, for reasons difficult to describe exactly, integral to the rhythmic effect of the essay.

Very few people who pick up this book will have seen the essay in question, as the reissue of *God and Man at Yale* was intended for a very small audience interested in historical curios. This is not so of the final essay in this book. That essay is on sailing, and is drawn from my book *Airborne*. The editorial condensation was done by the editors of *The New Yorker* magazine. I reproduce it here because it is the only thing I have ever written that everyone liked. I exaggerate. In this case it is fair to say that comments about it were in a number of cases ecstatic. I really don't know exactly why, surmising that it must be because so many sailors have had similar experiences and were inspirited by the knowledge that others had suffered the same vexations. But, strangely, many who wrote have never ridden in a sailboat, and they too were caught up in this essay. So here it is, to be read fresh by those who missed it and are curious; to be available for those who wish to read it again.

I was disappointed when my friend Mr. Walter Minton, the president of Putnam's, told me that my obduracy in including the two long essays on Yale and sailing meant that this book would be priced at more than twelve dollars, but I have learned to live with disappointments, and continue to hope that the extra dollar or two will, at least by a few, be spent without undue resentment. If it worked out that that extra dollar came to me, I'd gladly refund it to those who wrote to express their chagrin. Alas, the miserable authors have to get along with only 15 percent. If, in return for a dollar taken from the consumer, I returned him fifteen cents, I would be made to feel like the Federal Government and that, as so much of this volume attests, would be intolerable.

—WFB

Stamford, Connecticut
May 1, 1978

1. *The Struggle*

After Ten Years: A Toast on the 10th Anniversary of *The American Spectator*

November 1977

GEORGE NASH has done the best that could be done to chronicle the development of a movement. Several times in his book (*The Conservative Intellectual Movement in America since 1945*) he stresses that it is a *movement* he is talking about, and then, drawing copiously on his gifts for summary and contraction, he tells us what went into the mix: quite a gallimaufry, including economic distillations inspired by the Alpine air at Mont Pèlerin, a prayerful re-examination of the Declaration of Independence and the Constitution, searching questions about the responsibility of Socrates for his own elimination, the revival of the great tradition by Leo Strauss, empirical studies of the work of regulatory commissions, high colonic examinations of the internal cancer of the West, lyrical tributes to the good life as, for instance, by Richard Weaver, swash-buckling marches through the tortured ranks of our stuttering social scientists, the reassertion of form and the rejection of formalism by T. S. Eliot: all of this happened, and suddenly—little by little—we felt that there was—a brotherhood. Not quite so cohesive as that which grew up in response to the excesses of Orwell's Big Brother, or one whose members were bound to each other as men and women are bound who knew Gulag. But something of a brotherhood, and that is one of the principal differences between the struggle, then and now.

There was, even before *The American Spectator* was founded, way back in 1950 a "conservative" alliance. It was a legacy of inertial ideology from turn-of-the-century America. It was lubricated by profitable—and exploitative—relations—between business and its clients, between farmers and the state, between whites and racial supremacy. It had a certain sense of obligation to the old virtues, but it was, as we think back on it, highly unexplicated. The reasons for encouraging a private sector were wonderfully well known and advertised in the same classics to which we continue now to defer. But the new wave—a kind of secular modernism—was sweeping it all away, mostly in the classrooms of America, where the struggle was seen if not exactly in Marxist terms (Marxist rigor was never appealing to Americans at large), at least in neo-Marxist terms—the catalyst of my book, *God and Man at Yale*. Conservatives had a quintessential representative: Senator Robert A. Taft, whose strength derived from his integrity, his nimble (if less than profound) mind; and a considerable political agility. There was formal and even spontaneous enthusiasm for Senator Taft, even among young people: but never any sense of romance. Probably because conservatism was thought of, even by its friends, as something of a desiccated competitor in lusty ideological wars that had dominated the century: lacking in system, unlike fascism; in eschatology, unlike Communism; and in idealistic passion, unlike liberalism. Back in those days Whittaker Chambers wrote to me to warn that the hordes would not be stopped by fresh transcripts by Russell Kirk of the vaticinations of Edmund Burke.

There is no reason to suppose that the hordes will be stopped now, but every reason to suppose that the forces that stop them, if ever they mobilize to do so, will have been touched by that unbought grace of which the exegetes of Burke have reminded us. Could it be that the distinctive difference in the struggle, then and now, is that in the interim it has acquired grace? Is it not *grace*—most spectacularly celebrated in the final episode of Malraux's *La Condition Humaine,* when the older of the condemned men passes out his suicide pill to his two younger, frailer associates—that is the distinctive attribute of the movement now, as compared to then? In those days there was *1984*, but it was fantasy. Today, we have *The Gulag Archipelago*, and *One Day in the Life of Ivan Denisovich*; and *First Circle*—and by them we are annealed into a brotherhood, with a sense of mission marked by that grace which reminds us that, ultimately, we owe each other everything—even our private resources of self-destruction, of release. To read these books is to undergo a sacramental experience. I feel differently in the company of men who have read Solzhenitsyn. Solzhenitsyn was the solvent. He vested all that came before, all that George Nash wrote about, with a kind of unity which defined the struggle, even if it did not make self-evident the means of pursuing it.

On the tenth anniversary of this journal there are grounds for rejoicing. It is a journal of joy, reminding us in every issue of the reasons to celebrate the zest of combat, the joy of right thinking, the pleasure of language. I join this happy company in paying tribute to you.

Socialism and Freedom

April 1978

WHEN I WAS a boy at Yale, along about the time they were superannuating God, they were enshrining something called economic democracy. Many of my classmates, by the time they had gone through the typical ration of introductory courses in economics and allied fields, were ready to live and die, if necessary, to bring economic democracy to America. In those days anything attached to democracy was osmotically desirable, democracy having been postulated as the highest civic good. We had, then, not only economic democracy as a social desideratum, but its cousin, industrial democracy. Educational democracy enjoyed morganatic privileges, and of course social democracy was tantamount to eudaemonia. Henry Wallace could not give a speech without a dozen references to economic democracy, and of course it transpired that what was meant by the term was a progressive socialization of the economy. That which was capitalistic in form was disparaged quite consistently, especially by those who thought themselves progressive, as in the Progressive Party which fielded Henry Wallace as its candidate during my sophomore year.

But like executive supremacy, which was good when exercised by FDR and Truman, bad when attempted by Richard Nixon, the term democracy began to suffer and, *pari passu*, economic democracy. I like to think that the bubble burst when some scholar, who flogged himself through John Dewey's *Democracy and Education*, carefully annotated twenty-two distinct uses to which Mr. Dewey had put the words democracy and democratic. There was, of course, the postwar confusion caused by the establishment of such states as the German Democratic Republic, and the endless encomiums in the Communist and fellow-traveling press to the democratic arrangements in Stalin's Russia, which of course was what the Webbs and Harold Laski had hailed as the fountainhead of economic democracy. There were the noble dissenters—I think Sidney Hook was the most vociferous, not to say encephalophonic—who kept stressing the differences between true economic democracy and the kind of thing practiced in Russia. But doubts had begun to set in, reinforced during the 1960's by the advent of democracy in Africa. Democracy had been used, along with "independence," as an antonym for colonialism. And when it became clear that the expulsion of the colonizers in Africa would bring not democracy but merely an end to white rule, many Americans, rather than sort out their frustrations, simply stopped reading about Africa, even as one stops counting Bolivian coups. And I think it correct to say that the term economic democracy tiptoed out of the workaday rhetoric of progressive politicians who although generally the last group to recognize the uselessness of shibboleths, are sensitive to public ennui. Economic democracy was increasingly understood to be the progressive transfer of power from the private to the public sector. There is continuing enthusiasm for this, but it tends to be inertial and dogmatic. Looking again for symbols, I think of Peter F. Drucker who in his *The Age of Discontinuity* dropped the line that modern experience has demonstrated that the only thing the state can do better than society is inflate the currency and wage war. The experience of Vietnam brings one of those two claims for the state into question.

With the demythologization of the state as the agent of universal well-being came also a revived curiosity about what it is in democracy that is desirable. Begin by admitting that the democracy that brought us Perón and Hitler is an imperfect cathedral in which to worship, and you have come a long way. If democracy can substantially diminish human freedom, it is only casually interesting that that diminution of freedom was effected by political due process. Which brought to the attention of the curious, particularly among libertarians, the startling insight that it is altogether conceivable that in a given situation one might be faced with freedom and democracy as mutually exclusive alternatives. Not entirely so, because if you surrender democracy on the grounds that democracy is heading you toward a totalitarian abyss, you have indeed given up something. But that something which you give up is not necessarily more valuable than that which by giving it up you stand to retain. Burke said it most simply when he remarked that the end of political freedom is human freedom.

It is best, I think, to ruminate on these matters by reasoning *a posteriori*. Freedom *can* be quantified. Freedom is not, in an imperfect world, indefeasible. If, let us say, a society acknowledges (1) the freedom to write, (2) the freedom to own property, and (3) the freedom to practice one's religion, it is a better state than the state that grants only two of those freedoms. But the state that grants two of those freedoms is better than the state that grants only one of them. By extension, the republic with a vigorous public sector that protects the right of property and the attendant right of economic enterprise is one which understands democracy as primarily a procedural commitment—instructing us how to make such changes in public policy as are desired by the majority, but warning us that the use of that procedural authority for the purpose of limiting substantial freedoms is intolerable. It is plain that an increasing number of intellectuals, dismayed by contemporary experience, have stopped superordinating democracy to all other specified and specifiable freedoms. Having done that, it is easier to arrive at the conclusion that a vigorous private sector is necessary for the validation of democracy. Democratic socialism, as the venerable insight tells us, is all about A meeting with B for the purpose of deciding what C will give to X. To say that democratic socialism "works" in Scandinavia is merely to say that the individual who makes that statement would rather exchange those freedoms absent in Scandinavia for those social perquisites offered in Scandinvavia. If democracy is to be the servant of human freedom rather than the instrument by which to afflict the minority, then it must acknowledge the great self-denying ordinances which reasonably limit all other freedoms.

Alert intellectuals are in increasing numbers interested by what the lawyers anxious to preserve constitutional guarantees call the "slippery-slope" theory, the generic statement of which is, Give them an inch and they'll take a mile. The appetite of the socialist to govern tends to insatiability. Thus Freedom House, in the latest of its annual tables of political rights and civil rights, is instructive. The nations of the world are divided into three categories: the capitalist, the mixed, and the socialist. Only a single state is both socialist and politically free. For those interested in purple cows, that state is Guyana.

How Robert Redford saved us from the CIA

September 28, 1975

Three Days of the Condor has everything, and one thing too many, wherein alas lies its chic. But for the terminal protuberance, we would have an expertly directed, trimly jigsawed, adequately acted spy-suspense story which catches the viewer with the opening scene: What can that mysterious man in the parked car be about, checking off the names, one by one, of the half-dozen people as they saunter into the "American Literary Historical Society" on Manhattan's East Side to begin a day's work? Why, what he is doing is making sure there's a full house, because at lunchtime, he and his accomplices are going into that staid old building to shoot them all down in cold blood, made colder by the special ice pellets used—at least, that is one inference—by specially designed carnage-machines.

What was Robert Redford doing while his colleagues were being mowed down? He was out for lunch. Specifically, out to fetch lunch for his colleagues, it being his turn to go to the delicatessen. But, in order to avoid the rain, he ignores prescribed security regulations and bounds down the staircase and out the back door, which is closer to the deli; and anyway, it is time to establish him as a man of rather independent habits, who makes the boss of this supersecret CIA front perpetually uneasy ("Are you sure you are quite happy working for us, Turner?") with that roaming, restless intelligence. (The director, Sydney Pollack, is unwilling to blemish Redford's beautiful face with any of the scars of The Thinker, but makes the concession of having him, occasionally, wear glasses. He does not wear glasses when he makes love to Faye Dunaway, but then this is not a moment when his restless intelligence is his dominating concern.)

Redford's job at the "American Literary Historical Society" is to apply his encyclopedic knowledge and omnivorous curiosity to the scanning of routine material in search of surreptitious enemy activity. He has recently come on an anomaly: A certain bestseller has been translated only into Dutch and Arabic. So what, you say? So *you* would never qualify to work for the CIA because of *your* restless intelligence. Redford has sent down to Washington, through his superior at the Manhattan front, the datum, on which he frames a hunch which is mercifully unexplicated, and the lunch-hour carnage is the result. Redford had stumbled over an operation of international significance, and it is a lucky, lucky thing that it was his day to go to the deli and that he used the back door, else he'd be stone-cold dead, along with the boss, the beautiful Oriental secretary, and all the others.

On bringing in the hot dogs and finding everybody dead, Redford decides he had better report the event to Washington, but he is good and scared, and so are you in his behalf, I'm telling you. So when he calls Washington, and is told by the bigger boss which alleyway to report to at exactly what hour, Redford says, No sirree, I'm not going to report to any alleyway to meet up with a perfect stranger. How do I know I'm not talking to the chief killer himself? It is therefore arranged that the unknown boss will be accompanied by an old friend of Redford's from another division of CIA. Recognizing his old friend, Redford will say to himself—and would even if he *didn't* have a restless intelligence—"That's my old friend all right, so the guy with him must be O.K."

But what happens is that as soon as the three men get together, the boss suddenly whips out a pistol and in the general shoot-out Redford's friend is killed, the boss is fatally wounded, and Redford knows he's in real trouble. So he kidnaps Faye Dunaway, a perfect stranger of the kind Robert Redford would come upon, and over the next couple of hours the plot proceeds along its anfractuous way, and the viewer has a superb time as assassins come and go, and gets a true sci-fi thrill out of the display of intelligence hardware, of which my favorite is a machine that flashes a map showing the location of the telephone being used by the caller. However, Redford's restless intelligence at some point in his life put him on to everything anybody ever knew about telephones, and he manages to cross the lines of half the telephone trunks in the city and sits comfortably on a ganglion that makes a laughing stock out of the Central Intelligence Agency's telephone-spotting machine.

By now we all know that the Mr. Big who ordered the killings is very high up in government. Our government. Indeed, by the laws of compound interest, if the movie had endured another half an hour, one would have been satisfied only if the President of the United States, or perhaps even Ralph Nader, had proved to be the energumen behind it all.

Thus it goes, right to the smash ending, as unbalancing as Jimmy Durante's nose. The viewers would, at that point, have been left totally satisfied by a traditional double-agent theme—Mr. Big was really working for the Soviet Union; or, if that is not trendy enough for Pollack-Redford, a Chilean colonel. It transpires, however, that Mr. Big is a 100 percent American who had to eliminate all those people at the "American Literary

Historical Society" because they might have become privy to a contingent operation by following the lead turned up by Redford's restless intelligence.

Then, in a dramatic sidewalk confrontation, Mr. Junior Big explains to Redford that it is all high patriotism, working against a future national shortage of oil, and invites Redford to come back into the company and accept the requirements of orthodoxy in the modern world. But Redford says, taking off his glasses, No, never! This very day I have told everything to . . . the camera slithers up to a marquee above the two men who are talking and you see the logo of . . . the New York *Times*. The director failed only to emblazon under it, "Daniel Ellsberg Slept Here." Mr. Junior Big reacts like the witch come into contact with water. He snarls and shrivels away, and says, half-desperately: "Maybe they won't print it!" But Redford has by now seeded the audience with his restless intelligence, and *we* all know that the New York *Times will* print it, and we shall all be free.

The film's production notes state: "Over a year ago, Stanley Schneider, Robert Redford, Sydney Pollack and Dino de Laurentiis decided to create a film that would reflect the climate of America in the aftermath of the Watergate crisis." "The climate of America" is a pretty broad term. They really mean; The climate of America as seen by I. F. Stone, Seymour Hersh, Susan Sontag and Shirley MacLaine. One recalls Will Rogers, returning from the Soviet Union where he had seen a communal bath. "Did you see all of Russia?" he was asked. "No," Rogers said, weighing his answer. "But I saw all of *parts* of Russia!"

Redford-Pollack-de Laurentiis have shown us the climate in all of parts of America. It sure is cold out there.

II. *People, Characters*

The Long War Against McCarthyism

Lillian Hellman: Who is the ugliest of them all?

January 1977

WHEN *Scoundrel Time* (Little, Brown, $7.95) was first published, in the spring of 1976, only the cooing of reviewers was heard. Up front, in the most prominent seats, they applauded so resolutely, so methodically, that the sound of the metronome teased the ear. Solzhenitsyn, in the first Gulag book, writes about how, during one of the terrors, Stalin's agents would fan out from Moscow to give speeches to the satellite brass, hastily convened in crowded theaters in the outlying cities to receive the details of Stalin's hectic afflatus. After the speaker was done, the subjects would break into applause, and the clapping would go on and on, because no one dared be the first to sit down, lest he be thought insufficiently servile. Indeed, rather than wait for the speaker finally to beckon the whole assembly back to its seats, on one occasion someone did it—stopped clapping, though only after a boisterous while. That man was spotted, given ten years, and shipped off to a prison camp—where, perhaps, he was given to read from the collected anti-fascist *opera* of Lillian Hellman. . . . It seemed for a while the reviewers would be that way all around the town—the New York *Times*, the Washington *Post, Commonweal, America*, the Chicago *Tribune*. Then . . . then, in *The New York Review of Books*, Murray Kempton interrupted his own paean to Miss Hellman to make a comment or two which, however gentle, quite ruptured the trance. It was as if, in Paris during the occupation, an anonymous arranger had, by fugitive notation, insinuated the motif of the "*Marseillaise*" into a great Speer-like orchestration of "*Über Alles*." Others, after that, came rushing in. It would never be quite the same again for Miss Lillian.

Even so, one has to hand it to her. Though the book is slender, the design is grandly staged, in self-esteem as in presumption. To begin with, here is someone described in the introduction to her own book as the greatest woman playwright in American history. Now this is probably true. But a) Isn't that on the order of celebrating the tallest building in Wichita, Kansas? and b) Doesn't an introduction to oneself in such terms, in one's own book, by one's own chosen introducer, interfere with the desired perception of oneself as a hard-working artist ignorant, indeed disdainful, of the outside world of power-plays and flackery? and c) Aren't the auspices the most alien for making sexual distinctions? I mean, Garry Wills, the Last Kid, talking about the Greatest Woman Playwright as one would talk about the downhill champion on the one-legged ski team?

And here is a writer (Wills) introducing an autobiographical book by a woman who is publicizing now her complaint against an America that, as she might put it, victimized her because of her alleged championship of the regime of Josef Stalin. And what, then, does Wills go and do in his introduction? Quote from the author's pre-McCarthy works, to demonstrate the impartiality of her opposition to tyranny? Not at all. He goes on (and on and on—Mr. Wills consumes thirty-four pages with his introduction, one-fifth of the book), blithely—offhandedly—describing the era of Miss Hellman's travail as the era in U.S.-Soviet relations during which horrible old us, led by Harry Truman, promulgated a cold war against reasonable old them, the startled, innocent Communists, led by Josef Stalin. In *Commentary*, Nathan Glazer quoted from Wills's introduction: *"A newly aggressive Truman had launched the Cold War in the spring of 1947, with his plan to 'rescue' Greece and Turkey. . . . We had still a world to save, with just those plans—from NATO to the Korean War . . ."* And commented: "One reads such passages—and many others—in astonishment. Garry Wills [evidently] believes that Greece and Turkey did not need to be rescued, that one of America's 'plans' was the Korean War. It seems that he prefers the political condition of, say, Bulgaria and North Korea to that of Greece and Turkey." *That* introduction, which might have been written in the Lenin Institute, introducing *that* book, under the circumstances of Miss Hellman's apologia, was a venture either in dumb innocence (inconsistent with Hellman's persona), or in matchless cheek, on the order of Mohandas Gandhi writing the autobiography of a pacifist and asking General Patton to introduce it.

But the difficulties had only just begun for her. Is Ms. Hellman a nice guy? In a way, it shouldn't matter. A sentence from her book, much quoted, asks, *"Since when do you have to agree with people to defend them from injustice?"* By the same token, we shouldn't require that someone be endearing as a prerequisite to indignation at unfair treatment of her. But Ms. Hellman, author of *The Little Foxes*, is quickly spotted as being no less guileful than one of her characters. It's another case of Germaine Greer, filibustering against male chauvinism, while stripteasing her sexual biography across the magazine rack. Ms. Hellman, affecting only a disinterested concern for justice, twangs the heartstrings—with, however, more sleight of hand than craft. She had to sell her country house! She had to fire her cook and gardener! She had to give up a million-dollar contract! She had to take a part-time job in a department store! Her lover had to go to jail! If, unlike the earlier reviewers, you finish the book believing that you have read anything less than an episode in the life of Thomas More, you are either callous—or else her art has failed her.

She takes awful risks, entirely unnecessary. For instance, she exhibits hit-and-run contempt for Lionel and Diana Trilling—for the sin of believing in the sincerity of Whittaker Chambers. Nice people would have handled that differently. James Wechsler of the New York *Post* is denounced for being a *"friendly witness"* before the House Committee on Un-American Activities (he never appeared before HUAC: it was the McCarthy Committee, and Wechsler was hostile). Theodore White is dismissed contemptuously as a *"jolly quarter-historian"*—because he once wrote a book saying that Nixon was a complicated man (Lillian Hellman finds nothing complicated in evil incarnate). Elia Kazan, struggling to appease his conscience, in revolt now against his earlier complicity with the Communist movement, took a full page in the New York *Times* to run his palinode—characterized by Miss Hellman as *"pious shit."*

All in all, her performance is about as ingratiating as a post-Watergate speech by Richard Nixon, and so we quite understand it when Murray Kempton is driven to saying, in concluding his review, that, really, he would not want Lillian Hellman "overmuch as a comrade." Thus, the scaffolding of the book is pretty shaky. It is, after all, implicitly entitled, *"The Heroism of Lillian Hellman during the Darkest Days of the Republic*, by Lillian Hellman." It would have been a little seemlier if her book had gone out as "*Scoundrel Time*, by Lillian Hellman, as told to Garry Wills." Or—why not just *"Scoundrel Time: How Lillian Hellman Held Her Finger in the Dike and Saved American Freedom and Self-Respect*, by Garry Wills"? He would not have needed to increase the size of his contribution by all that much. In any event—an artistic point, and with apologies to Burke—this martyr, to be loved, should be lovelier.

Then there is the problem of factual accuracy, best captured in the author's unguarded reference to Whittaker Chambers and the pumpkin papers.

Here is what Miss Hellman wrote:

"Facts are facts—and one of them is that a pumpkin, in

which Chambers claimed to have hidden the damaging evidence against Hiss, deteriorates."

Now here is a sentence that might have been written by Eleanor Roosevelt. It sounds strange coming from the greatest woman playwright in American history, and is incredible when proffered in support of the proposition that facts are facts.

Yes, it is a fact that pumpkins deteriorate.

But they do not deteriorate appreciably overnight, which is how long the Hiss films reposed in the pumpkin.

As for *"in which Chambers claimed to have hidden..."* nobody questions that Chambers hid the films there, not even Alger Hiss. Not even Stalin. Nor could she have intended to write, *"in which Chambers hid the* allegedly *damaging evidence."* Because it wasn't *allegedly* damaging, it was just plain damaging, which indeed is why all the fuss. The films went a long way to establish Chambers's credibility, and therefore the guilt of Hiss. What she presumably *meant* to write was, *"in which Chambers hid the damaging but, it now turns out, meaningless evidence."* Earlier in the book she had constructed an explanatory footnote from which the sentence in question coasted, to wit: *"In 1975 the secret pumpkin papers were found to contain nothing secret, nothing confidential. They were, in fact, non-classified, which is Washington's way of saying anybody who says please can have them."*

Facts are indeed facts. But Miss Hellman's rendition of the facts caught the attention of one of her fans, Congressman Edward Koch of Manhattan. He read her book, and wrote the author a letter of fawning praise reciting his own sustained effort to kill the House Committee on Un-American Activities. But Edward Koch has a streak of Yankee inquisitiveness, even as it is advertised about Miss Hellman that she is curious. John Hersey has written about her—his dear friend—"Miss Hellman's powers of invention are fed by her remarkable memory and her ravenous curiosity. Her father once said she lived 'within a question mark.' She defines culture as 'applied curiosity.' She is always on what she calls 'the find-out kick.'" Well, not quite always. Not on those occasions when she begins a paragraph with the phrase, "Facts are facts." (Like the *Daily World*'s ritual introduction of a lie: "As is well known...")

Congressman Koch wrote to the Library of Congress to ask

about Miss Hellman's description of the pumpkin papers, and simultaneously wrote to Miss Hellman asking for an elucidation. The lady who lives within a question mark didn't reply. But the lady at the Library of Congress did. As follows: "The footnote statement is inaccurate. On July 31, 1975, Alger Hiss was permitted to see the 'pumpkin papers,' which consists of five rolls of microfilm. One roll, as Mr. Kelly reports, was 'completely light-fogged.' Two other rolls were pages from apparently unclassified Navy technical manuals. The other two rolls, however, contained Government documents 'relating to U.S.-German relations before World War II and cables from U.S. observers in China.' Documents in these two rolls were marked highly confidential. Of the five rolls of microfilm, only these latter two had been used as evidence against Hiss in the trial which led to his conviction for perjury in 1950."

Miss Hellman's reputation as a literary precisionist (she is said to write and rewrite her plays four, six, ten, twelve times) leads one to expect a cognate precision in those of her books and articles that bid for the moral attention of the Republic; so that one is inclined to take literally such a statement by her as, *"Certainly nobody in their* [*sic*] *right mind could have believed that the China experts, charged and fired by the State Department, did any more than recognize that Chiang Kai-shek was losing."*

But whom is she referring to? Who is it who was *"charged and fired"* by the State Department for such an offense? The controversial John Carter Vincent was three times *cleared* by the State Department's Loyalty Security Board, and when the Civil Service Loyalty Review Board found against him, Dulles *overruled* that Board, though accepting Vincent's resignation. McCarthy's target, John Paton Davies, was *cleared* by the State Department. John Stewart Service was, granted, finally dropped by the State Department, but only because the Civil Service Loyalty Review Board ruled against him, not the State Department's board, which repeatedly cleared him. And Service was otherwise engaged than merely as a diplomatic technician predicting the ascendancy of Mao. His emotions in the matter were hardly concealed. He had provided his superiors, from the field in China, such information as that "Politically, any orientation which the Chinese Communists may once have had toward the Soviet Union seems to be a thing of the past . . . they are carrying out democratic policies which they expect the United States to approve and sympathetically support." And Service's case was further complicated when he was arrested for passing along classified documents to the editor of *Amerasia*, a Communist-front publication. But of course the principal architect of our China policy, singled out by the Senate Internal Security Subcommittee, hadn't even been a member of the State Department, exercising his influence on policy through the Institute for Pacific Relations. The blurb printed on Owen Lattimore's book *Solution in Asia* went further than merely to predict the downfall of the Kuomintang. "He showed," the book's editors compressed the author's story, "that all the Asiatic people are more interested in actual democratic practices such as the ones they can see in action across the Russian border, than they are in the fine theories of Anglo-Saxon democracies which come coupled with ruthless imperialism. He inclines to support American newspapermen who report that the only real democracy in China is found in Communist areas."

We have learned about democracy in the Communist world. What have we learned about Miss Hellman's credibility?

Nor is she entirely candid in describing the nature or extent of her own involvement with the Soviet Union. She vouchsafes, in a subordinate clause that could be interpreted as contritional, only this much: *"Many* [American intellectuals] *found in the sins of Stalin Communism—and there were plenty of sins and plenty that for a long time I mistakenly denied—the excuse to join those who should have been their hereditary enemies."* (Interesting, that one. Is she talking about American Jewish socialist anti-Communists? Who else?) Later she says, *"I thought that in the end Russia, having achieved a state socialism, would stop its infringements on personal liberty. I was wrong."* Isn't there something there on the order of, "I thought that, on buying the contract of Mickey Mantle, the Yankees would go on to win the World Series. I was wrong . . ."? But the ritualistic apology was not enough to satisfy. Soon after Mr. Kempton broke the spell, one began to notice the misgivings of others. William Phillips in *Partisan Review*, Melvin Lasky in *Encounter*, Nathan Glazer in *Commentary*, most notably Hilton Kramer in the New York *Times* (ardently defended by Arthur Schlesinger, Jr. in the letters section), and even Irving Howe, in *Dissent*.

Forsooth, Lillian Hellman's involvement in the Communist movement was not comprehensively divulged in her offhand remarks about her concern for justice and peace, and her stated disinclination for politics. Miss Hellman went to Russia for the first time in 1937, where her ravenous curiosity caused her to learn enough about the Soviet system to return to the United States confidently to defend Stalin's purges and denounce John Dewey and his commission for finding Stalin guilty of staging the show trials during the great purge. She devoted much of her professional career during that period dramatizing the evil of brown fascism. *Watch on the Rhine*, staged in 1941, is devoted to the proposition that *"the death of fascism is more desirable than the lives and well-being of the people who hate it."* When, a quarter-century later, in 1969, she criticized, in a letter to the New York *Times*, the novelist Kuznetsov for fleeing Russia and seeking asylum in England, having first secured an exit visa by "cooperating" with the Soviet Union by giving an obviously fabricated and useless deposition against fellow dissidents, Kuznetsov replied that Miss Hellman's attack on him, "like that of a few others," was "prompted by some surviving illusions about Russia." "The Soviet Union," he explained to Miss Hellman, "is a fascist country. What is more, its fascism is much more dangerous than Hitler's. It is a country which is living in Orwellian times. . . . Tens of millions of bloody victims, a culture destroyed, fascist antisemitism, the genocide of small nations, the transformation of the individual into a hypocritical cipher, Hungary, Czechoslovakia. In literature—nothing but murder, suicides, persecution, trials, lunatic asylums, an unbroken series of tragedies from Gumilev to Solzhenitsyn. Is that really not enough?" There is no recorded reaction from Miss Hellman.

During the war, she traveled to the Soviet Union and was received there as a celebrity. She returned the hospitality in first-rate mint: an article in *Collier's* magazine about the heroism of the Russian people and the Russian soldiers. In that article there is a passage of triumphant irony. She has been implored by her guide to ask more questions. She records her reply: *"I said, 'The first week I was in the Soviet Union I found out that if I did not ask questions, I always got answers. . . . Tell your people to tell me what they want to. I will learn more that way.'"* (Life within a question mark.) And, indeed, she learned everything Stalin and his agents wanted her to learn, and came back to America to share her knowledge, and to despise those of her fellow Americans who insisted on asking questions.

In 1948 and 1949 she was, for a non-politician, very active. She backed Henry Wallace's bid for the Presidency on the Progressive Party ticket, and was visibly amused on being asked privately by poor old Mortimer Snerd if it were true that there were Communists in positions of power in his party. *"It was such a surprising question that I laughed and said most certainly it was true."* She then put in a call, convening the top Communists in the Progressive Party, and said to them at that meeting, Look, why don't you go paddle your own canoe in your own party? There cannot have been such dumb amazement in Christendom since Lady Astor asked Stalin when would he stop killing people.

A few months later, Lillian Hellman played a big role in the famous Waldorf Conference—the Cultural and Scientific Conference for World Peace. In her book, her running guard Mr. Wills treats most fiercely those who attended the meeting for the purpose of "disrupting" it—such redbaiters as Mary McCarthy and Dwight Macdonald, and officials of the Americans for Democratic Action who, at a press conference, raised with the wretched Russian superpawn, Dmitri Shostakovich, head of the Soviet delegation, questions about the fate of his cultural and scientific colleagues back home, Russian writers, intellectuals, and musicians who had disappeared from sight after the most recent choler of Josef Stalin. Miss Hellman does not allude to any of this. Her quarrel with American intellectuals is over their failure to devote the whole of their time to criticizing J. Parnell Thomas. Presumably, criticism of Stalin could wait until Miss Hellman was personally satisfied that, now that he had established state socialism, he had in fact failed to introduce human freedom.

Indeed, her attitude is ferocious toward those who, looking back on their complicity with Communism, wondered more inventively than she how to make amends. By writing books? (Koestler.) Cooperating with congressional committees? (Kazan.) Doing both? (Chambers.) Miss Hellman, who wrote about how the cause of anti-fascism was bigger than anything, seemed to have lost interest in tyranny, preoccupied now with her material well-being, and that of Dashiell Hammett, her relationship with whom is jovially described by one reviewer—"She was then and had long been a friend of Dashiell Hammett—more than a friend: a wife, off and on, but for the paperwork." In that spirit one could say that thus had been Lillian Hellman's relations with the Communist movement—a marriage, but for the paperwork. If one feels that paperwork, the formal exchange of vows, is essential to a sacramentally complete union, then perhaps Lillian Hellman was not married to the Communist movement any more than she was married to Dashiell Hammett. But the investigating committees, like Miss Hellman's reviewers, were interested in de facto relations.

So off she went to Washington, for her great moment before the congressional committee. There has not been such a prologue since the *Queen Mary* weighed anchor in Manhattan in order to move to Brooklyn. Her device was simple. She wrote to the committee to say she would not answer questions about anybody's activities other than her own, and unless the committee agreed not to ask such questions, she would take the Fifth Amendment. Implicit in her position was her sacred right to be the sole judge of whether her acquaintances in the Communist world were engaged in innocent activity. The committee of course declined to permit her to define the committee's mandate, so she took the Fifth, and wants us to celebrate her wit and courage every twenty-five years. The committee treated her with civility, did not ask Congress to hold her in contempt, and is hardly responsible for the decline in her commercial fortunes. She, not the committee, dictated the script that got her into trouble with Hollywood.

Yet the lady is obsessed with the fancy that she and her common-law husband were specific victims of the terror. "Dash" floats in and out of the book disembodiedly, but always we are reminded that he actually spent time in jail—for refusing to divulge the names of the financial patrons of the Civil Rights

Congress, a Communist front (Dashiell Hammett was not a dupe, at least not in the conventional sense: he was a Communist). Miss Hellman makes a great deal of his victimization. Murray Kempton, who would not send Caligula to prison, at this point has had enough. He writes, "We do not diminish the final admiration we feel owed to Dashiell Hammett when we wonder what he might have said to Miss Hellman on the night he came home from the meeting of the board of the Civil Rights Congress which voted to refuse its support to the cause of James Kutcher, a paraplegic veteran who had been discharged as a government clerk because he belonged to the Trotskyite Socialist Workers Party. But then Hammett was a Communist and it was an article of the Party faith that Leon Trotsky, having worked for the Emperor of Japan since 1904, had then improved his social standing by taking employment with the Nazis in 1934. Thus any member of the Socialist Workers Party could be considered by extension to be no more than an agent of Hitler's ghost. Given that interpretation of history, Paul Robeson spoke from principle when a proposal to assist the Trotskyite Kutcher was raised at a public meeting of the Civil Rights Congress. Robeson drove it from the floor with a declaration to the effect that you don't ask Jews to help a Nazi or Negroes to help the KKK." The voice of Paul Robeson lives on, speaking from the same principle: "Oct. 7, 1976. Lillian Hellman, author and dramatist, will receive the third annual Paul Robeson Award tomorrow at 12:30. The award is presented by the Paul Robeson Citation Committee of Actors' Equity for 'concern for and service to fellow humans.'"

The self-pity reaches paranoia. Edmund Wilson once wrote an entire book the thesis of which silts up as suggesting that we went to war in Vietnam for the sole purpose of increasing his income tax. Miss Hellman is vaguer on the subject of motivation, but denies her reader any explanation for bringing the matter up at all, leaving us to suppose that Somebody in Washington singled her and Dash out for Special Treatment. Thus Hammett goes to jail for contempt of Congress (for six months). *"That was a tough spring, 1952. There were not alone the arrangements for my appearance before the Committee, there were other kinds of trouble. Hammett owed the Internal Revenue a great deal of back taxes: two days after he went to jail they attached all income from books, radio, or television, from anything. He was, therefore, to have no income for the remaining ten years of his life. . . . That made me sad."* And again, *"Never in the ten years since the Internal Revenue cut off his income—two days after he went to jail—did he ever buy a suit or even a tie."* As for herself, *"Money was beginning to go and go fast. I had gone from earning a hundred and forty thousand a year (before the movie blacklist) to fifty and then twenty and then ten, almost all of which was taken from me* [note, "taken from me"] *by the Internal Revenue Department, which had come forward with its claim on the sale of a play that the previous Administration had seemingly agreed to."*

La Précisionniste rides again. a) It is, of course, the Internal Revenue *Service*, not Department; b) if she means to say that her companion Dashiell Hammett should have been excused from paying the same taxes other people pay on equivalent income (perhaps because, as a Communist, he was entitled to preferential treatment?), then let her *say* that; c) the IRS doesn't "agree" to the sale of a play, but might have agreed to accept a taxation base: in any event, the tax levied by IRS was on profit; to say nothing of the fact that d) Lillian Hellman is not Vivien Kellems' sister. The latter was the authentic American Poujadiste, and when *she* complained about taxes, she spoke from the bowels of principle. When Lillian Hellman complains about high taxes, she is complaining about the monster she suckled.

What does one go on to say about a book so disorderly, so tasteless, guileful, self-enraptured? The disposition to adore her, feel sorry for her, glow in the vicarious thrill of her courage and decency (her favorite word, "decency": she is apolitical now, she says, desiring only "decency") runs into hurdle after hurdle in the obstacle course of this little book. Consider. It is 1952, and she is living in her townhouse in New York, and the buzzer rings. *"An over-respectable-looking black man. . . stood in the elevator, his hat politely removed. He asked me if I was Lillian Hellman. I agreed to that and asked who he was. He handed me an envelope and said he was there to serve a subpoena from the House Un-American Activities*

Committee. I opened the envelope and read the subpoena. I said, 'Smart to choose a black man for this job. You like it?' and slammed the door."

Ah, the decent of this earth. The same lady who in her book tells us that she will not style her life to political fashion, now refers to her visitor, back in 1952, as "black," when of course that word was unused in 1952. Miss Hellman was brought up in New Orleans where, paradoxical though it may seem, the same class of people who institutionalized Jim Crow never (I speak of the decent members of that class) humiliated individual members of the Negro race. It is difficult to imagine suggesting to a Negro bureaucrat who has merely performed a job assigned to him that he is collusively engaged in anti-Negro activity; impossible to understand a civilized woman slamming the door in the face of someone—a messenger—executing a clerical duty. Truly, the lady's emotions are ungoverned, and perhaps ungovernable. She seems to like to advertise this. *"I have a temper and it is triggered at odd times by odd matters and is then out of my control."* And, elsewhere, talking about her "black" nanny, she reveals that she was given *"anger—an uncomfortable, dangerous, and often useful gift."* To be used against black messengers bearing instructions from Washington, but on no account against white messengers bearing instructions from Moscow.

The author, though she attempts to project a moral for our time out of her own travail, does this less avidly than most of her critics, who seized greedily on this mincing tale of self-pity as the matrix of a passion play. It doesn't work. The heart of her failure beats in a single sentence. *". . . whatever our mistakes, I do not believe we did our country any harm."*

"Dear Lillian Hellman," the socialist Irving Howe writes, "you could not be more mistaken! Those who supported Stalinism and its political enterprises, either here or abroad, helped befoul the cultural atmosphere, helped bring totalitarian methods into trade unions, helped perpetuate one of the great lies of the century, helped destroy whatever possibilities there might have been for a resurgence of serious radicalism in America. Isn't that harm enough?"

What were we supposed to defend, William Phillips of *Par-*

tisan Review, himself an ex-Communist, asks. "Some *were* Communists, and what one was asked to defend was their right to lie about it."

The message of Lillian Hellman, says Hilton Kramer of the New York *Times*, is rendered in "*soigné* prose," causing one to wonder if one ought to be less sensitive than Khrushchev in denouncing the work of his predecessor. But it was Providence that provided the epilogue, the ironic masterstroke. Lillian Hellman, best-selling author of the diatribe against the Hollywood moguls who discriminated against her after she was identified as a Communist apologist. When Miss Hellman finally brought herself to criticize the Soviet Union, she singled out for special scorn Soviet censorship. *"The semi-literate bureaucrats, who suppress and alter manuscripts, who dictate who can and cannot be published, perform a disgusting business."* And lo! the publishers of Miss Hellman's book, Little, Brown, instruct Diana Trilling to alter an essay on Miss Hellman in her manuscript. Mrs. Trilling declines, and Little, Brown breaks the contract—does its best, in effect, to suppress her book. "Miss Hellman is one of our leading successful authors," said Arthur Thornhill, president of Little, Brown. "She's not one of the big so-called money makers, but she's up there where we enjoy the revenue." The principled Miss Hellman, who condemns Hollywood for its base concern for profit, has not severed her relations with Little, Brown, never mind that they sought to suppress and alter a manuscript—in deference to *her*! But, don't you see, the vertebral column of her thought finally emerges. *She* can do no wrong. *"There is nothing in my life of which I am ashamed,"* she wrote to the chairman of the House Committee on Un-American Activities, setting herself, by that sentence, in a class apart from her fellow mortals. Well, it took a long time for her to learn about Communism. She is elderly, but there is time yet, time to recognize that she should be ashamed of this awful book.

Tail Gunner Joe

February 24, 1977

IN THE LATE Fifties, Richard Rovere published a book on the late Senator Joe McCarthy which was greeted as deliriously as Lillian Hellman's recent book, *Scoundrel Time*, the implicit thesis of which is that anybody who thought ill of Josef Stalin before she did, which was some time after he died, was, well, a scoundrel. Rovere's book was called "a brilliant essay in contemporary history" by Professor Arthur Schlesinger, Jr., "one of the most distinguished political documents of the year" by Eric Goldman, and, by Walter Lippmann himself, "the definitive job . . . I can't imagine what else there is to say about him."

In that book, published seventeen years before the networks thought to come up with a dramatization of the Joe McCarthy story, the resourceful Mr. Rovere found Senator McCarthy "a cheap politician" "a guttersnipe" "a seditionist" "a crook" "a foul-mouthed bum" "a mucker" "a liar" "a ranter" "a screamer" "a faker" "an ogre" and "a rattlesnake." Reviewing that book in England, Mr. Evelyn Waugh judged it favorably, but confessed to some misgivings about certain uncompleted bits of narrative. What actually had happened to McCarthy's victims? "There is a curious raggedness . . . in the accounts of the various inquiries which seem to have ended without findings and of the various men who appear and disappear in the story without acquittal or prosecution. What happened to everyone? I wish Mr. Rovere would re-write the book for us ignorant islanders giving us the simple story. We can make the comments."

I wrote to Mr. Waugh at the time and told him that if he was concerned to know such facts, I would send them to him, but I warned that they would distract from the unleavened judgment of McCarthyism in which the Western world basked; and which now, with the television spectacular "Tail Gunner Joe," has been revived. He wrote and asked for the material, and I sent him the book written by Mr. Brent Bozell and me in 1954 called *McCarthy and His Enemies*.

In due course he acknowledged it: "McCarthy is certainly regarded by most Englishmen as a regrettable figure and your *McCarthy and His Enemies*, being written before his later extravagances, will not go far to clear his reputation. I have no doubt that we were sent a lot of prejudiced information six years ago. [I.e., at the height of the McCarthy era.] Your book makes plain that there was a need for investigation ten years ago. It does not, I am afraid, supply the information that will convince me that McCarthy was a suitable man to undertake it. Rovere makes a number of precise charges against his personal honor. Until these are rebutted, those who are sympathetic with his cause must deplore his championship of it."

This, of course, is the crucial point now that anti-McCarthyism has become, once again, the rage. The thrust of the television spectacular was that McCarthy was a mountebank. And indeed by the rules of logic Mr. Waugh could be correct. It could transpire that the anti-McCarthy legend based on his role and the government's in the matter of internal security is altogether false—and still it could stand that McCarthy died of drink, cheated on his taxes, lied in his election campaigns, malingered in the marines—that he was, in Mr. Rovere's elegant word, a Rattlesnake.

But of course, these distinctions are not being observed. There is no significant discussion of Owen Lattimore in "Tail Gunner Joe," none of the successful lengths to which the Communist propaganda machine had gone in convincing such as Lillian Hellman that Stalin who presided over the show trials was a hero, and John Dewey who accused him of staging the trials, a scoundrel. During the Fifties, the Soviet Union consolidated its hold on Eastern Europe, the Chinese Communists theirs on the mainland, our atomic secrets were stolen and exploited, a small group of American Stalinists mounted a major political movement under the titular leadership of Henry Wallace; and now, looking back on the Fifties, NBC devotes itself to the character of Joe McCarthy. It is more than a great cop-out. It is a grand feint. And the most pathetic victims of it are those who write so exultantly about "Tail Gunner Joe."

Mr. John Leonard of the New York *Times*, reviewing the television spectacular, writes that during the McCarthy years "we seemed willing to believe that there were more Communists—in the army, in the clergy, in the State Department, in the glove compartments of our cars—than there were Americans. Books were burned and teachers were fired and writers went to jail and intellectuals cultivated their own gardens..."

Now those readers so unfortunate as not to be familiar with the work of Mr. Leonard should know at least this about him, that Tom Wolfe aside, he is the funniest writer in America, the hottest epigrammatist in the language, with a sense of irony the equal of Murray Kempton's, a prose rich as Rimsky-Korsakov—but he suffers from a sad failure quite to connect with reality, notwithstanding a precocious flirtation with conservatism in his early twenties. Hyperbole is one of his wonderful strengths. "One can't disagree that We the People made McCarthy," he writes, "any more than one can disagree with the proposition that death is sad or that sex is less so. But are such pious observations very helpful? On television, there is no shortage of natural gas."

Ah, our tortured poets! But those who believe that Mr. Leonard's delirium is a particular disease have forgotten the history of the era, where the excesses were far less McCarthy's, than his critics'. In those days there actually convened in plenipotentiary sessions six professors at Haverford who dubbed themselves "The Unterrified," and plotted how to rescue America from McCarthy. And there was of course the rabbi who preached that the student panty-raids were the result of the internalization of student exuberance caused by the Terror. There were those wonderful attempts at openmindedness, of which my favorite remains the Dalton School's response to a girl who complained that McCarthy's side had not once been given. In the spirit of free inquiry, the dean thereupon scheduled a debate on the topic, "Resolved, That McCarthy's Un-American Activities are Justified."

Lord Bertrand Russell actually said that McCarthy had made it unsafe for Americans to read Thomas Jefferson. Mr. Robert

Hutchins actually said that so cowed were we all by McCarthy that it took courage to contribute support to Harvard University (where Mr. Leonard was incompletely educated—could it have been the shortage of funds caused by McCarthy?).

McCarthy, up through the Tydings investigation which gave him the notoriety off which "Tail Gunner Joe" coasts, named—and only when required to do so by the Tydings Committee—a total of forty-four persons, whom with a single exception (Owen Lattimore) he designated as loyalty risks.

The writers who went to jail are the Hollywood Ten, for committing exactly the same offense for which Judge Sirica sentenced Gordon Liddy to twenty years in jail, getting for himself in return the Man of the Year award from *Time* Magazine: contempt of a duly constituted government board of inquiry. The loudest protestor, Mr. Dalton Trumbo, subsequently revealed *sua sponte* that, what do you know, he had indeed been a member of the Communist Party during the period under investigation.

If anyone undertook today to write a screenplay about the fraternity of teachers, intellectuals, and writers who smeared as fascists or warmongers anyone in America who criticized Josef Stalin, railed against the Hitler-Stalin Pact, defended the innocent at the purge trials, denounced the repatriation of 16 million East Europeans to their death in Soviet camps—that play would likely not be produced. And if by chance it were, it would either be *ho-hummed* to death, or rigorously denounced, probably as McCarthyite. It is more fun to laugh with Woody Allen at those Americans who resented the greatest diplomatic reversal in human history than to wonder, darkly, about the extent to which we were responsible for the Gulag Archipelago.

Let those who amuse themselves by asking that McCarthy be judged by the deficiencies in his character get on with it—this is after all the season for judging Thomas Jefferson on the basis of the mulattoes he sired. But in the process, we are coming very close to judging the decade of the Fifties as one in which the great moral divide was between the McCarthyites and the apologists for the Soviet Union. The substantial anti-McCarthyite, anti-Stalinist liberals received such disdainful treatment as was awarded them in the Lillian Hellman book—

which is historically, morally, and intellectually destroyed by Professor Sidney Hook in the current issue of London's *Encounter* magazine. There were some foolish things done and said by McCarthy and some of his supporters during the Fifties. But they cannot hold a candle up against the continuing excesses of McCarthy's critics.

I remember Paul Hughes

March 5, 1977

I HAD RESOLVED to give up for Lent any mention of Paul Hughes now that we have been catapulted back into a general discussion of the McCarthy years. But this proves impossible now that I have seen a statement by Mr. Alfred Friendly, retired managing editor of the Washington *Post*, indignantly denying any wrongdoing in his association with Paul Hughes. The Hughes story is probably the single most embarrassing thing that happened in the Fifties to the liberal Establishment. The success of their subsequent cover-up is the kind of thing Nixon dreams about in his prison at San Clemente. Mr. Friendly, in his reminiscences about the McCarthy years, notes that the "best book" ever written about McCarthy is Richard Rovere's (*Senator Joe McCarthy*, 1959). When *National Review* exposed the Hughes case in 1956, the editors teased the court historians for failing to write about it. Mr. Rovere replied huffily, "I agree . . . that the Hughes case is full of import. I know that I shall deal with the Hughes case in [my forthcoming book]." But Paul Hughes was not mentioned in the book.

Paul Hughes was a young confidence man. He represented himself, in 1953, to Joseph L. Rauh, Jr., the civil rights lawyer; to Clayton Fritchey, then editor of the official journal of the Democratic Party; and to Alfred Friendly, representing the Washington *Post*, as a disaffected member of Senator Joe

McCarthy's Senate staff, willing to feed Rauh, Friendly, *et al.* confidential information about McCarthy. Rauh's opposition to secret informers vanished overnight, and there was cranked up surely the strangest transmission belt in modern history, establishing a credulousness among top American liberals that would make John Birchers blush.

He gave them "evidence" of a secret alliance between Eisenhower and McCarthy; of tantalizing rivalries between the staffs of the Internal Security Committee and the McCarthy Committee; of imminent plans to enter into forbidden communication with Igor Gouzenko, the Soviet defector in Canada; of marital problems developing between Senator and Mrs. McCarthy; of a clandestine White House conference at which a smear campaign against the Demcoratic Party was programmed; of McCarthy's informers in the White House, in the Louisville *Courier-Journal*, in the New York *Post* (the cooking editor); excruciating teasers about informants whose identity had not been disclosed; and (my very favorite) news that Senator McCarthy had amassed an arsenal of pistols, Lügers, and submachine guns in the basement of the Senate Office Building. All this wrapped up in a chaotic package of notes, official memoranda, interoffice communications, secret transcripts, some illiterate, some eloquent, always steaming with drama and emitting a sex appeal irresistible to the professional anti-McCarthyites.

Now this association continued with, and a sum of almost $11,000 was paid over to, a man who had written what nowadays might be called a premature Huston Plan. The memo dated December 1953, from Paul Hughes to Clayton Fritchey, prepared for Joseph Rauh, said: "Phone taps can be utilized [against McCarthy] . . . Don't discount the tremendous values in just bargaining power of recorded phone discussions . . . A program of this type, although not nice, can result in harm to no one except [McCarthy] . . . As mentioned earlier, being nice, too ethical, or squeamish, will accomplish less than nothing . . . I don't see the necessity for us to send a boy to do a man's work."

Eventually, after *nine months* of association, on the eve of publishing the definitive exposé of McCarthy, researchers for the Washington *Post* went to work and discovered that the whole thing was a phony. There was a trial: at which the jury refused to take the word of Hughes's employers, freeing him and disgracing them. But you won't read about it in the history books, let alone see it dramatized in "Tail Gunner Joe." (You can, however, get the whole story in "The Case of the Secret Informer, *or*, The Terrible Disappointment of Joseph L. Rauh," *NR*, Feb. 8, 1956.) I say it again, the story of McCarthy cannot be told without telling the infinitely more complex story of his enemies.

Commemorating Paul Robeson

February 14, 1976

THE DEATH of Paul Robeson was widely noticed, and his accomplishments, as an athlete, young lawyer, singer and actor, widely remarked. Then there was, to be sure, that other business. Here is how *Time* magazine handled it. ". . . Always he felt hemmed in by the constraints upon blacks. . . . In the mid-1940's and 1950's, he was an outspoken champion of civil rights. He moved for a time to the Soviet Union where he thought that blacks had more freedom and where he sent his only son to school. Condemned at home in the McCarthy era as an admirer of the Soviet Union and a friend of Communism, Robeson went into a clouded decline from which he never emerged. Stricken by a circulatory ailment in 1963, he spent his last years in seclusion . . ."

Now the editors of *Time*, who are high practitioners of literary precision, know that the clause, "Condemned at home in the McCarthy era as an admirer of the Soviet Union and a friend of Communism," is intended to denote a fuller understanding than the mere words convey. The statement is intended to be read, "[Falsely] condemned at home in the [hysterical] McCarthy era as an admirer of the Soviet Union and a friend of Communism [which of course he wasn't]"—and it makes one muse ruefully that Senator McCarthy never attempted in his lifetime as much historical revisionism as some of his detractors commit in his name.

Now take Robeson. In 1947, he earned $104,000, singing and acting in America. In 1948, the great decline began. All of America stopped listening. "But for the $30,000 he got for a 1949 concert tour in England, he really might have starved to death," Carl Rowan wrote in the late 1950's, interviewing Robeson.

Now, what happened in 1948? Did Joe McCarthy eat Mrs. Roosevelt? Did he call Shirley Temple a Communist? Did he demand that anyone who defended civil rights for Negroes should be banned from the recital halls of the nation?

No, as a matter of fact. In 1948 Senator McCarthy was totally unknown, a junior senator from Wisconsin who was poking around the edges of one or two controversies, none of them related to Communism. But here is what *did* happen in 1948. The Soviet Union staged a coup in mid-day, collapsing the freedom of Czechoslovakia, for which freedom the British, in 1938 and 1939, promised to fight if necessary by war.

In 1948 the fury of Stalin's purges was becoming known in the West, as defectors wrote about life under his terror. In 1948, crucial atom bomb secrets were delivered to Russia by Soviet agents. In America, the Communist Party mounted a Presidential candidate, dubbed by Mrs. Luce as "Stalin's Mortimer Snerd." By the time the vote came, Henry Wallace was so discredited for his obvious manipulation by Moscow that he got the vote of a mere handful of people.

Senator McCarthy began his notoriety in Wheeling, West Virginia, in 1950. By that time, Robeson was already a pariah in America.

Because of his outspoken championship of civil rights?

Robeson never cared for civil rights in general. He was prophetically right in denouncing Jim Crow. He said he desired civil rights for American Negroes. But it cannot even be assumed that there was a genuine purity in his attachment to black rights, for all his talk about his identification with black people everywhere in the world. Because when such African states as he praised—Ghana, in particular—systematically denied civil rights to their black citizens, there was no protest from Robeson.

Robeson was, quite simply, a Communist fellow-traveler, whose service to the Soviet Union began in the mid-Thirties, who took his son there to school in the late Thirties, who accepted a Peace Prize from Stalin in 1952, who denied in 1946 that he was a Communist but a year later invoked the Fifth Amendment when asked the question again; who was denied a passport when Dean Acheson was Secretary of State—Acheson being the premier anti-McCarthyite in government; who, even when the State Department authorized him to visit Canada, was denied entrance into Canada.

In 1963, a Reuters dispatch from London reported rumors "that the singer would give up Communism." These were denied by Robeson.

Contributions to *Time*'s morgue will be gratefully received.

Honoring Linus Pauling

September 30, 1975

THE BOSTON *Globe* is positively shimmering with pleasure over the award given by President Ford to Professor Linus Pauling. The writers call their editorial "Tardy Honor," and they speak in it of the belated recognition by the President of Dr. Pauling's "contribution to society" which goes "further than his accomplishments in either chemistry or politics."

Why was the honor belated?

Because Dr. Pauling "was considered a dangerous radical—a Communist sympathizer, even—by such authorities as Senator Joseph McCarthy, Herbert A. Philbrick, Louis Budenz and William Buckley."

My dear friends on the Boston *Globe* have never before referred to me so matter-of-factly as an "authority," and I really do appreciate it. But candor requires that I share the honor, however belatedly, with others.

In 1961, the Senate's Internal Security Subcommittee issued an extensive report on the activities of Linus Pauling. The report concluded: "Dr. Pauling has figured as the No. 1 scientific name in virtually every major activity of the Communist peace offensive in this country. He has participated in many international organizations and international conferences sponsored by the Communist peace offensive. In his statements and his attitudes, Dr. Pauling has displayed a consistent pro-Soviet bias."

That report was accepted unanimously by: Senators James Eastland, Estes Kefauver, Olin Johnson, John McClellan, Sam Ervin, John Carroll, Thomas Dodd, Philip Hart, Edward Long, William Blakely, Alexander Wiley, Everett Dirksen, Roman Hruska, Kenneth Keating, Norris Cotton.

The editors of the Herald Tribune also should share in the honor. In an editorial in the 1960's they said "The Linus Paulings of the world have . . . made themselves not only nuisances, but dangerous nuisances." *Life* magazine's editors also deserve credit. When the Nobel Committee gave Pauling its peace prize, the editors denounced the choice as "A Weird Insult from Norway."

In New York alone, the *Wall Street Journal, The World Telegram and Sun,* the *Daily Mirror,* and the *Daily News* remarked similarly on the activities of Linus Pauling. And it wasn't just Americans who were authorities on Linus Pauling's activities. The Australian Consolidated Press during that period said about him that though no one doubted his scientific ability, in fact "he is the very model of the fellow-traveler of the type who willingly adds respectability to Communist frauds. He signs Communist petitions, he speaks from Communist platforms, he has his speeches published by Communist presses. He has, however, never been heard to say one word of criticism . . . of Soviet terrorism or of the lack of freedom for Soviet scientists."

The Court of Appeals in New York upheld a jury verdict for the New York *Daily News*, sued by Linus Pauling for calling him a Communist sympathizer. Judge Friendly, in his opinion, said in effect that surveying the evidence a jury could reasonably conclude that Dr. Pauling was that: a Communist sympathizer.

We authorities on the subject were influenced by Pauling's organizational affiliations, of course, but also by other things. By his telegram to President Kennedy denouncing Kennedy's Cuban missile crisis ultimatum as "horrifying," "recklessly militaristic," "warlike." We noticed it when he said about President Truman, for deciding to proceed with nuclear testing as necessary, that Truman was "irrational, ignorant or unscrupulous, or any combination of each." And we noticed the telegram he sent to President Kennedy on March 3, 1962, denouncing him for resuming nuclear testing after the Soviets resumed theirs: "Are you to go down in history as one of the most immoral men of all times and one of the greatest enemies of the human race?" And Pauling's support of M. S. Arnoni's publication which compared President Kennedy adversely to Hitler, and described Kennedy as a "bully who knows himself to be a bully."

The Boston *Globe*, which gave its readers the impression that President Ford was righting great historical wrongs against Dr. Pauling, did not bother to give the citation on the Medal of Science, so this authority on Linus Pauling called down to the White House and got it. It reads, in its entirety: "To Linus C. Pauling, for the extraordinary scope and power of his imagination, which has led to basic contributions in such diverse fields as structural chemistry and the nature of chemical bonding, molecular biology, immunology, and the nature of genetic diseases." If President Ford gives William Schockley one of those Science Medals, will the *Globe* write that this vindicates his genetic theses?

A Tory's Tribute to Hubert Horatio Humphrey

December 1977

WHAT IS HAPPENING to Hubert Humphrey is unparalleled in my memory. The apocalyptic word was used by the doctors after his latest operation—he suffered from a "terminal" illness. In what seemed no time at all, he reappeared on the public scene. Scooped up from the clinic by Air Force One, he was to find the entire nation celebrating him like Lindbergh come home. A huge new federal building was named after him. The House of Representatives invited him over from the Senate to give a speech—unprecedented in congressional annals—and he came, occupying the podium used by Presidents of the United States when addressing joint sessions of Congress. He was visibly withered by his experience at the clinics, but otherwise he was unchanged. The same horizon-to-horizon smile, the twinkle in the eyes, the unabashed reference to his longtime ambition to occupy the podium *ex officio*. He was cheered as lustily as anyone in memory, cheered by everyone, on both sides of the aisle, notwithstanding that he has political enemies on both sides—a few on the Democratic side, everyone on the Republican side. It did not matter. There was the familiarity of the figure. His renowned good nature. The tear-drawing physical heroism. The indomitable cheerfulness.

Moreover, the tribute was for a man as partisan as ever sat in the Senate. But it didn't—doesn't—matter. It is worth asking why. To do so requires examining the ideological and intellectual opposition to Senator Humphrey, his works and his ways, if we are to plumb the deepest of the mysteries: How is it that *we* feel this way about him?

We write, all of us, on the assumption that Hubert Humphrey is going down. It is, of course, possible; indeed, in the larger context, probable. All of us who visit the doctor after a certain age do so to frustrate, but only temporarily, a degenerative ineluctability. It is so even for Hubert Horatio Humphrey. The only political promise he neglected to make to his constituencies—and he speaks nowadays to the grandchildren of those he addressed back when he was running for mayor of Minneapolis—was that a vote for the Democratic Party would bring eternal youth.

But having said that, a proper skepticism is in order respecting Hubert Humphrey. He may frustrate the laws of probability, yet again; and surely there is nobody in the world better practiced than he at defying the laws of logic—that being, of course, his profession; and, I assume, not an inconsiderable reason for his appeal. To exercise the politics of joy, it is required to release one's constituency from the depressing restraints of reality and reason.

Dear Lord, you must understand when—many years hence we all devoutly hope—your servant Hubert appears before you that he is *different* from most of your creatures. Deal kindly with him, on the Day of Judgment, and above all, do not instruct the registrar to read back to you any of Hubert's political speeches. We are dimly aware, down here, of the divine tension between the demands of mercy and justice. But so help me, God, if you listen to one of his speeches, the demands of justice are going to get the better of you. And although I am a Tory, born and bred, with absolutely no ambitions to transcend that estate, I do not wish, for Hubert Humphrey, exemplary justice. I will try to explain.

The last coast-to-coast speech by Senator Humphrey was delivered at Madison Square Garden, on July 13, 1976, to the Democratic National Convention gathered together to nominate Jimmy Carter as candidate for President of the United States. The night before had been opening night, with several speeches, the first by keynoter John Glenn. Concerning that speech, the less said the better. One might call it (indeed, on the occasion, one did) "Senator Glenn without Houston Control." Democratic choreographers, clearly worried about the prospective ratings after reading the text of Senator Glenn's speech, scheduled their oratorical Big Bertha, Barbara Jordan. She was airborne by her native eloquence, which is lucky—because for all that the lady stirred the Convention, in fact she had nothing to say, never mind that, when she was done, everyone cooed that here had been a "great oration" (almost everyone's evaluation, including Barry Goldwater's).

I would be surprised if anybody, an hour later, could have written a fifty-word précis of what Mrs. Jordan said with such rapture. But she used with abandon one of the Senator's favorite rhetorical devices, namely paralepsis, with which Hubert Humphrey, the sometime graduate student in political science, is no doubt formally familiar. "I could easily spend this time praising the accomplishments of this party and attacking the record of the Republicans. I do not choose to do that," said Mrs. Jordan, proceeding to do exactly, and lengthily, that. The television cameras focused on Senator Humphrey, seated in his box, beaming. His beam was required over a very long evening, but it did not begin to tax his reserves—Hubert Humphrey could have beamed, start to finish, through the Hundred Years War.

George Wallace had a speech to make, in which he denounced the "monstrous bureaucracy" in Washington that had recently forbidden a father-son dinner at one of HEW's pads, on the grounds that such exclusivity violated the rights of women. Hubert Humphrey was pensive during that one—his jaw resting in his right palm, the striated fingers of wisdom partially covering mouth and cheek. On and on. Jerry Wurf spoke about the need to enfranchise civil servants, and Humphrey nodded his head in solemn assent. Edmund Muskie spoke about the need to "say yes to fair labor standards" as if everywhere in America man was in chains. Barbara Jordan's central point—not entirely unfamiliar to students of political oratory—was that the great American people are possessed of great common sense. This they demonstrated that evening. The Nielsen raters the following day disclosed matter-of-factly that the great Democratic spectacle, covered by all three networks, reached fewer Americans in the New York area than the film *Casablanca*, shown for the tenth time on an independent channel, and filmed in 1942, about the time that Hubert Humphrey, who would be featured on the following night, was deciding to give up academic studies in order to enter politics.

Tuesday evening, as I say, was Hubert Humphrey's. It was generally assumed by the crowd that he would do his very best, which, under the aspect of the heavens, is of course his very worst. From time to time acrid political commentators are inclined to say, after a bad experience, that *this, "surely,"* ranked as the "worst speech" in "political history." No one, of course, can pretend to the requisite experience to say such a thing with authority. About Hubert Humphrey's speech on July 13 one could only say that it was so triumphantly awful that he reached the darker partisan heart of his audience, who gave him a standing ovation.

"Do you know how I became mayor of Minneapolis?"—Hubert Humphrey twinkled the technique a generation ago to a former fellow graduate student at a cocktail party. "He spoke *delightedly* on the subject," my professor-friend recalls, without any trace of irritation, let alone condescension. He quoted Humphrey. "Well, I spoke *every* Saturday, and *every* Sunday, at the parks in Minneapolis—there are lots of parks in Minneapolis, you know. And, after the crowd would gather, I would pick up the microphone, and I'd begin to talk. Then—suddenly—I'd stop. And I'd say: 'Wait a minute. Wait a *minute*, I want to see the kids here up front. They're the future of the nation, folks, let's face it, *your* kids. Now come on up here. Don't be shy! That's it . . . right up front, sit down and make yourselves comfortable. Right. Now, as I was saying. . . . But I have to say *something else* first. You know, I've been around. I know the great state of Minnesota the way few folks know the state of Minnesota. But I know other states of the Union too, and let me tell you something, ladies and gentlemen: these kids here have got to be the *most* beautiful, the most *wonderful*-looking, the *healthiest* kids I have ever seen . . . *anywhere!'*

"The parents," Humphrey exclaimed to his friend, "would look up at me . . . *adoringly*! Then you know what?"—he put his arm over the professor's back—"*Later* in the *same* afternoon, speaking to *another* audience, at *another* park, at *another* end of the city, I would say . . . *exactly the same thing*!" The miracle of the multiplication of the loaves!

I doubt that anyone in the days ahead will devote much attention to a textual analysis of Hubert Humprey's speeches. It would be an unfriendly thing to do, and infinitely unprofitable. And, of course, it would miss the point about Humphrey, the point being that he is a great human figure (like Eleanor Roosevelt), never mind that if any civil constitution should ever be written as a congeries of deductions from Humphrey's Laws, the citizenry would all be smiling at each other in a federal zoo that disdained to distinguish between a mole and a giraffe.

At Madison Square Garden—as I say, his most recent coast-to-coast political oration—he began with that brazen defiance of reason that levitates an audience by vacuuming off all sense of reality. What Senator Humphrey said, at the Democratic Convention after the one that nominated for President a Democrat who proceeded to lose every state in the Union save Massachusetts—what he said, referring to the forthcoming election, was: "And once again, [after Carter's victory] the American people will have a friend in the White House, and majority government will have been restored." The sweep of such presumptuousness is its indispensable yeast. It is like the meeting of a Communist International at which the keynote speaker begins by saying, "As everyone knows, the United States is the last surviving imperialist power on earth." It has always been indispensable to Humphrey-the-orator that distinctions, qualifiers, taxonomic niceties, must *never* stand in the way of the Main Purpose. Hubert Humphrey has *never* been publicly distracted by mere events. The San Francisco fire would not have interrupted a tribute by Humphrey to California fire laws. He is out of this world.

But insufficiently so, as we see, with ineffable grief, the workings of the mortal coils, transfiguring his physical image.

No, nothing publicly disturbed Humbert Humphrey's famous equilibrium, in sickness or in health. Even his famous walk-out in the 1948 Convention seems rhythmic, in retrospect. And then twenty years later, late on the Saturday night before the tumultuous Convention in Chicago that finally nominated him for President, Humphrey appeared on the "Irv Kupcinet Show." The show had been taped. In the course of elaborating to Kupcinet the great triumphs of President Johnson's foreign policy in Europe—never mind for a moment the problem of Vietnam—Vice-President Humphrey said happily that, just for example, the East European nations were by now "relatively autonomous." Unhappily, between the time Humphrey spoke those words and the time, one week later, that they were broadcast, the Soviet union sent tanks into Prague to dispose, for good and all, of any autonomous blooms of the Czechoslovakian spring.

When Mr. Humphrey became Vice-President, he had campaigned on the Atlantic City Democratic platform. "We pledge unflagging devotion to our commitments to freedom from Berlin to South Vietnam." A few days after the Kupcinet show, in the debris of Chicago, Hubert Humphrey managed, with consummate skill, to address successfully the Convention, one-half of which had wanted to nominate Eugene McCarthy, on the Vietnam War. The shadow on his right was President Lyndon Johnson, whose inflexibility on the subject of Vietnam had been validated by a parliamentary majority of the Convention after bitter debate. Without Johnson's support, Candidate Humphrey would never make it to the White House. The shadow on his left was Eugene McCarthy. Without propitiating him and his followers, Humphrey would never make it to the White House.

The performance was superb. Candidate Humphrey got his biggest cheers by insisting he would devote himself to ending the war in Vietnam. What he actually said about his devotion to peace in Vietnam wasn't anything different from what Candidate Nixon—or, for that matter, Superhawk Barry Goldwater—would have said. But Humphrey said it with inflections so wonderfully, so endearingly acquiescent to the shadow on his left, that he succeeded in appearing to draw over his stout shoulders the lonely cloak of righteousness, thus giving the impression that he spoke for the desolate minority, against the obdurate majority. When, listening to his oration, one began to ask oneself, might he be annoying, irritating, that unforgiving shadow on his right?—somehow he would manage a compensating inflection, something on the order of "winning is not worth a compact with extremism," being careful not to identify extremism (let Gene McCarthy think he was talking about Mayor Daley, and let LBJ think he was talking about Gene McCarthy).

But Hubert Humphrey, privately, is no more immune to the irritations of the season than his body is to the impartial appetites of the runaway, roustabout human cell. It was about a year later that ex-President Lyndon Johnson, in one of those exclusive interviews with CBS, said to Walter Cronkite that in Johnson's opinion Humphrey had lost the Presidency by "backing down" on Vietnam in his speech in October at Salt Lake City. A colleague of Humphrey, who had been with him that evening listening together to LBJ, later quoted Hubert's private reaction. It was colorful, definitely not for Kupcinet's show, most definitely not right for a speech to a Democratic National Convention. Turning off the switch, Humphrey said heatedly to his friend, "I really wish I *was* President. Because if I *was*, I'd dispatch the Israeli Army to Cairo to pick up Cleopatra's Needle, take it to Johnson City, and stuff it up the biggest ass-hole in Texas." One always suspected that Hubert's red corpuscles were exercised other than by the universal need for more jobs, better housing, better health care, and equal treatment under the law.

Hubert's animadversions have almost always been general, rather than private. To speak about Republican scoundrels was always easier on his good nature than to speak about individual Republican scoundrels. Fighting for his political future against George McGovern in the California primary in June 1972, Humphrey began their public debate with an apology. Earlier in the week, he explained, he had said that people who believe in confiscatory taxation are foolish. On reflection, he feared that some people would think that he had said his colleague George McGovern was a "fool." Such people would be wrong, and if he had given them that impression, he wanted here and now to "apologize." Political exchanges are not models of syllogistic form. Granted that in a classroom, Professor Humphrey would have been obliged to put it this way: (1) People who believe in confiscatory taxation are fools. (2) George McGovern believes in confiscatory taxation. Therefore, (3) George McGovern is a fool.

But Hubert Humphrey's career has been spent in ignoring the mute reproaches of logic. In September 1968, Candidate Humphrey intoned before a convention of the B'nai B'rith that Nixon had chosen to join forces with "the most reactionary elements in American society," by which he meant George Wallace, whose third-party candidacy was impinging on Humphrey's Democratic support. One year earlier, Vice-President Humphrey had been photographed arm-in-arm with Governor Lester Maddox in Atlanta, Georgia. On that occasion he had said, "The Democratic Party is like a big house and has lots of room for all of us. I am happy to be in the presence of a good Democrat."

And so on, year after year, sponsoring a bill to outlaw the Communist Party in 1954, expressing himself as devoted, to the end, to South Vietnamese freedom in 1968, preparatory to saying in 1972 that he was in favor of cutting off the South Vietnamese "flat" because they were "in my judgment" "capable of their own defense." When the need would come to dodge on an issue, as in the California primary on the question of busing, he would say deprecatingly that busing "is only *one* of the many tools to effect integration," which was to say something as illuminating as that paper is only one of the constituents of pornography.

Ah, but that final speech at Madison Square Garden, when Hubert Humphrey, having lost the primaries to Jimmy Carter, must have reasoned—his physical health aside—that he had had his last crack at the Presidency. But he would rouse the Convention, after the torpor of Monday night. First, as we have seen, he denied the democratic credentials of the incumbent Administration, which required merely that his audience ignore an electoral victory of 521 to 17. Then he would find just-the-right-word for the Republicans in power, taking care to make no mention that the legislature, which passed all the bills, and spent all the money, and caused all the inflation, was solidly Democratic. He found a new word, or at least one I had not heard him use before. They were . . . "Tories."

"These modern Tories repudiate the magnificent legacy of Andrew Jackson and Woodrow Wilson; of Franklin Roosevelt and Harry Truman; of John Kennedy and Lyndon Johnson.

"There was no room for the Tories in Philadelphia in 1776. And I say there is no room for them in New York in 1976 or in Washington, D.C. in 1977!"

I know, I know. You know. *He* knows. The Tories in Philadelphia, *mutatis mutandis*, were the people who wrote the Constitution. But what does that matter, when the clamor of the crowd rings in the ear, when you know they will shout We Love Hubert! and the band will play, and everyone will rush to congratulate him. "That was a great speech!" the television viewer heard Bob Strauss, National Democratic Chairman, say. Perhaps Strauss had been singularly moved by Herbert Humphrey's passage, "After eight years of phases, freezes, and failure, of start-ups and slow-downs, of high prices and fewer jobs, we are still being asked 'just a little more time and patience.' Go slow, not now, no, no, veto—this is the Republican theme. This is their policy. Well, we've had enough of this defeatism!"

Ah, that causes the analytical blood to tingle with excitement!

Or was it the peroration?

"America looks to new leaders who can make our country both dynamic and just, who have a sense of compassion, but also dedication to individual initiative—leaders who can inspire and are inspired by our history, but who sense that our greatness is in the future.

"America's best days—America's great days—have only just begun!"

They speak about those marvelous new machines that one day will identify each one of us as surely as if they possessed our fingerprints, by scanning a stretch of prose. Hubert's will be unmistakable. Such prose as sets up dynamism and justice as dissonant, let alone antithetical; as suggests that compassion and initiative are disjunctive human impulses . . .

But how futile is the exercise, when we are engaged, in fact, in trying to console ourselves against the inconsolable reality, which is that this preposterous man, this man of majestic intellectual imprecision, this demagogue of transcendent gall, may not be with us forever. What is it about him that causes this sadness to well up, even in those Tories he has sought so diligently to exile?

I confess I do not have the answer. There are emotions—and quite properly so, is a Tory insight—that defy the taxonomic enterprise. Why do we care for him so? Why does his Las Vegas smile in fact light up the room? Why do we sit down and do our knitting, and let our eyeglasses slide down our nose, permit ourselves to smile—when Hubert is on TV, saying all those silly things? Why, when you talk to him, is there that inexplicable rise in human temperature, that makes *you* want to smile, like a blithering Democratic idiot making time at Madison Square Garden? Could it be that all that talk about civil rights and health care and old people and employment and slums and decent housing and nursery care and good education has, imperceptibly, but no less surely, sensitized the public conscience? So that we . . . *feel* more strongly than we used to do before Hubert called us to sit in the front row, and told us we were positively the prettiest children in town—and feel more keenly that concern for each other which, although it was enjoined by Jesus without cosmetics, lights, bands, or Potomac fever, never occupies us as devoutly as it should—is *that* what we love him for?

My experiences with him have been few, but one of them presses the memory. The forward compartment of the Pan Am 747 was very nearly empty. I think there were only eight or ten of us, but when the movie went on there was palpable excitement, because it was to be *The French Connection*, and we unhappy few hadn't seen it. What came on the screen was a frozen oscilloscope of sorts. After several attempts to fix it, the chief stewardess pronounced her apologies—something was wrong with the machine. There is within me, notwithstanding a lifetime's effort to suppress it, an impulse to intrusive do-gooding which from time to time simply takes me over, so that before my wife could succeed in manacling me to the seat, there I was, advising the chief stewardess that if she would get a screwdriver, I would be glad to draw the curtain on the insides of the machine and see if I could not put things right. I did not tell her that a screwdriver in my hand is less useful than a computer in the hands of an aborigine. My unexplicated rule of thumb is that screwdrivers have numinous powers when applied to the tangled webs of technology.

But after I unscrewed the underside panel of the machine and shone the flashlight up on the workings of the projector, acutely conscious of my expectant audience, my heart sank. I stared, as I'd have done at rows of Chinese calligraphy, when the voice under me spoke. "Come on, Bill. Get out of the way. You reactionaries wouldn't know how to fix a broken wheel." I took the flashlight out of my mouth, slithered back down the large intestine of the machine, and handed the light, and the screwdriver, to Hubert Humphrey, until two years earlier Vice-President of the United States. Taking the flashlight, he slid up into the darkness with total confidence, and began to bark orders to me. Screwdriver. Pliers. Something long and thin—"like a giant needle." At my disposal now was the 747's vast tool box, and I strove to please.

In the course of an hour he asked for everything except a Scotch and soda, with which, in my position as apprentice, rump on the staircase, head inside the projection bulkhead, I consoled myself. Hubert chattered on endlessly, reading aloud the arcane instructions that surrounded the tortuous passage the 16-millimeter film declined to follow. Finally the stewardess told me that dinner was being served, and I bellowed the information up to the spelunker, who was chatting away about how, finally, he was confident he had located the difficulty. Eventually I announced that I was capitulating, but that the entire inventory of tools was now within his reach. "You go ahead and eat, Bill. I'll have this licked in a minute."

It was two hours later that, defeated, he climbed wearily down, and exuberantly attacked his cold dinner. But meanwhile I was distracted. The captain of the airship had sent down word: Would I care to witness an instrument landing? He was a fan, and was waiving the no-spectator rule. Excitedly, as the sun came down over London, I strapped myself into the little extra chair in the cockpit, to witness the great technological feat. We were on the final descent when the dialogue was interrupted by a knock. The engineer opened the door slightly, and there was—Hubert Humphrey. "I wonder," he said beaming, "would it be all right if I also peeked?" My wife had given out the word of my whereabouts, and Hubert Humphrey was not about to go through life admitting that he had never witnessed an instrument landing even though a Tory had done so. The situation, in the tight little cockpit, was socially embarrassing because there was no extra seat, and the effort to proffer my own was acrobatically impossible. "No no no no no. I'll just squat down right here." Which he did, and, together, we witnessed that workaday miracle, a 747 making a perfect touchdown under the guidance of electronic hands. My companion, they say, is headed for another touchdown, under the guidance of other hands, but they will look after him, I feel certain, and smile at his inability to fix the machine on the 747, merely one more in a long series of terrestrial failures, but God knows he tried.

David Niven Recreates Hollywood*

September 1975

THIS IS A BOOK about Hollywood and incidentally a masterful self-portrait. Inasmuch as what David Niven recalls is mostly what he saw, smelled, and tasted, you wonder, after putting it down, how he managed to bring it off without making it sound like a book starring David Niven produced by David Niven directed by David Niven from an original screenplay by David Niven. This does not happen because of a talent for self-effacement which is one of the many things Niven did not learn in Hollywood, the others being a resolute amiability and thoughtfulness. That talent serves him now as a pillar supporting what must easily be the best book ever written about

**Bring On the Empty Horses*. By David Niven. G.P. Putnam's Sons. New York, 1975.

Hollywood. A volume, moreover, that is not likely to be challenged on its own terms because there is no other survivor of the scene from 1935–1960 a) who knew everybody Niven knew and b) who can write the way Niven can write. He is a fine actor and comedian. He is an even better writer.

How does he manage to keep the focus away from himself? Watch. "One Fourth of July he [Douglas Fairbanks] and Sylvia chartered a motor cruiser and invited a small group, including Norma Shearer and Irving Thalberg, to sail with them to Catalina. The idea was to anchor on arrival alongside Cecil B. DeMille's sleek white three-masted schooner. Our captain had an ominous name—Jack Puke . . ." *Our* captain! Is there a neater way to all but inflect oneself right out of an episode?

Yet in ghosting himself out he limns, unconsciously, a portrait that superbly complements the hilarious autobiography of his youth, *The Moon's a Balloon*. One comes to know David Niven as one might one's brother; so to speak, by feel. Hear him again, writing—this time—about Cary Grant. "Through the years to come he made generous efforts to straighten out my private life by warning me of the quirks and peculiarities of various ladies, by giving me complicated advice on how to play a part in a film I was making with him, by telling me which stocks to buy when I could not afford a phone call to a broker, and by promising that he could cure my liking for Scotch by hypnotizing me." We have learned something about Cary Grant, and at least as much about David Niven.

A book for grown-ups about Hollywood and the lives of Hollywood stars? But the skepticism ends with the first chapter. There is a narrative tension from the beginning, and an ear for piquancy, an eye for the amusing and absurd and the poignant. The compulsion of the entertainer, in Niven's case a blend of exuberance, skill, and good manners (it is after all rude to be dull, if one knows how not to be), keeps the book moving like an Olsen and Johnson production. Even so, he will now and then defer to meticulous but illuminating detail. "He [Edmund Lowe] . . . drove me around the cozily named 'Back Lot'—a 200-acre spread upon which stood the permanent sets, including New York streets, New England, French, and Spanish villages, medieval castles, a railroad station complete with rolling stock, lakes with wave-making machines and rustic bridges, a university campus, an airliner, a section of jungle and another of pine forest, a Mississippi steamboat, a three-masted schooner, native canoes, a submarine, a stretch of desert with ruined fort and, in case anything was missing, several acres of carefully dismantled, docketed and stored streets, villages, cathedrals, mud huts, dance halls, skating rinks, ball parks, theaters, vineyards, slums, Southern plantations, and Oriental palaces."

Thus the paraphernalia of Hollywood. There is much more about the beast. A two-part chapter—he calls it "Our Little Girl," withholding from the reader, for once, the identity of the principal—describes the physical and psychic torture of stardom by giving two days in the life of one star, hour by hour, compressing a decade's exhilaration and decomposition as imaginatively and evocatively as Robert Nathan describing the evolution of a young girl in his *Portrait of Jennie*. David Niven has no illusions about the Hollywood that died in the late Fifties, even if he has not quite yet compounded an antidote to paganism. "[It] was hardly a nursery for intellectuals, it was a hotbed of false values, it harbored an unattractive percentage of small-time crooks and con artists, and the chances of being successful there were minimal, but it was fascinating, and IF YOU WERE LUCKY, it was fun." In a curious sense, David Niven continues to be starstruck, but the reader finds himself—caring. Not because the reader is involved in mankind, but because he actually finds himself involved in Errol Flynn! That makes David Niven something of a sorcerer.

Douglas Fairbanks furtively revealed to him his fear of growing old. George Sanders confided in 1937 that at age sixty-five he would commit suicide, which he did. Errol Flynn suggested the uses of just a touch of cocaine on the tip of the penis. Greta Garbo swam naked in his pool. (Their enduring friendship Niven is required modestly to concede, even as he describes her pathological fear of friendship, recalling Robert Montgomery's acid remark on being snubbed only weeks after co-starring with her, that "making a film with Garbo does not constitute an introduction.") Ronald Colman, noblesse oblige, speeded to his side in his launch and narrowly rescued him from a shark. Clark Gable began by giving him his catch to clean when Niven, broke, worked as a sportsfisherman's assistant—and was soon agitating to get him a screen test. Fred Astaire, a clumsy social dancer, ripped off a wild routine in his living room. Tyrone Power dressed as Santa Claus for his children. Miriam Hopkins acknowledged a Christmas gift of two handkerchiefs by giving him a Studebaker. Charlie Chaplin described in a throwaway paragraph how to contrive to make truly comic a fat lady approaching a banana peel. Charles MacArthur, resentful over the second-class status given by the big producers to writers, took revenge by elaborating to L. B. Mayer the fictitious talents of a London garage mechanic who happened to be entirely illiterate, and landing a thousand-dollar-a-week contract for him. Scott Fitzgerald was numb with gratitude when Niven matter-of-factly offered him the use of his refrigerator for the Coca-Colas Fitzgerald briefly besotted himself with while trying to exorcise demon rum . . .

The book teems with that kind of thing but the incidents are not carelessly catalogued, like a book of jokes by Bennett Cerf. Some of the portraits—of Clemence Dane, for instance, and Errol Flynn—approach art, and easily surpass entertainment. The sentiment, which abounds, stops (usually) short of sentimentality. The descriptions are agile, terse or profuse as the situation demands. And all this the work of an *undertaker*. Because although David Niven is still acting, and hit movies are still being made, the phenomenon of Hollywood has passed, and David Niven has no desire to resurrect it, though in fact he has done so.

James Jackson Kilpatrick Celebrates Scrabble, Va.

December 22, 1977

SOME WRITERS take awful chances, and in doing so many of them fall on their . . . (I have just committed what the verbal technicians call *aposiopesis*). If I or Arthur Schlesinger, Jr. were to attempt to write a book about life in the country, about dogs and flowers and winter and summer, we would both be led ungently to a cell block in which no paper, pen, pencil or typewriter was permitted. While such a confinement would in the one case spare the United States a terrible ongoing affliction, it would, in the other case, deprive the Republic of its principal moral and political gyroscope. All the more reason to wonder, with awe and gratitude, at the accomplishment of James Jackson Kilpatrick.

Everyone knows Kilpatrick as a political commentator.

There is no one else who can do such profiles as he has done of Presidential candiates, or political Conventions. That he is the most widely syndicated political columnist is the highest tribute that can be paid to the editors of American editorial pages. He never fails to instruct and to delight. He can be angry without being sour, critical without being catechistic, lyrical and never sing-song. He can see through the least dictum of a Supreme Court Justice and conjugate its strategic mischief before the rest of us have even noticed it. One would assume such a man would be satisfied to have achieved his proconsular rank in American political letters, but no, he has to go and write a book about country life.

Buy it. Letters of gratitude to me for calling attention to it cannot be acknowledged. It is called *The Foxes' Union*, and is published by EPM Publications Inc. of McLean, Virginia. It costs $9.95, and is guaranteed to give you a fix of serenity and pleasure unequaled by any other book of the season.

Kilpatrick was born in Oklahoma, but traveled to Virginia as quickly as he could. It is unimaginable that he was ever other than a Virginian. There he rose to prominence as editor of the Richmond *News Leader*, which he quit after twenty years of hard and distinguished labor to become a syndicated columnist, television commentator, and lecturer. He and his wife Marie, an artist, happened on a stretch of land in Rappahanock County, eighty miles from Washington, and went the way of Mr. Blandings, building his dream house. Happily, he did not permit his new life to remain an entirely private affair.

Many things have happened to him since writing from Scrabble, Virginia, and they happen also to the reader of his book. For instance: in Virginia, people don't really know how to cope with those episodic snowfalls which are routine business in, say, Minneapolis. When the first one came, Kilpatrick and his wife fought it instinctively.

"Then a second thought struck home: accept it. The thought has recurred many times since. In the sum total of man's brief span upon the earth, what would be missed? Truly missed? So the choirboys would not rehearse, nor the Kiwanians convene that day, and the schoolboys of Culpeper would miss the parsing of their sentences. For the time being, there would be no further work upon the new stone wall; but the wall could wait. Somewhere a local court had closed; but justice would be done tomorrow, or the day after, or next week."

These stretches of privacy, in the isolated hills of Virginia up against the Blue Ridge Mountains, have cultivated in the author a consciousness of his natural surroundings that stimulates deep artistic resources. He notes the coming of the spring and the profusion of flowers. Among them "the trillium, loveliest of them all, [which] kneels as modestly as a spring bride, all in white, beside the altar of an old oak stump. If you're not familiar with the trillium, imagine the flower that would come from a flute if a flute could make a flower. That is the trillium, a work of God from a theme by Mozart."

The Foxes' Union is an experience in sensitization. Hark, the spring! It "tiptoes in. It pauses, overcome by shyness, like a grandchild at the door, peeping in, ducking out of sight, giggling in the hallway. 'Heather!' I want to cry, 'I know you're out there. Come in!' And April slips into our arms. The maples do not come forth in green; they are flowering red, soft as slippers, in tassels like a jester's scepter. The flowering almond is pink, absurdly pink, little-girl pink, as pink as peppermint and cream. The apples display their milliner's scraps of ivory silk, rose-tinged. All the sleeping things wake up—primrose, baby iris, candytuft, blue phlox, the Scotch heather that had seemed dead beyond resurrection. The earth warms—you can smell it, feel it, crumble April in your hands." But you can smell and feel this engrossing and enchanting book, and be grateful alike to nature and to its poets.

III. *Abroad*

The Panama Canal: An Opening Statement, Debate with Ronald Reagan

January 1978

MR. CHAIRMAN; ladies and gentlemen: If Lloyds of London had been asked to give odds that I would be disagreeing with Ronald Reagan on a matter of public policy, I doubt they could have flogged a quotation out of their swingingest betting-man. Because, judging from Governor Reagan's impeccable record, the statisticians would have reasoned that it was inconceivable that he should make a mistake. But of course it happens to everyone. I fully expect that, some day, *I'll* be wrong about something. Ronald Reagan told me over the telephone last Sunday that he would treat me very kindly tonight, as he would any friend of his suffering temporarily from a minor aberration. He does not, in other words, plan to send the Marines after me. Perhaps he is saving them to dispatch to Panama.

I find myself, Mr. Chairman, in your company, and in the present company, disarmingly comfortable. I have sat in Saigon with Ellsworth Bunker and heard him confide to me that in his opinion we should militarily cut off the Ho Chi Minh Trail. I have sat in Hawaii with Admiral McCain when, as commanding officer of CINCPAC, he fretted privately over our failure vigorously to work our will on the Vietnamese. Admiral Bud Zumwalt, on "Firing Line," deplored *three years ago* the progressive deterioration in American military strength. Patrick Buchanan is probably the author of every truculent anti-Communist statement uttered by Richard Nixon—the old Nixon—over a period of ten years. Roger Fontaine is that anomaly in the academic world, a scholar whole-heartedly devoted to the anti-Communist enterprise. George Will is probably the most consistent journalistic critic of the SALT treaties, insisting that they play into the hands of the Soviet Union. And my colleague James Burnham is, after all, author of *The Struggle for the World*, and has been the leading anti-Communist strategic prophet in the United States, whose books and articles have illuminated the international understanding of the global threat of the Communist world beyond those of any other scholar. . . . And yet here we are, disagreed on a matter of public policy impinging on our common concerns.

We should, I think, make this dispute as easy on ourselves as possible. We are here to ask the question: Should the treaty submitted by the President to the Senate be signed? If I were in the Senate of the United States I *would* sign that treaty. So would Will. So would Burnham. So would Zumwalt. So would Bunker.

Now this does not commit us to saying anything more about that treaty—or, more properly, those treaties, because as you know there are two of them, one governing the role of the United States in Panama until the year 2000, one governing the role of the United States after that time—than that we would vote *for* them, rather than against them. To vote for them is not to endorse the foreign policy of President Carter. To vote for them is not to renounce the foreign policy of Theodore Roosevelt. To vote for them is not to say that we are frightened by any threat directed at us by Omar Torrijos. To vote for them is not to say that we are in the least influenced by the desires of the United Nations, which is dedicated to the decolonization of any part of the world not under Communist control.

I think I speak for my associates when I concede that the means by which we achieved our present position in Panama were a part of what one might call pre-Watergate international morality. But then, if we look about us at the activity during that period of our sister states, we do not—those of us who do not suffer from the sin of scrupulosity—think ourselves historically unique. Indeed—here I should perhaps excuse my colleagues from any identification with my own views on the subject—*I* happen to believe that there is a great deal to be said historically for the achievements of colonialism. Even so rigorous a critic of Western practices as Professor John Kenneth Galbraith manages to change the subject when you ask him whether he believes it was a good thing that Great Britain entered India in the nineteenth century. If anybody wanted to raise the banner of colonialism at this moment in Cambodia or in Uganda, I would salute him and start sounding like a bagpipe. So that what I am saying is that I for one am singularly unmoved by lachrymose appeals to pull out of Panama on the grounds that our presence there is "the last vestige of colonialism." My instinctive response to assertions put to me in those accents is: Maybe we should have a little *more* colonialism, not less of it.

Nor does our belief that it is wise to sign these treaties suggest that we harbor any illusions about the character of the head of government of Panama, or the stability of his regime; or that we find that the thirty-two governments that have ruled over Panama since it became an independent state are tending toward creeping stability because the current government has lasted almost ten years. And, finally, we are not unaware of the friendship struck up by General Torrijos with Fidel Castro, the premier barbarian of this hemisphere. What we are maintaining is that the United States, by signing these treaties, is better off militarily, is better off economically, and is better off spiritually.

Why militarily? The question needs to be examined in two parts. If there is a full-scale atomic war, the Panama Canal will revert to a land-mass, and the first survivor who makes his way across the Isthmus will relive a historical experience, "like stout

Cortez when with eagle eyes he stared at the Pacific—and all his men looked at each other with a wild surmise—silent, upon a peak in Darien."

In a situation of hostility short of the exchange of missiles, we would desire mobility through the Canal. That mobility is more easily effected if we have the cooperation of the local population. As matters now stand, 75 percent of the work force in the Canal is Panamanian. It is frequently asserted that the natural economic interest of Panama is sufficient to keep the Panama Canal open and operating. Those who come too readily to that kind of economic reductionism fail to take into account great passions that stir not only in the breasts of members of the Third World, but also in our own. The same man who built the Panama Canal once spoke, in the spirit of Robert Harper, of millions for defense, but not one cent for tribute. Theodore Roosevelt would not have been surprised by the closing of the Suez Canal in 1967 even though the loss of revenues to Egypt was roughly comparable to such a loss to Panama. The Panama Canal is responsible for 12 percent of the gross national product of the Republic of Panama. Subtract 12 percent and you have 88 percent left over—in addition to your pride. I hope that Governor Reagan will not tell us tonight that Panamanian pride is not involved in the matter of the treaties. He may tell us that Panamanian pride must in this case be subordinated to the national interest: and if he convinces me that the national interest requires subordination of Panamanian pride, I shall side with him. But he must not tell us that pride does not count. He must not tell us that the Panamanians should not be expected to share those passions which moved Egyptians a decade ago to make huge sacrifices, closing their canal. And he ought not to suggest that American pride is one thing, Panamanian pride quite something else.

I take it, then, that the cooperation of the 2 million people in whose territory the Canal lies, whose personnel already do three-quarters of the work required to keep the Canal open, is, to put the matter unobtrusively—desirable. At the same time, I deem it essential, along with Admiral McCain, that the United States should continue to exercise responsibility for maintaining access to the Canal, and I note therefore with satisfaction that the first treaty reaffirms the absolute right of the United States to defend access to the Canal and to continue to garrison our troops in Panama until the year 2000; and I note with satisfaction that the second treaty reaffirms the right of the United States to defend the Canal and to guarantee access to it even after the Canal itself shall have become the physical property of the Republic of Panama. It is appropriate to reflect at this moment on the words of William Howard Taft, reiterated by Theodore Roosevelt in another context. Taft said: We do not want to own anything in Panama. What we want is a canal that goes through Panama.

I should add, before leaving the military point, that if we cannot secure access to the Canal after the year 2000 from bases outside Panama—i.e., if our power is so reduced that we cannot control the waters at either end of the little Isthmus of Panama—it is altogether unlikely that the situation would change in virtue of our having the right to bivouac a few thousand Marines within the territory of Panama.

Why would we be better off economically? Because under the first treaty, the revenues from the use of the Canal flow to the United States. The royalty retained by Panama is, at 30 cents per ton, approximately 25 percent of the tolls, plus a share in the profits not to exceed $10 million. Ancillary economic commitments do not spring directly from the treaty, by which I mean our extra-treaty commitment to help Panama achieve credits from the Export-Import Bank, from AID and OPIC; and our commitment to give it, over the term of the treaty, $50 million of military equipment for the purpose of relieving us of expenses we currently shoulder. Those who have made a huge production over the financial price of these treaties—which figure approaches $60 million a year, the whole of it derived from Canal revenues—are perhaps most easily sedated by comparisons that come readily to mind. One billion, 290 million dollars to Spain during the last twenty years—I know, I know: we are paying Spain for the privilege of protecting Spain, such are the burdens of great nations. Or there is Turkey. For the privilege of protecting Turkey from the Soviet Union, we have spent 2 billion, 878 million dollars, and are now committed to spending an extra 1 billion over the next four years. Dear Turkey. Lovely people.

And unlike the Canal, Turkey provides us with no offsetting

revenues. Perhaps we should send Mr. Bunker to Ankara to argue that we should receive a royalty on every pound of heroin sent out from Turkey for sale in the streets of the United States. And there is Greece—1 billion, 800 million, with 700 million committed over the next four years—plus reversion to Greece of U.S. military installations. Or the Philippines, which is asking for a cool billion. I do hope and pray that Mr. Reagan, whose propensity to frugality with the public purse is one of his most endearing characteristics, will not devote an extravagant amount of our time tonight to telling us how ignominious it is, under the circumstances, to cede 40 or 50 million dollars a year—out of revenues—to the Republic of Panama.

I said we would be better off spiritually. Perhaps—I fear it is so—this is the most provocative point I have made, particularly in this company. That is so, Mr. Chairman, because we are most of us agreed that the people who have been responsible for United States foreign policy during the postwar years—Republicans and Democrats—have tended to suffer from grievous misconceptions concerning what it is that makes a country popular, or prestigious. The conventional wisdom is that we earn the respect of the world by prostrating ourselves before the nearest Cherokee Indian, and promising to elect Marlon Brando as President. The factual situation suggests that the world works very differently. General Torrijos has criticized the United States far more than he has criticized Fidel Castro. American liberals accept solemnly plebiscites conducted in Panama when they see validated something they want validated, while scorning plebiscites conducted in Chile when they see validated something they don't want validated. I happen to believe that the surest road to international prestige is to pay absolutely no heed whatever to foreign opinion. However, in order to do this successfully, it helps—though it is not required—that you be a gentleman. Nikita Khrushchev had no problems whatever in getting himself admired by Nehru, the great ethical heart-throb of the century: not even when Khrushchev took to expressing his crotchets by sending Russian tanks to run over Hungarian students who wanted a little liberty. In the corridors of the United Nations, the representatives of the anti-colonialist world don't rise and walk out in indignation when the Soviet overlords walk into the room, or the Chinese:

they don't pass resolutions calling for freedom of Tibet or of Lithuania, let alone Poland—which, we were advised last week by our pleasantly befuddled President, shares American principles and ideals.

No, we do not believe, those of us who favor this treaty, that it is to be favored because it will cause the president of Libya to smile upon us as he lubricates his megaphones with expropriated American oil, happily joining a consortium of extortionists whose respect for the United States—interestingly enough—diminishes as we agree to pay the price they exact from us as a reward for our defective diplomacy.

No, it is another kind of satisfaction we seek—I mean the approval given by reflective men and women to nations that disdain a false pride. Nothing should stand in the way of our resolution to maintain United States sovereignty and freedom. And nothing should distract us from the irrelevance of prideful exercises, suitable rather to the peacock than to the lion, to assert our national masculinity. We have great tests ahead of us: Are we going to disarm unilaterally? Is our word to our allies a reliable covenant? Do we really believe in human rights? Do we really believe in sovereignty? even in sovereignty for little countries, whose natural resources, where and when necessary, we are entitled to use, but not to abuse? The kind of satisfaction a nation truly consistent in the practice of its ideals seeks for itself is the kind of satisfaction, at this moment in history, we can have—by ratifying treaties that, at once, enhance our security, and our self-esteem.

On Hating America from Abroad

January 22, 1976

DR. ROBERT MCAFEE BROWN is Professor of Gloom at Stanford University where, in the Department of Religious Studies, he weeps over American sinfulness. This is all very well, but recently Dr. Brown went abroad to do this, and clearly spoiled the meeting of the World Council of Churches at Nairobi which, like almost every other meeting of that Council, is called for the purpose of indulging one of the principal pleasures of this world: criticizing the United States. He gave a pre-emptive talk about American guilt, so full of mortification, so copious with grief over our sins, that when the time came for the Third World speakers to berate America, they looked as though they had been summoned from the rear of the bus. Everything was anticlimax.

The Third World now has yet another reason for being anti-

American: American spokesmen fan out across the globe, frustrating anti-Americans by beating them to the punch.

What specifically did Dr. Brown say? Well, the usual things, one gathers: about warring against the peasantry in Vietnam, and all those other sins of the postwar period during which we spent almost 200 billion dollars trying to help people and keep them more or less free. Dr. Brown summarized his case. "I am ashamed of [America] particularly for what it has done, and continues to do, to so many of your countries." He said that many in the Third World are starving because "American business exploits them economically."

In the current issue of *Commentary* magazine, Professor Peter Bauer of the London School of Economics, who has written extensively on many matters relating to the developing countries, African in particular, makes a number of points which, in turn, would spoil Dr. Brown's fun, assuming he could read without paralysis to his nervous system.

Professor Bauer concedes that the popular notion that rich America is ruining things for the poor nations of the Third World is "axiomatic." In fact, he advises us, this is not only untrue, but more nearly the opposite of the truth. Our acceptance of these axioms has, however, "paralyzed Western diplomacy, both toward the Soviet bloc and toward the Third World, where the West has abased itself before groups of countries which have negligible resources and no power."

Item. When the West descended on the Third World countries, the polarization did not then begin. "The West was [already] far ahead of the present Third World when it established contact with these regions in recent centuries." But surely it is fair to conclude that the underdeveloped nature of much of the Third World is the result of Western depredations? . . . Well, as a matter of fact, no, it is not fair to conclude any such thing. "Some of the materially most backward countries in the world never were colonies (Afghanistan, Tibet, Nepal, Liberia)."

Are trade relations stunting the development of domestic economies in the underdeveloped world? Not at all. "It is paradoxical to suggest that external economic relations are damaging to development."

But doesn't such trade take more and more from the poor nations for the benefit of the rich nations? No. The opposite.

What about the enormous amount of consumption by, for instance, Americans? Well, it's true that we overindulge ourselves—witness Dr. Brown's appointment to Stanford. But the relevant economic index is quite different. "Per capita production in America exceeds production in India by more than the difference in consumption, allowing it not only to pay for this consumption, but also to finance domestic and foreign investment as well as foreign aid."

But Westerners have been responsible for racial and religious discrimination? Yes, but "colonial governments . . . have usually protected the minorities and not persecuted them; and [anyway] discrimination long antedates colonialism."

And a conclusion: So far from the West having caused the poverty of the Third World, contact with the West has been the principal agent of material progress there. Indeed, the very *idea* of material progress is Western.

These are sad tidings for such as Dr. Brown. All his life he has, apparently, shielded himself from them.

The United Nations

Experiencing Carter

March 22, 1977

THANK GOODNESS there was one red corpuscle at the tail end of President Carter's speech to the United Nations, because up until then it was the worst treacle yet served up by Jimmy Carter, and is best ignored, which it will be. Toward the end he made a concrete suggestion—that we move the Human Rights Commission from Geneva, to New York, where it would probably accomplish nothing. But it is a good idea, because if you're going to ignore human rights, which is the principal activity of the United Nations, you should ignore them in plain view, and that means in New York, not Geneva.

The late Professor Willmoore Kendall of Yale University gave it as his cynical opinion twenty-five years ago that American Presidents should be elected for life terms—on the grounds that every President feels free to lose *one* continent or subcontinent to the Communist world, and the incumbent having already used up his ration, it would be better to hang onto him. By the same token, every President of the United States appears to feel compelled to give one silly speech to the United Nations, and we can be grateful that President Carter, who has four and perhaps eight years more to serve, will not feel any further obligation to appear before the UN to pronounce such inanities as he pronounced there on Thursday.

On top of the banalities, there was the strange awkwardness of the prose. Listening to the speech, one suspected that perhaps the speech writers from whom Mr. Carter wrested the limousines are retaliating by a kind of syntactical slowdown. Listen:

"Poverty, inequality of such monumental scope that it will take decades of deliberate and determined effort even to improve the situation substantially." The hybrid metaphors, the vermiform appendices, the redundancy and alliteration, are bad enough—but on top of that, the sentence does not make sense. The world "substantially" was clearly intended to be "slightly."

Listen again. Mr. Carter wants to "maintain peace and to reduce the arms race." How do you reduce a race? By making it shorter?

Again: "We must seek to restrain inflation and brings ways of managing our domestic economies for the benefit of the global economy." Whaaat? How do you go about bringing ways?

And on and on. But then the thought matched the syntax:

"In Southeast Asia and in the Pacific we will strengthen our association with our traditional friends..." Our traditional friends in Southeast Asia are mostly dead.

"We recognize our parallel strategic interests in maintaining stability in Asia, and we will act in the spirit of the Shang-hai Communiqué."

Do we have an interest in "maintaining stability" in Asia? We have the same interest in maintaining stability in Asia as George III had in maintaining stability in the colonies, with the rather important difference that George Washington and his gang of fifty-six who signed the Declaration of Independence revolted against conditions which, by contrast with those that continue to enslave 800 million Chinese, were mere bureaucratic inconveniences. If Mr. Carter is interested in human rights, as he does not cease to tell us is the case, he can hardly be interested in maintaining a stability of Asian servitude.

"Throughout the world," Mr. Carter went on, "we are ready to normalize our relations and seek reconciliation with the states which are ready to work with us in promoting global progress and global peace." But of course that sentence is pandemonium. We are in fact seeking good relations with the Soviet Union, which however is promoting global disruption and global strife: in Africa, in the Caribbean—in the situation room at the White House, if we continue to dismember our security apparatus at the current rate.

But let us console ourselves that an important speech by a Chief of State to the United Nations has yet to be delivered. So let us forgive our President, confident that just as his listeners probably don't remember today what he said, neither, probably, does Mr. Carter remember today what he said.

Experiencing Andy Young

June 2, 1977

EVERYWHERE THEY ASK: "What do you think of Andrew Young?"

1. He is said to be a most engaging man. So was Harvey, the wonderful, fanciful rabbit whose creator was everybody's best friend. I will go to see *Harvey* as long as James Stewart revives it on Broadway. Andrew Young is, in the judgment of this observer, somewhere between an innocent and a naïf. Only an innocent could explain his apparent indifference to world Communism by saying he never felt threatened by it. I doubt he was ever threatened by smallpox, but you would like to think he would nevertheless react intelligently to a world epidemic. And of course he is naïve if he believes that stabilization

is what happens when Soviet-dominated troops enter a territory. This is true only in the sense in which you can say that the Communists stabilized Czechoslovakia in 1948, the Nazis stabilized the Sudetenland in 1938, and the Ku Klux Klan stabilized the South after the Civil War.

2. His negritude, worn on his sleeve, is not merely distracting. It is counterproductive, and racially offensive. The whole purpose of the civil rights movement in America is to bring on equality. It is, to use the Court's phrase, intended to make the country color-blind. Andrew Young sometimes supposes himself to be the representative of the black American community in the United Nations. He isn't. Daniel Patrick Moynihan wasn't a representative of the Irish community when he served in the United Nations. But Andrew Young, who arrived in Africa giving the Black Power salute, identified himself not only with American blacks, but with a relatively small segment of American blacks. About as many American blacks give the Black Power salute as sing in minstrel shows. Moreover, the rhetoric he used in Africa is straight out of the old song books of the Black Panthers. "... When you talk about the infant mortality rate, when you talk about the presence of disease, when you talk about the malnutrition that is the result of systematic oppression and death dealing, then you have to relate the violence of a military situation... to the total violence of the situation." That was Young in Africa.

Elsewhere he found Idi Amin and Ian Smith "similar" which is the same as saying that Jan Smuts and Papa Doc Duvalier were similar. Throughout his tour, he was a Catherine wheel of black bombast, suggesting boycotts here, comparing Jimmy Carter to Afrikaners there, announcing that in the United States the racial climate was in some ways more "brutal" than in South Africa until recently. He was, so to speak, SNCC's representative to Africa, which is not what he was appointed to be, or what he is paid to be.

3. It is both reassuring and alarming that, under the circumstances, he has become not a fighting word in America, but something of a pet. A pet bulldog. *National Review*, a fortnight ago, reproduced the first sentence of an editorial in the New York *Times*—"Ambassador Andrew Young announced in Michigan today that he would continue to speak out can-

didly . . ."—under *National Review*'s own headline: "TERRORIST THREAT of the WEEK." In Europe, during January and February, Andy Young got big headlines in the scary sections of the papers, together with accompanying editorials of hushed and apprehensive gravity, all of which asked the same question: Does Andy Young represent the President of the United States?

Eventually, the White House tactfully dissociated itself from Young sufficiently to quiet this particular worry. The press went on to Phase II: Isn't it scandalous, they would now say, that the President has an ambassador who so regularly is an embarrassment to him and says things that clearly the President would not himself say? But a scandal, if it goes on and on, becomes, somehow, less scandalous. And this is especially so in the current situation because

4. Mr. Young is ambassador to an organization that is so morally inert, it is hard to tease a scandal out of it. The United Nations, a writer who served there recently observed (it was I), is the most impacted institutional hypocrisy in the history of the world. Ostensibly dedicated to enlarging human freedom, it is not only silent but sycophantic toward those powers that practice most diligently the repression of human freedom. To this assessment of the United Nations there is increasing agreement, from Right to Left. Andy Young becomes just plain Harvey in virtue of the increased disposition of Americans simply not to care what our ambassador to the United Nations says about anything.

So What *Is* Wrong with Great Britain?

May 9, 1976

WELL, to begin with, what's *different* these days about Britain? At least one convention is changing. It is uncharacteristic, not to say unthinkable, for Englishmen to wonder just what it is that foreigners may be thinking is wrong with them, and unheard of formally to solicit their opinions on the matter.

That kind of thing has for generations been an American copyright. We have begged non-Americans to tell us what is wrong with us for more than a century. And we consider that they have earned their keep only if they tell us how thoroughly unsatisfactory we are. Oscar Wilde and GBS would have spoken to empty houses in America if they had arrived with the whispered news that America's achievements, rather than her derelictions, were compulsively the subject of any discussion about America.

The trouble with Britain, I suppose, is that too much is expected of her . . . why should any country continue forever to be "Great"? I remember a dazzling moment with Harold Macmillan when a student panelist on a television program asked him whether it might not sadly be concluded of Great Britain that she no longer was generating great leaders.

He turned on the young lady (rather than to her), and in not more than a few sentences huffily-avuncularly reminded her that England was an island of barely three million people when she defeated the Armada and began, over a period of three centuries, to put three-quarters of the globe under her flag.

But always during those years, Macmillan said, there was talk, talk, talk of the imminent end of British greatness. Indeed, as a young man he remembered being at White's the day Bonar Law died, listening to an elder statesman at the bar bemoan the loss of indispensable and irreplaceable Great Englishmen. "Bonar Law gone . . . Lloyd George . . . Asquith . . . now," he shook his head sadly, "there are only a few of us left."

Macmillan's serenity was electrifying, and you could hear the strains of "Amazing Grace" in the studio. He was testifying, so to speak, as an Old Boy from British History; rock-sure that when the williwaws were done, the air, so preter-naturally clear in the sceptered isle, would breathe fresh life into this remarkable breed. As it had done—one of the great prodigalities of history—when simultaneously producing men who could defeat the Armada, and poets who could enshrine St. Crispian's Day. That afternoon I'd have followed Macmillan anywhere—except to the sanctuary of his thesis.

What's wrong with Great Britain is its class structure. The conventional criticism of it is that it keeps Britons separated, frustrates mobility and encourages an abjectness of the spirit. I view the problem differently. The class structure in Great Britain is a tropism, the obsession with which draws Britain to internecine war with itself.

Socialism, that hoary vision of a factitious fraternity which gave theoretical respectability to an untutored generation's superstitions (collective ownership will breed collective satisfactions), fired its enthusiasts only in part because they were seduced by its eschatological pretensions. It didn't take very long to establish that socialized industries tend to produce inferior products at high prices by dissatisfied workers.

You can get a smile even at Brighton—maybe even from Barbara Castle, if the sun is shining—by quoting *Krokodil*'s charming little heresy about socialism ("'What happens when the Soviet Union takes over the Sahara Desert?' Answer: Nothing for fifty years. After that, there is a shortage of sand.")

It isn't that the socialists desire, really, to own the steel companies; it is that they desire that the people who owned the steel companies should cease to own them. One part is envy, but a much more important part is resentment, and the fury of the emotion is, I think, magnified at the polls precisely by virtue of that docility which a tradition of good manners enjoins at home and at work.

The character in fiction who, on his day off as fawning valet to "Milord," marches with the most radical pickets demanding an end to wealth and privilege isn't a character from Shaw. He is Colonel Blimp's stepson.

A guide who took my son and me a few years ago around Copenhagen rattled on about the accomplishments of his remarkable little State and, arriving at the peroration, said rather breathlessly: "Here we have a 99 percent tax on the highest brackets of income." He beamed with pleasure, as if no one could now deny that Denmark had achieved the high-water mark of Western civilization. I remarked that Britain was not far behind, and he said patronizingly that yes, Britain with its 85 percent tax was doing pretty well.

But of course Britain is not doing pretty well, and it isn't only the ravages of a tax rate so preposterously high as to encourage economic stupidity. It is the implicit mandate behind such plutophobic tax rates.

A rate of 85 percent against the most productive members of society, quite apart from what it does to discourage savings, investment and the intelligent allocation of resources, a) abrogates any plausible theory of equal rights under the law (we are *not* all Englishmen; we are, in an involuntary way, servants and masters); b) stimulates a sense of bitterness by a victimized class; c) robs Britons of the morale that makes partnership of endeavor an act of spontaneity (the genius of Switzerland); d) encourages outright defiance of parliamentary authority thus undermining political democracy; and e) causes a few sensitive and important Britons to feel that their only defense is to take residence outside Britain.

Anthony Burgess is not moved primarily by materialist emotions. He feels it an indignity to live in a country that does not need his paltry surplus, but *declines* to let him have it.

Something is wrong with any society a significant number of whose luminaries feel that, Procrustes having taken their measurement, they are found guilty of being too tall; and so, walking past the immigration authorities, they tiptoe out of the country, lest they rouse Harold Macmillan from his reverie.

Revisiting the Soviet Union

Russia *contra naturam*

December 27, 1975

Moscow—IN THREE YEARS, the people of Moscow are better dressed, slightly better housed, slightly less harassed, it would appear. There isn't any reason for this that issues out of any recent access of Soviet efficiency or benevolence. The top rulers of the Soviet Union aren't sadists, like their predecessors. But cruelty does not particularly disturb them, if they can think up uses for it, and there are plenty. It is useful for staying in power, maintaining a worldwide force of menacing potential, and suppressing any organized effort to provide the Russian people with an alternative life. What progress the Russian people have made in recent years can be said to have leaked through. If 95 percent of the bureaucracy retired tomorrow, along with their rules and regulations, the Russian people would prosper as never before.

One hears, in the West, about the few conspicuous Soviet dissenters. Most notably, now that Solzhenitsyn has gone, Sakharov; echoes, every now and then, from Amalrik, who gave one interview too many to a CBS correspondent, producing that distribution of justice to which we have become accustomed: the CBS man was booted out of the country, sentenced to life outside the Soviet Union. Amalrik was sent to a labor camp, with special treatments at a neighborhood psychiatric asylum that specializes in blowing the minds of dissenters. But it has been four years now since an American correspondent was tossed out of the country. And although they are monitored as keenly as ever, they do not, any longer, disguise their movements as diligently as they used to. They reason as follows: if the Kremlin is going to permit traffic with the dissidents, as journalists they must go ahead and pursue those contacts. If the dissidents, knowing they will be observed, want to take the risk, why there isn't very much the foreign correspondents can do about it. It is an entirely unpredictable matter when, on what pretext, or in what numbers the dissidents will be rounded up and sent off to torture. Those who collect the benefits of détente like to think that official Russo-American amity serves as something of a life insurance policy for the dissenters. This needs to be said slowly, carefully. Because no one believes that the Soviet mind has been lobotomized and is incapable now of doing spasmodically what yesterday it did routinely. But some American observers continue to believe that the uneasy toleration of dissent is traceable to a new self-consciousness about Soviet barbarism, induced by détente.

For instance—one foreign correspondent pointed out—there was the scene a year ago that shook the artistic world: a bulldozer running through an outdoor exhibit of unlicensed Soviet artists. The repercussions in the art world were damaging to Soviet authorities, who noiselessly permitted a subsequent exhibit, on a smaller scale, to proceed without interference; and indeed it is reported that one or two of the offending artists have been invited into the Artists' Union. This is revolutionary indeed; or, more properly, counter-revolutionary, it never having been previously supposed that the day would come when any Russian artist would be permitted into the Artists' Union.

For the rest, détente has meant little to Soviet citizens. The rise in the standard of dress and consumption is a tribute not to the relaxation of tensions, but to the sophistication of the so-called counter-economy. Although the standard of living in Russia is very low—less than one-half our own—there is a good deal of cash income around, for the very good reason that for years there has been nothing to buy with it. American tourists shopping in Russia can patronize shops out of bounds to native Muscovites. Having come to these oases, you can buy a) caviar and vodka, b) a fur cap, or c) an enameled box. The techniques of the counter-economy are designed to find something to buy with the money you save. A license to buy a car. Blue jeans. A silk scarf. A short-wave radio. A record by the Rolling Stones. The right to live in Moscow (price: marry somebody who already lives there, divorce him/her, pay him/her off). The counter-economy is beginning to thrive in the Soviet Union. It is nature's defense against totalitarian socialism, and the antibodies thrive on corruption, bring a small measure of contentment to the fortunate few among the Soviet people. The Soviet Union would be infinitely better off if corruption were absolutely universal. It would remain, then, only to declare corruption to be legal—and you would approach a free market system.

Sunday in Leningrad

December 30, 1975

Leningrad—FORGET GULAG for a moment. In Russia it is also the little things. You are much better off traveling here in groups, because the Soviet state thinks macrocosmically.

Twenty, thirty, a hundred people are palpable. One is a nuisance. But the trouble now was a subgroup. Twelve of us wanted to go to church on Sunday. This is not, by the way, a Provocative Act for a foreigner in Russia—he is free to attend church, and leave the country peacefully.

We are at the newest, largest hotel in Leningrad, a city of 4 million people. You would suppose that the lobby is bustling at 8:30 in the morning. It is not. You look outside the door, into the Arctic dark, and there is no taxi line. You go to the desk where the sign tells you they will call a taxi for thirty kopeks, but there is no one there. You go to one end of the main desk, and the lady hears you out; and then points to another woman, at the other end of the desk—*she* is the one who speaks English. You go through it again. She tells you you must go to Information on B Floor. You go to Information on B Floor. There is nobody there. You return to the main desk. She tells you to talk to the lady on your own floor who keeps the room keys. You complain that she does not speak English. You are told she will understand you. You go back to Floor 5 and explain that you desire f-o-u-r taxis, counting the fingers on your hand as in This Little Piggy Went to Market, to take t-w-e-l-v-e people to church. She nods, and picks up her telephone. But it does not work. She says something in Russian which has got to be earthy. FLASH! She reaches for a key, obviously to an unoccupied guest room, halfway down the hall. In two minutes she is back, and scribbles the number of a cab which will come to the door of the hotel in a matter of minutes. What about the other three cabs? Go down, she says, and advise four members of your party to occupy the cab with number 76-30. Then come back here, and I will tell you the number of the next cab.

You go to the elevators, but four of them are out of order, and three are not enough to handle rush hour traffic, which has now begun. So you run down 4, 3, 2, 1, PAST THE MYSTERY FLOOR—nobody knows what's there; perhaps Howard Hughes has hedged his bets—B, A, bark your orders to four communicants, and bound back up the six flights. She is at her desk. As you reach her, she hears the telephone ring, bounds down the hall, returns with the number of the second cab, and instructs you to rush down and Fire Two. You ask if you might not simply wait downstairs as all the taxis arrive, and she says No! Under no circumstances! How would you know what the number is of the cab that is dispatched for your use? You do not argue in Russia. I expect you would not argue even if you knew how to argue in Russian. The logical gears are non-reciprocating. On the other hand, the management of the largest hotel in the most cosmopolitan center of Russia finds nothing abnormal in organizing something like Houston Control to round up four taxis at nine in the morning on Sunday. On the other hand, you have the feeling that if you had appeared at the main desk and asked for six B-52s, you would not have been required to make any extra exertions.

We got there. There were perhaps two hundred parishioners. The priest was venerable, and he spoke to a congregation that must have been born, every one of them, before the revolution. The priest read extensively in Russian—from the Scriptures, one supposes. You take fugitive delight in calculating that there probably isn't enough religion left in Russia to attract the attention of the new liturgists.

So the old priest spoke the Mass in Latin, in the old rite, and the old women, and a few men, bowed their heads. Behind the altar is a huge florid painting of the romantic school, the cross figuring large with the legend, IN HOC SIGNO VINCES: *by this sign, ye shall conquer*. You sigh under the weight of all that is undone, in Russia, and outside Russia, before the Church can be called triumphant; but then you ponder the fact that it—the little tatterdemalion church—is still there; and ponder even the demisemiquaver of a miracle—that all twelve American tourists got there. And anyway, after a half-century's experience with Communism in Russia, impatience with chiliastic Christianity is childlike. Someday, when the statues of Lenin are as windblown as his thoughts, the major shrine in Leningrad will probably be that little Christian church, that went on and on, Sunday after Sunday, as if nothing had happened.

Restoration in Russia

January 1, 1976

Leningrad—IN HIS BRILLIANT forthcoming book *(The Russians),* Hedrick Smith of the New York *Times* confirms the worst we have suspected, namely that the exhilarating movement of the dissidents in the Soviet Union has been skillfully choked back by the Communist nobility, to ghostly proportions. It is reduced to three superstars, on whom brilliant but episodic lights continue to shine as they sweatily perform their death-defying trapeze acts in a progressively sequestered ring of the huge auditorium, once filled with an elated constitutency of artists, intellectuals, poets, and pilgrims; who for the most part are absent now when, with increasing frequency, the act goes on. The crowds are back in their crowded quarters, queueing up for a fresh orange, reading—or not reading—the Soviet press; dolefully appeasing the ugly demands of their ugly society, even though this requires them to join in ritual denunciations of the three great dissenters among them, Solzhenitsyn, Sakharov, and Medvedev.

They take you, in Leningrad, to Peter and Paul Fortress, built in the beginning of the eighteenth century when Peter the Great decided to Westernize Russia through a resplendent new capital. The prison cells at P & P bear the pictures and biographies of the latest occupants before the revolution, the most celebrated of whom are the older brother of Lenin, and the poet Maxim Gorky. The guide will tell you in catch-throated sentences about the horrors of prison life under the czars. He then tells you that the prisoners were seldom incarcerated for more than six months, dying thereupon on the gallows, or of tuberculosis; or, subsequently, of overexposure in Siberia. It is true that Lenin's brother died on the gallows. His infraction was that he contributed his scientific knowledge to the production of a bomb designed to explode the czar. The bomb, however, misfired. "Upon his death," the guide tells you, "we lost a young genius, already at twenty-one recognized as the leading young light of Soviet science." Those who have followed the vicissitudes of Soviet science will understand that its provenance was a misfired bomb.

But that observation apart, it is hard to get worked up about the execution of somebody who tried to blow up his emperor eighty years ago. We will deal with Squeaky with condign severity.* The other prison cells record matter-of-factly the death dates of their former occupants—in the '30's and '40's of this century, for the most part—comfortably escaping execution, TB, and terminal experiences with Siberia.

The craze in Leningrad, so greatly devastated by the German siege of 1941–44, is for *restoration*. The exquisite palaces of the czars and czarinas of the past 200 years are recreated with brilliant eye and numinous hand, and there is nowhere in the world such repristinated splendor of decorative detail, achieved by a society that will hang a sign: *DO NOT TOUCH!* on a hard marble staircase, which sign it would not hang over the genitalia of political dissenters, dragged into the torture chambers for interrogation; unavailable for inspection by American tourists.

There is something about the past of Russia that modern Soviet Russia cannot let alone. The exception is intriguing. It is the desolate palace of Nicholas and Alexandra, the last czars. They will drive you right by it to Catherine's Palace, only 300 yards down the road. You need to make a major scene to slow the bus down to let you look at the one unreconstructed palace in the great complex around St. Petersburg. When, finally, the guide sulkily consenting, the photographs are taken, she divulges "our resentment" that "so many Americans" should be "interested" in the habitation of the last czar. "For us," she says—I would guess she was born twenty-five years after the czar and his family were murdered—"the Czar Nicholas is not history, he is still evil, he did much to hurt Russia. . . . How would you like it," she asks, "if I went to New York and took a picture of, of—the Bowery?"

*[Squeaky Fromme received a life sentence for attempting the assassination of President Ford—W.F.B.]

Her audience was greatly amused, and one of them suggested she would probably get a prize from the National Endowment on the Humanities, provided the picture were gruesome enough.

Why, one wonders, do they fear so much the memory of that pallid, awkward, maladroit monarch, drawing curtains over his relatively modest palace, while restoring busily every gilded filigree in every antechamber of his ancestors? Is it a psychic fear of illegitimacy? Anastasia-in-the-closet? The felt need to immure the link between the fastidiously restored past, and the gruesome present? Lest Restoration should become more than a craftsman's passion.

The Beauty of Chinese Shadows

November 5, 1977

THERE IS LITTLE in politics that is truly beautiful. A great oration, every now and then—one or two of Churchill's qualify. A vignette that transcends politics—as Solzhenitsyn did in *One Day in the Life of Ivan Denisovich*. A cry from the soul: this has come to us now from a Belgian Sinologist trained in the appreciation of art. He has written a book of such searing beauty about what Mao Tse-tung has done to China it is safe to say that people will be reading *Chinese Shadows* by Simon Leys after Mao Tse-tung is reduced to fetid memory, occupying a common grave site with Hitler, Stalin, and Caligula.

Mr. Leys's lyre is his wit, and his passion. He began his love affair with China, with its people, with its history and art, at nineteen, devoting himself for twenty years entirely to the study of China, its language and its culture, living there, indifferent to politics. But the Cultural Revolution aroused him, and as he surveyed its ruins—contemporary China—he wrote, sadly, this volume. Sadly because he knew that its publication would bar him forever from revisiting "the country I love more than my own." His book is the only bloom of the Cultural Revolution.

He describes the evening banquets presided over by Chou En-lai (I attended six of these in 1972, and any co-survivor will corroborate Mr. Leys's description, while envying his wit). "Each table seats 12. How the places are chosen and where everyone sits is the result of some complex algebra that would have fascinated the Duc de Saint-Simon: it takes into account the rank of each guest as well as the degree of warmth in relations between China and his country.

"These delicate equations are not easy to solve, and one can easily understand that the civil servants in charge of etiquette do not want to repeat such mathematical efforts too often: this means that once you have been given a seat at one table, you will always have the same fellows with you, barring death or transfer, in all subsequent events. After a few such evenings, the conversational topics are exhausted (provided, of course, that a common language made it possible to converse in the first place, which is not always the case). During lulls, there is music: a band from the People's Liberation Army plays at regular intervals, like a well-oiled music box, from its vast repertory of about a dozen tunes."

Alexander Pope would not have done better. But transcending the anger, there is something that approaches dumb grief—as he describes, for instance, the architectural ruination of Peking. And, riding in the train from Peking to Shanghai, he looks out the window at Mao's new China, the latest hobby of the Ideological Smart Set, from Shirley MacLaine to Barbara Tuchman.

"In the harsh Shantung countryside I rediscovered for the first time the graves scattered in the fields, marked by a stele, an old tree, or a copse, that are such a feature of the Chinese landscape. Instead of our death-ghettos, our corpse quarters, here the whole earth is a vast and welcoming cemetery: the dead nourish the earth that had nourished them, and their tombs, like a protecting presence, witness the work of their offspring from generation to generation. The new regime—both for technical and economic reasons (regrouping the fields, levelling the countless tumuli that prevented continuous plowing) and for political and ideological reasons (the fight against 'superstition,' the desire to break the old clan ties, woven around the tombs of common ancestors, that bridged the class differences between 'poor farmers' and 'rich farmers')—started long ago to expropriate the dead, and has generally succeeded, despite desperate peasant resistance. Shantung was about the only place that I could still find some remnants of this celebration of the mystical union between life and death, between man and earth, which once could be seen all over China."

George Orwell in his book *1984* fascinates Simon Leys. "Re-reading this book, written before the People's Republic was founded, one is aghast at its uncanny prophetic quality. Without ever dreaming of Mao's China, Orwell succeeded in describing it, *down to concrete details of daily life*, with more truth and accuracy than most researchers who have come back from Peking to tell us the 'real truth.'"

Mr. Leys's book, published by the Viking Press, is as engrossing and as beautiful as *1984*. But the heart stops at the awful realization that it is not a work of fiction.

The Chastened Dollar

May 13, 1975

Geneva—THE FRIGHTENING stories you hear about prices in Europe are largely true. It will require a major change in the American mind to revise the fiction that Europe is where you go to have a cheap vacation. A generation's experience with a dollar swaggering down the European marketplace taking a little of this, a bunch of that, filling the basket to overflowing is now as remote as the Paris of Hemingway.

A few concrete examples. I and my six bags and briefcases needed, this afternoon, to get from Geneva to Montreux, which is superhighway all the way, about sixty miles. Price? Three hundred francs. The easiest way to translate Swiss francs into what we used to call Real Money is to multiply by four. It comes to $120—for an hour's car ride. (I write these words on the train.)

Two weeks ago I spent one night at the Dolder Grand in Zurich, a lovely hotel I have known since childhood. I asked for the smallest suite. The bill was $160. A few months ago, driving by night to the mountains and having gagged at the food proffered on the airplane by BEA, my wife and I found a country inn, ordered two sandwiches each and a bottle of the local wine. Twenty dollars.

The Swiss will tell you, quite politely and quite cogently, that, really, it isn't their fault. Only two and a half years ago you could take a $10 bill to a bank and get forty-three francs for it. At that rate the hotels, taxis, and ham sandwiches in Switzerland have risen only by that almost universal 10 percent a year that everybody seems to get used to. But when you add to that 10 percent two devaluations of the dollar, you get a polarization that makes travel in Switzerland—and France, and Germany—terribly expensive. It is, I think, not an exaggeration to say that travel within America is substantially cheaper than in Europe. Our gasoline is half as expensive. Our typical motel rooms are half as high. Except for the fancy spots in the fancy cities, our cuisine is, I would guess, about three-quarters as high. Inflation, as Lord Keynes reminded us, is a most evil disease not least because its consequences are so subtle, so pernicious, so difficult to track down. The United States has gravely mismanaged its economic affairs, but it is only lately that we begin to realize that all that scope we thought we had in virtue of our dizzying per capita wealth is very largely illusory.

Everyone knows, of course, that the richest per capita state is one of those places in the Persian Gulf, where there is an oil pool per goat-herder. And this is true—specifically, of Kuwait, which has a per capita gross national product of $11,000. But surely we are next, and well ahead even of the Europeans?

No. The second richest country (I use per capita income, of course) is Switzerland, at $7,270. After Switzerland comes Sweden, with $6,840. Then Denmark ($6,800); and only after that, the United States with $6,595. We are only a little way ahead of West Germany ($6,215) and France ($5,390). We are just a hair ahead of Canada, after which come Norway, Australia, Belgium, the Netherlands, Libya, Austria, and Japan.

The big dip comes at this point with Great Britain at $3,385.

Recently Mr. Denis Healey, the Chancellor of the Exchequer, proudly announced that the government is spending $2,400 per year on every member of the working population. He doesn't have very far to go before he spends more on Englishmen than Englishmen earn.

But not to stray from the point: the United States is massively rich because it has a huge capital plant geared to produce for 200 million people. That capital plant can accomplish marvels: it can land people on the moon, produce 10 million automobiles, provide a huge percentage of the foodstuffs of the entire world. But it is powerless to defend itself against the depredations of politicians who abuse it: by taxing it into premature senility; by improvident fiscal and monetary policies. And by a kind of disgust-with-it-all, of which the best expression was the formative book of Professor Galbraith, *The Affluent Society*. The United States has done more than any country in the world to lift its own people and—by the export of capital and technology—other people out of material misery. But a few days in Europe, with humiliating trips to the money changer's window, reminds us that an era is over.

Airline Update

February 8, 1977

Rio de Janeiro—IT HAS BEEN a while since I filed one of my occasional reports on air travel, but now I must caution against flying by Viasa, the Venezuelan airline, if you are among those who a) desire to read aboard an airplane; or b) prefer not to eat lunch at three in the afternoon; or c) tend to prefer the company of an amiable crew. It is probably unfair to file a report based on a single experience, but it is equally unfair to fail to pass along the word after two consecutive experiences.

To be sure, waiting at the airport in Rio de Janeiro is especially trying. The other day the temperature there was 110°. The airport is not air-conditioned. There is a single room there that is cooled, but access to it requires that you call twenty-four hours ahead to reseve a seat. This may strike you as unreasonable, since in the United States we are not accustomed to going to airports for the purpose of going to waiting rooms. But it makes a certain amount of sense in Rio where—just to begin with—the habit of mind is bureaucratic. At that same airport, if you want to check a bag in the baggage room, a form must be completed in quadruplicate, including your passport number. But the main reason for waiting at the Rio airport is, presumably, because flights by Viasa don't usually land on time. Why then not wait at home, or in your air-conditioned hotel, knowing that the flight will be late? Because there is no way of ascertaining whether a particular Viasa flight will be late: You see, Viasa does not answer its telephone.

Two and one-half hours late, the flight to Buenos Aires finally took off, and since it had turned dusk, the handful of passengers on board turned on their reading lights. A faint glow issued, rather like wartime London protecting itself against the blitz. Questioned, the stewardess tells you blithely that no one has ever complained before. You respond that, as of this moment, the record is broken, but she does not smile with you. FLASH! Why not go forward to the compartment with the table in the first-class lounge!

You do so, and the light is gratifying. But, in a moment, in storms the Jefe de Cabina. "This lounge is reserved for the crew."

Surely not, you say: it is clearly an amenity for all the first-class passengers?—and nothing less than an oasis for those who have work to do, and need light to do it? Besides, there are approximately 104 empty seats on the plane, wherein, provided they don't want to read, the crew could relax? The steward retorts that the crew has been working for nine hours. You retort that *you* have been sitting two and one-half hours in Rio, and, before that, worked seven hours, and that it is not *your* responsibility that the airplane is late. Whereupon—the ultimate weapon!—the Chief of Cabin, who ought to be featured in Viasa's next series of advertisements, turns off the overhead light by master switch, leaving you in the dark. Ah so. The Jefe de Cabina does not know something; I can type in the dark!—which I am now doing.

Three months ago, I boarded Viasa in Panama at 2:30 P.M. for a three-hour flight to Caracas. A Teutonic stewardess with brushed-back blonde hair plunked assorted cold matter in front of me at 2:45, and I observed that having lunched at 1:00, I had no appetite at 2:45, but would be grateful for the sustenance at, say, 4:30. She *harrumphed*, as if I had made an improper proposal, that refreshments were being served *now*, and not again! There is of course no point in eating when you are not hungry—unless you are a bear preparing for hibernation: so I passed. But I did observe the lady who, a good two hours before landing at Caracas, everyone having been served, reclined in her chair, there being nothing to do. Save possibly hate passengers. If her thought turned to contempt for patrons of Viasa, I must concede that she was intelligently occupied.

By and large, Venezuelans are the most hospitable people in the world. But there are some who become positively Russian in their attitude toward customers. The Russians, as readers of Mr. Hedrick Smith's wonderful book will recall, actively resent patronage of any facility by which they are employed. My own experience suggests that the Teutonic lady, and the Jefe de Cabina of Viasa, will be happy only when their airplanes are entirely empty of passengers. They may not have long to wait.

IV. *Manners, Morals, Mannerists*

Auction Time at the ACLU

June 30, 1977

THE ASSOCIATED PRESS brings us an item on a recent fund-raising auction in New Orleans. Let me relieve the suspense—the auction was a success. It brought in about $3,000, which, apparently, is average.

The custom in such matters is for tradesmen to be invited to contribute items which are then auctioned off. But the ACLU deals in a different métier, so that instead of collecting color television sets, round-trips to Israel, two-ounce bottles of Sortilège, and dinners for two at Antoine's, it offered a smorgasbord of professional services from all those people who hover around the ACLU taking advantage of the liberties it secures for us. The most exciting contribution—the most generous, one gathers—was: one free abortion.

That contribution was, presumably, by a practicing abortionist—a doctor. Last week, you will remember, the Supreme Court ruled that it is not required that states pay for abortions out of tax money, and this caused a great hue and cry, with the suggestion that from now on only Doris Duke can get an abortion; everyone else will need to go to the nearest Snidely J. Whiplash in a grimy basement, or—as in the movie *The Other Side of Midnight*—to a clothes-hanger. Well, spirited bidding in New Orleans resulted in a selling price of $30. That must have disappointed the folks at the ACLU. Who knows, it may have embarrassed the doctor. If you make a grand gesture before an appreciative house where, moreover, the tradition calls on the bidders to be extra generous in their donations—which are usually tax-deductible—then you normally get bloated prices. But $30!

An economist, taking this datum, would authorize one of several inferences. The first and most obvious is that $30 is the true free-market rate for an abortion in New Orleans by a licensed practitioner. If that is so, it teaches us a great deal about the hysteria of those who have said that, with abortion no longer paid for by the government, it will be priced out of the popular market. Just about everybody can afford $30. And since you can't have an abortion more often than once every couple of months, you can keep a special piggy bank for the purpose.

There is, a properly trained economist would insist, the alternative explanation: perhaps in New Orleans there is no demand for abortions. The old problem of selling refrigerators to Eskimos. But common sense suggests otherwise, New Orleans being a city of passionate people, and, although heavily Catholic, by no means exclusively so. No—it has got to be that science has brought down the price of abortions to a very low level.

Speaking of very low levels, another item auctioned by the ACLU was a free divorce. This went for $19. Now, understanding this requires a little more concentration. A licensed doctor administering an abortion is engaged in a pretty routine event. The objective is absolutely straightforward: kill the fetus. But divorces are, to a certain extent, artistic instruments. There are all those little points of bargaining, and evidently the bidders at the ACLU auction feared that the lawyer offering the free divorce was an ambulance-chasing type, not up to looking after the sophisticated demands of such classy people as attend ACLU auctions. As much might explain why free legal services for driving while intoxicated brought only $10. The explanation is not only reasonable, it is charitable. The entire price structure of the legal fraternity would collapse if divorces sold for only $19, and drunken driving defenses for ten bucks.

The leadership of the ACLU has shown considerable originality. Next year it might auction a free defense for rape. If they maneuver the very best lawyer in New Orleans into making that contribution, then the successful bidder might figure he has in effect bought himself one free rape. In the land of noblesse oblige, the same bidder might also buy the free abortion voucher—which he could then stuff down the dress of the girl.

The implications are fascinating. I do wonder, though, whether there aren't some problems here the ACLU hasn't thought through. Suppose the intoxicated driver runs over the guy with the free rape and abortion vouchers, and they are discovered among his assets. Who pays the estate tax? The ACLU? But surely the ACLU would find that unconstitutional. If the ACLU really wanted to jazz up its fund-raising, it should auction off the reconstitutionalization of prayer in the schools. Or would that demean the spirit of their auctions?

The Trials of Christianity

May 29, 1976

Time magazine's biennial essay on the vicissitudes of the Roman Catholic Church is launched with an epigraph attributed to an "elderly woman parishioner of St. Thomas Aquinas Church, Ames, Iowa": "I hope I die soon so that I can die a Catholic." The lady expresses the misgivings of many Catholics, here and abroad, though the statement of her frustration is philosophically perplexing. Rather like the story of the man whose doctor informs him that he has terminal cancer, and asks what he proposes to do. The patient reflects for a moment, and then says he will join the Communist Party. "Better one of them should go than one of us."

The travail of the Catholic Church is of continuing interest to non-Catholics, for reasons analogous to the curiosity Republicans feel about Democratic sentiment, in the historical knowledge that their own platform of a few years hence is being written. As Catholicism is, so to speak, Protestantized, so is Protestantism. If you find Catholics wondering out loud about the doctrine of the Trinity, you will find more Protestants like the famous Unitarian who believes in "at most one God." At the same time, you find a growing hunger for the formal stuff of Christianity. That formal stuff is really quite simply stated in the Apostles' Creed, or whatever they decided to rename it at Vatican II when, on a rainy afternoon, they ran out of more subversive ideas. It is of course the notion of the Incarnation—that's about it; all the rest is derivative, and interpretive.

Much has been written about the Christianity of Jimmy Carter. Everything evil is being imputed to his Christian belief, short only of the allegation that he is a secret Catholic. Ten years ago, they'd have been saying *that* about him. But nowadays to be a secret Catholic is no more arresting politically than to be a non-secret Catholic. People do not seem to care, because Catholicism has lost so much of its distinctive flavor. "The Catholic Church of today," Clare Boothe Luce says, resignedly, "isn't the same Church I joined." That is certainly true, and as its moorings weaken, so, *pari passu*, do the dogmatical moorings weaken of the coordinate Christian religions. Again, with the exception of fundamentalist Christianity, which it is widely assumed is what Jimmy Carter subscribes to.

What are the implications of that faith? For a President of the United States? It is very difficult to say. Consider the most pressing question a President might need to answer: whether to use nuclear force to defend the independence of the United States. How would a Christian answer that one differently from a non-Christian? Well, we all know that there are Christian pacifists. But there are also non-Christian pacifists. Pope Pius XII said that some things were of "such great value"—for instance, the freedom to worship—that they should be defended "at any cost." That was interpreted as a papal blessing on the use of the atomic bomb under certain circumstances. It is not recorded that the Pope's sanction affected in any way American policy on the use of the bomb. When that statement was uttered, we were committed to building a substantial nuclear arsenal with which to defend this country and even some of its allies.

Suppose that the Soviet Union succeeded with a first-strike against our counterforce weaponry, leaving us merely with nuclear submarines which we would petulantly dump on the Soviet Union, killing off a half-hundred million Russians but leaving us then exposed to a retaliatory strike against our population centers. Leaving the Russians with the last laugh, to put the thing into the jargon of black humor. Is there a distinctively Christian response? Or is it unfair to construct the deductions after positing a successful first-strike by the Soviet Union? Would the Soviet Union risk a first-strike if they knew the American President would instantly put his submarines into action? Is it possible for a President a) to convince the Russians that that was exactly what he intended to do, while b) secretly committing himself not to initiate mutual slaughter, if it came right down to it? Is there a shaft of Christian reason that illuminates the problem? Is it explicable in the vocabulary of fundamentalist Christianity, or, for that matter, of Jesuitical casuistry?

What does it mean to be a Christian is easier to answer, and Christ, the authority on the matter, did so repeatedly, usually in the form of a parable. But there are no parables that quite fit the apocalyptic responsibilities of a President. With the important single exception that the life we lead here on earth is not the final experience of the human being. Though on this much everyone would gratefully agree, that it is certainly our last political experience.

His New Prayer

November 17, 1977

THOSE OUTSIDERS (I am not an Anglican) who have been following the agony of that Christian communion oscillate between feelings of sorrow and anger. It is conceivably a part of the Lord's design to torture His institutional representatives on earth, and of course it is generally conceded that the special object of His displeasure in the past decade has been His old favorite, the Roman Catholic Church, which He has treated with stepfatherly neglect. But as if some providential version of equal treatment under the Law were guiding Him, it has been recently the season of torment for the Anglican Church, which indeed is now riven in factions so resolutely opposed to one another that schism itself has set in.

This last was precipitated by the question whether to ordain women priests. There is an Episcopal bishop in New York who is given to extreme formulations in any field whatsoever. About a year ago he was anathematizing businessmen who were driven from New York having looked at their ledgers and decided that, on the whole, they and their flock would be better off in an area in which the tax overhead was less, and also the incidence of murder, rape, and mugging. Bishop Moore would have lectured Moses himself on his lack of civic pride in departing Egypt in search of greener pastures. Well, the Bishop not only came out for ordaining women, for which there is at least a coherent argument, he proceeded to ordain a self-professed lesbian, which struck his flock as less a gesture of compassion, than of defiance. Anyway, when last heard from, entire individual churches were busy renouncing their ties to the central church.

This morning, the Church of England has issued its rewording of the Lord's Prayer. Now, the head of the Church of England, at least titularly, is the Queen of England. She continues to be addressed with all the euphuistic pomposity of Plantagenet prose, but now they are modernizing the form of address appropriate to God. One continues to refer to the Queen as Your Majesty, and as "Ma'am," but for God, "Thee" and "Thou" are—out. The Lord's head has been placed on the Jacobinical block. He is not quite yet addressed as Comrade, or even Big Brother: but He is definitely made to feel at home in the modern world.

It now goes not, "Our Father, Who art in Heaven, hallowed be Thy name"—but "Our Father in Heaven, hallowed be Your Name." Granted, they have left the capital letter in "Your," which must have been done after grave debate in the relevant councils. But clearly it was felt that "Thy" was simply—too much. Who does He think He is? The Queen of England?

It goes on, "Your will be done on earth as in Heaven."

One wonders what has been gained by that formulation over the traditional formulation, which read, "Thy will be done on earth as it is in Heaven." There is transparent here something on the order of a Parkinsonian imperative: A venerable passage will be reworded by a rewording commission insofar as a commission to reword possesses the authority to do so.

Is it suggested that more people will understand the phrase in the new formulation? In the first place, we are hip-deep in the aleatory mode when we say, "Thy will be done"—since we all know that it is very seldom done; and, indeed, some would go so far as to say that it is most unlikely that it is being done by the Royal Commission on the Vulgarization of the Book of Common Prayer when they take such a sentence as "Thy will be done on earth as it is in Heaven" back from the alchemists who worked for the Lord and for King James, and beat it into the leaden substitute which they have now promulgated.

One wishes that were all, but there is no sin of omission for which we might be grateful. "Lead us not into temptation, but deliver us from evil" has been changed to, "Do not bring us to the time of trial, but deliver us from evil." Why? For the sake of clarity? (That is the usual answer.) I know, because every sense in my body informs me, and every misinclination of my mind, what is temptation, from which we seek deliverance. But *"the time of trial"?* That sounds like the Supreme Court is in session. I grant that is a time of trial. But what are we doing bringing in old metaphors in the name of clarification?

Perhaps it was ordained that the Anglicans, like their brothers the Catholics, should suffer. It is a time for weeping, and a time for rage. Do not go gently into the night. Rage, rage against the dying of the light. That would be the advice of this outsider to my brothers in the Anglican Church. They must rage against those who bring upon Christianity not only indifference, but contempt.

Feminism: Unsex Me Now

April 29, 1976

WHAT DO Mary McCarthy, Joyce Carol Oates, Muriel Spark, and Joan Didion have in common?

Ans. They are first-class writers. If you like, you can say they are "first-class woman writers." But it must be somewhere along the line communicated that by that you mean that they are first-class writers who are women. Otherwise there is a patronizing residue, as in "he is a first-class junior skier." Ironically, one of the reasons these ladies (patronizing? All right, these women) are first-class writers is that they would shun like the plague such exhortations as are being urged on all writers by the National Council of Teachers of English (NCTE), in the name of eliminating sexism.

As a rather agreeable surprise, the latest bulletin from the anti-sexist league is itself fairly literate. We are told: "The man who cannot cry and the woman who cannot command are equally victims of their socialization." The trouble is that by the time they are through with their recommendations, they make everybody cry who cares for the mother tongue.

Unhappily, there is no way in the English of Shakespeare, Milton, Pope, and Faulkner, to get rid of the synecdoche "man," which, as in "mankind," means man and woman. Clifton Fadiman wrote years ago that the English language is wonderfully resourceful, but that "there are some things you *just can't do with it*." One of them is to replace "man" in some situations. Consider the efforts of the NCTE.

The common man becomes *the average person*, or *ordinary people*. Try it out . . . "The century of the average person." No. Why? If you don't know, I can't tell you. Ditto for "The century of ordinary people." Here, at least, you can point out that ordinary has several meanings and that whereas common does too, the conjunction of *common man* instantly excludes all but the Henry Wallace use of the word common; whereas the conjunction *of ordinary man* does not exclude such a sniffy remark as, say, Lucius Beebe might have made about vulgar people. Clarity is one of the objectives of good writers, which is why Mary McCarthy would never write about "the century of ordinary people."

The bulletin offers you a typical sexist slur: *The average student is worried about his grades*. Suggested substitute: *The average student is worried about grades*. There again, you will note a difficulty. The two sentences do not mean exactly the same thing. In the first, the student is worried about his (or her) grades. In the second, the student is worried about grades as a generic concern. Perhaps he is worried about, say, the role that grades play or do not play in getting into graduate school. Anyway, there is a residual indistinction, and English teachers shouldn't be teaching people how to write imprecisely.

The bulletin notes that English does not have a generic singular common-sex pronoun, the convention being to use the male. This will be proscribed . . . *If the student was satisfied with his performance on the pre-test, he took the post-test*. This becomes, *A student who was satisfied with her or his perfor-*

mance on the pre-test took the post-test. That is called killing two birds with one stone. You eliminate the generic male singular, and reverse the conventional sequence (her and his). The distortions ring in the ear.

At one point, the NCTE wants us to validate improper usage. Here we are asked to rewrite *Anyone who wants to go to the game should bring his money tomorrow* to *Anyone who wants to go to the game should bring their money tomorrow;* and I say anyone who does that kind of thing at this point should not be hired as a professional writer.

So mobilized are these folk that they do not stop at a war far from the cosmopolitan centers, designed to wipe out little pockets of vernacular resistance. *Gal Friday* has to become assistant. A *libber* must become a *feminist* (here I think they have dealt from the bottom of the deck: what's inherently sexist about libber?). A *man-sized job* becomes a *big* or *enormous* job. Question: How do you describe a job that requires physical exertion beyond the biological powers of wopersons?

It is comforting to know that this effort to correct the language will precisely not succeed because the genuine artists among woman writers are more concerned for their craft than for fashionable sociological skirmishes. Nothing more persuades the general public of women's inferiority (which doctrine is of course preposterous) than efforts at equality achieved by indicting good prose.

Personal

Does anyone know Elton John?

September 6, 1975

EXCUSE ME, but does anybody out there know someone called Elton John? This is very important to me, and maybe you can help. . . .

A little girl called Maria came to live in our household with her mother about ten years ago. In those days she spoke only Spanish, though her deceased father was American. But now, after ten years of schools in New York City she speaks Spanish, however perfectly, with some reluctance. She is entirely American. The other change is that she has grown into picture-book beauty. She is just now fourteen, and one has to go back to *National Velvet*, to the fourteen-year-old Elizabeth Taylor, to find a face as breathtakingly lovely. I don't know how Elizabeth Taylor was at that age, though I suspect the worst; but Maria is entirely unspoiled, the least demanding of God's creatures, so that when, a week ago, my friend and I, drinking iced tea in the sun, engaged her in conversation, she was her characteristic reticent, undemanding self.

Marvin asked her what she wanted for her birthday. She replied that she wanted nothing, nothing at all.

Marvin, who has the tough-Jewish sentimentalist's way with children, accepted the challenge. "Suppose," he said, "you could have anything you wanted in the whole world, what would you choose?"

She giggled self-consciously and said she didn't need anything.

Undeterred, Marvin said: "How about a Lear jet?" She laughed, like Alice in wonderland.

"How about Queen Elizabeth's jewels?" She broke out in a bright smile, flashing her pearl-teeth.

"How about the S.S. *France*—you can get it cheap now, you know?"

Now she began to laugh, joyously.

Marvin told her she had twenty-four hours to decide what she wanted for her birthday, and the next day, driving to church, I asked her gravely if she had come to a decision.

I knew this would take a good deal of wrenching, but after several times repeating that there was nothing in this world she needed or wanted, I got her to say, "Except maybe one thing."

"What?"

"Well, never mind—sir."

It required two more assaults before she blurted it out. "I'd like to meet Elton John."

Now, Elton John is one of my many lacunae, along with institutions like the Dallas Redskins, and 90 percent of the people talked about in the hagiographical pages of *Rolling Stone*. Since at this point Marvin and I had privately resolved to devote ourselves entirely to realizing Maria's dream knowing her to be sensible enough not to commission a raid on the Tower of London to extract the coronation jewels, I was stunned by my impotence.

Between us, Marvin and I know Jerry Ford, we know somebody who knows the Pope, and Golda Meir. But we don't even know somebody who knows somebody who knows Elton John. Moreover, it required great delicacy at once to participate in her idolatry, and to fix exactly the identity of the man Maria loves. Marvin asked if Elton John was the young blind singer who just got 13 million dollars from a single contract, and Maria said no, but he wears big glasses, so—her delicacy here was very nearly paternalistic—she could understand it if we thought him to be blind. Well, where does Elton John live? Maria didn't know. In America, she thinks. Marvin whispered to me that he has the impression that Elton John is English. I seem to remember a cover story in *Time* magazine on, I think, Elton John, and make a note to look it up—but it is missing from our collection.

We managed to get her ten Elton John records for her birthday. My wife plunged collusively into the picture and came up with an Elton John sweat shirt and an Elton John pin, of sorts. I am surprised there are no Elton John toothbrushes—or perhaps there are? But, when you come down to it, we are not delivering on our great macho-swaggering boast, and we have let Maria down, which is why I reach out and ask you, please, to help. Maybe you are his brother. . . . His mother (born without original sin?). . . . His agent, sweetheart, banker, best friend, lawyer, stockbroker. . . . Could you please arrange it? I would do anything in return. Teddy—Teddy! You are wanting maybe a little interference, right-wise, in 1976? . . . It isn't as if Maria had asked, as a birthday present, to meet Howard Hughes. Or is it?

Up from misery: Kenneth and AA

January 27, 1977

A FRIEND OF LONG standing who has never asked me to devote this space to advertising any enthusiasm of his has now, diffidently, made the exception. He does not want to do anything less than what he can do, through his own efforts and those of his friends, to pass along the word that, within walking distance of the great majority of Americans, there is help waiting which can lead them out of the darkness, as indisputably as an eye surgeon, restoring sight, can lead someone into the sunlight.

Kenneth (we'll call him) is a cocky feller, something of a sport, tough-talking, an ace in his individualistic profession, who remembers getting drunk at college in the late '20's on the night he won an important boxing match, but at no other time during his college career. Emerging from college into the professional world, he revved up slowly, hitting in his late 30's his cruising speed: two or three martinis per day. These he was dearly attached to, but not apparently dominated by: He would not, gladly, go a day without his martinis, but neither, after the third, did he require a fourth.

Then in the spring of 1972 his gentle, devoted (teetotaling) wife had a mastectomy, the prognosis optimistic; but with a shade of uncertainty. So, to beef up his morale, he increased the dosage just a little. When, later that year, the doctor called to tell him the worst, he walked straightaway to the nearest bar. After she died, he began buying a fifth each of bourbon and gin on Saturdays, a week's supply to eke out the several martinis he had been drinking at and after lunch. Fascinated, he watched himself casually making minor alterations: "Make that quarts" was the modest beginning. Then the resupplying would come on Friday; then Thursday. In due course it was a quart a day.

In the morning he would begin; one, then up to five snorts before leaving for the office—later and later in the morning. Before reaching the door he would rinse out his mouth. But always—this fascinated him, as gradually he comprehended the totality of his servitude—he would, on turning the door handle, go back: for just one more.

At night he would prepare himself dinner, then lie down for a little nap, wake hours later, go to the kitchen to eat dinner—only to find he had already eaten it. Once he returned to a restaurant three hours after having eaten his dinner: he forgot he had been there. Blackouts, he called the experiences.

On the crucial day it was nothing special. He walked home

from the office, full of gin, and vomited in the street (this often happened), struggling to do this with aplomb in the posh backdrop of the East 60's. On reaching his apartment he lurched gratefully for the bottle, sipped from the glass . . . and was clapped by the hand of Providence as unmistakably as any piece of breast was ever struck by a lance.

He heard his own voice say, as if directed by an outside force, "What the hell am I doing to myself?" He poured his martini into the sink, emptied the gin bottle, then emptied the bourbon bottle, then went to the telephone and, never in his life having given a second's conscious thought to the organization, fumbled through the directory and dialed the number for Alcoholics Anonymous.

One must suppose that whoever answered that telephone call was as surprised as a fireman excitedly advised that a house was ablaze. Kenneth would like to . . . inquire—but perhaps AA was too busy tonight, perhaps next week sometime? . . . What? Come today? How about tomorrow? Do you have a meeting every week? You have *800 meetings in New York a week?* . . . Scores every night? . . . Okay. Tomorrow.

Tomorrow would be the first of 250 meetings in ninety days with Alcoholics Anonymous. AA advises at least ninety meetings in the first ninety days. Kenneth had assumed he would be mixing with hoi polloi. Always objective, he advises now that "on a scale of 1–10"—incorporating intelligence, education, success, articulateness—"I would rank around six or seven." He made friends. And he made instant progress during those first weeks, quickly losing the compulsion for the morning drinks. But for the late afternoon martinis he thirsted, and he hungered, and he lusted. He dove into a despair mitigated only by his thrice-daily contacts with AA. His banked-up grief for his wife raged now, and every moment, every long afternoon and evening without her, and without alcohol, were endless bouts with the haunting question: What is the point in living at all?

And then, suddenly, as suddenly as on the day he poured the booze into the sink, twenty-seven weeks later, he had been inveigled into going to a party. Intending to stay one dutiful hour, he stayed five. On returning, he was exhilarated. He had developed anew the capacity to talk with people, other than in the prescribed ritualisms of his profession, or in the boozy idiom of the tippler. He was so excited, so pleased, so elated, he could not sleep until early morning for pleasure at re-experiencing life.

That was two months ago, and every day he rejoiced at his liberation, and prays that others who suffer will find the hand of Alcoholics Anonymous. And—one might presumptuously add—the hand of the Prime Mover, Who was there in that little kitchen on the day the impulse came to him; and Who, surely, is the wellspring of the faith of Alcoholics Anonymous, as of so many other spirits united to help their fellow man.

Mrs. Ford on chastity

August 16, 1975

ONE HATES to respond, or even comment, on the casual effluvia of spouses of important people, but what, really, is the alternative other than to take it lying down, a posture recommended by Mrs. Ford for young unmarried American women? Mrs. Ford's interview (on CBS's "60 Minutes") was in fact an act of aggression. What she did was to use her high office as First Lady, achieved by a concatenation of romantic and felonious coincidences, to rewrite the operative sexual code of Western civilization. It is bad enough to hear the same kind of thing from Margaret Mead, returned from a winter in Samoa and overwhelmed by the spontaneity of it all; or from Dr. Kinsey, whose iron rule was that if 50 percent plus one of the people do it, it is okay. But the role of the civic leader is to defend standards, even if the barbarians are at the gate; which they most definitely are. Her husband's policies of détente with the Soviet Union may, by some, be excused as a necessary capitulation to overwhelming force. But Hugh Hefner does not dispose of hydrogen bombs, leaving Mrs. Ford without a practical reason for insouciantly undermining the traditional presumption in favor of chastity, and fidelity.

What she did *not* say was that if her daughter Susan had an affair, she would understand, and forgive her. What she said was that she would not be "surprised"; that, in effect, she would approve, subject—here was a strange qualification—to an investigation of the boy-lover who took Susan to his bed. "I'd want to know pretty much about the young man that she was planning to have the affair with—whether it was a worthwhile encounter or whether it was going to be one of those . . ."

One of those what? What qualifications would Mrs. Ford look for, in a suitor who aspired to be the lover of her eighteen-year-old daughter? That he be a moderate Republican? Surely not—that would be politically strait-laced. That he be a WASP? That too would be atavistic—HEW would not approve of any such discrimination, nor would the 14th Amendment, or the Supreme Court. That the young man should be genuinely attached to eighteen-year-old Susan? I cannot imagine whom that would exclude, Susan being attractive and nubile. That he be rich? Or—at the opposite extreme—poor, and therefore otherwise unindulged? That he be handsome and attractive? But surely Susan is the exclusive arbiter of those qualities in any courtship? One concludes—happily, in this case—that Mrs. Ford really hasn't thought the matter through, and one is left ignorant of whether she is capable of thinking the matter through.

President Ford, who was suddenly cast into the role of poor John Mitchell a few years ago, authorized a spokesman to say limply that he had always encouraged his wife to "speak her mind." Well, clearly the Republican platform of 1976 should commit the President to discouraging his wife from speaking her mind. It is a rationalist and psychological superstition that it is always a good thing to speak your mind. It is nothing of the sort. If we all always spoke our minds, the situation would be entirely chaotic.

Civil behavior requires exactly the opposite: that we often *refrain* from speaking our minds—in deference to the sensibilities of others. In the last season there has been a good bit of breast-beating in the intellectual journals by writers who confess that they have always really disliked blacks. Under carefully controlled auspices it is permissible to discuss this kind of thing: but always with the understanding that it is a failing. Of the people who have thus written, I know none who would intentionally affront a black. It makes no difference that they might continue to harbor prejudice against blacks, any more than it makes any difference at all that all of us are sinners and that sexual permissiveness is in vogue. Hypocrisy, La Rochefoucauld said, is the tribute that vice pays to virtue.

Mrs. Ford's evangelistic and dismayingly superficial view of women's rights was not to be curbed that day on CBS. Asked about abortion, she commented that the Supreme Court's decision to legalize abortion was "the best thing in the world . . . a great, great decision." Now as a matter of fact, even lawyers who are enthusiastic in their belief that a woman should have the right to abort her child, agree that it was a very poor decision. But the quality of judicial thought aside, the enthusiasm of Mrs. Ford was a disastrous breach in tone. To apply to a Supreme Court decision affirming the right of a woman to abort, the kind of cheering-section enthusiasm Mrs. Ford gave it, is dismayingly insensitive. As if the head of the World Population Council were to appear and report gleefully that one million Biafran children had starved, thus relieving the population problem in West Africa. A moment's thought should have sufficed to inform Mrs. Ford that the Supreme Court was not endorsing abortion in *Roe* v. *Wade*. It was merely explicating its understanding of rights exercisable under the Constitution. That which is permitted is not *ipso facto* commendable; nor is that which is practiced *ipso facto* desirable.

It is very surprising, and very bad news, that Mrs. Ford abused her husband's position by speaking out in contravention of ethical values established, according to her husband who not infrequently invokes His assistance, by an authority higher even than the Supreme Court.

Please don't eat the daisies

October 14, 1975

THEY HAVE MADE a pretty good effort in recent months to adjust to the problem of the anti-smoker, so that now when we board an airplane we are politely asked, "Smoking or non-smoking, sir?" I have been giving routinely the answer, "I don't smoke, but I don't mind it if others do"—the only answer I could plausibly give, unless my wife and I occupied separate dining rooms.

Of course such an answer is the horrible equivalent of saying at a cocktail party, when asked, "What can I bring you from the bar?"—"Anything. Anything at all." People who say that mean to be accommodating. Actually, they merely confuse and exasperate. I'd rather a guest asked me for a Brandy Alexander than for "anything at all." To be sure, I would have to learn to make a Brandy Alexander.

But there remain uncrystallized civil accommodations, notably the typewriter. Now I am, for reasons unknown and irrelevant, the most instinctively undisruptive of men. I even hesitate to hang on the doorknob outside my hotel room the sign that says DO NOT DISTURB without first attempting to write in, "Please." It horrifies me as much as the English that we decorate our national parks with such barbed-wire phrases as "KEEP OFF THE GRASS." I'd have made a very good Jap. All the above on the understanding, of course, that when the bugles sound, I am ready and dressed to defend Pearl Harbor.

Like other journalists, I am saddled with the problem of The Typewriter. Wherever I go, I must use it. No, I don't mean at restaurants, or at public receptions at the White House, or at funeral processions. But other times: notably, on planes and trains.

The other day, traveling New York to Washington, I elected to go by Amtrak, thinking to have my dinner and begin typing my notes for a television program that would begin at 9:00 in the morning, followed by a second program beginning at 10:15. I chatted with a friend during the brief dinner hour, then went to work. I had no sooner begun to type than I was accosted by a tall middle-aged man with the bearing of an ex-colonel, who approached me and said in tones loud enough to sound over the hundred MPH noise of a train whistling through the night on tracks laid down during the Grant Administration: "I want you to know," he said without any introductory civility, "that I think you are the rudest man I have ever seen. My wife and I paid over $60 to travel on this train and to have a little peace and quiet, and all we get is the sound of your typewriter." He marched away, and all eyes were on me. Did I want to move? the porter asked me. Move where? I replied—the car was full.

I resumed typing but, actually, I found that I was not concentrating on my work. Suddenly every stroke of a key sounded like an acetylene torch triggered under a honeymooner's bed. It is a psychological cliché: the ticking of a clock that is entirely unnoticed can be made—in a movie, say—to sound like the rumbling of a juggernaut merely by having somebody say casually, "When that clock reaches midnight, London will be destroyed."

Every note I tapped sounded louder than the others. Every pause between strokes sounded like a provocative attempt at cacophony. People around me who had been dozing or reading, utterly unaware of the sound of the typewriter, were suddenly looking at me malevolently. This I'd have understood easily enough if they knew what I was writing. But for all they knew, I was copying out "Twinkle Twinkle Little Star" . . .

I don't like rules, but they can be liberating. If the sign says, "Smoking Permitted Aft of These Seats," then it is only a matter of ascertaining which way is aft before lighting up; and nobody has a legitimate case against you. You guessed it. I think they should get around to signs that say "Typing Permitted Aft of These Seats." Aft of *those* seats could put you with one foot in the baggage compartment, but at least you would have your own turf.

Some will say that, really, we are asked to make too many concessions: that people should try to curb their sensibilities. There is a case for this too. I don't like magenta. Should I have said to the gentleman on the train: "I'll make a deal, pal. I'll stop typing if you will tell your wife to go to the ladies' room and come back dressed in another color—any other color." "Magenta Permitted Aft of These Seats." To be sure, we are left without a solution for the man aboard an airplane who can't stand wings.

Just call me Bill

October 28, 1975

VERY SOON I will be fifty, a datum I do not expect will rouse the statisticians, or revive the fireworks industry. I reflect on it only because of a personal problem of general concern I had not solved twenty years ago, the nature of which keeps . . . changing, as you grow older. It is, of course, the first-name problem.

My inclinations on the matter have always been formal. In part this was a matter of inheritance.

I heard my father, days before his death at seventy-eight, refer to his best friend and associate of forty years as "Montgomery"; who, in deference to the ten-year difference in their ages, referred to him only as "Mr. Buckley."

I grew up mistering people, and discovered, after I was fully grown (if indeed that has really happened), that in continuing to do so, I was bucking a trend of sorts: the obsessive egalitarian familiarity which approaches a raid on one's privacy.

So on reaching thirty, I made a determined effort to resist. Even now, on the television program "Firing Line," I refer even to those guests I know intimately as "Mr. Burnham," or "Governor Reagan," or "Senator Goldwater." (This rule I simply had to break on introducing Senator Buckley, but even then the departure from the habit was stylistically troublesome.) The effort, I thought, was worthwhile—a small gesture against the convention that requires you to refer to Professor Mortimer Applegate as "Mort" five minutes after you have met. Jack Paar would have called Socrates "Soc."

I came on two difficulties. The first was the public situation in which mistering somebody was plainly misunderstood. Or, if understood at all, taken as an act of social condescension. For a couple of years I would refer, on his program, to "Mr. Carson." In due course I discovered that the audience thought I was trying to put on an act: Mr. Carson does not exist in America. Only Johnny does.

The second problem, as you grow older, lies in the creeping suspicion of people a little older than yourself that your use of the surname is intended to accentuate an exiguous difference in age. If you are eighteen and the other man is twenty-eight, you can, for a while, call him Mr. Jones without giving offense. But if you are forty and he is fifty and you call him Mr. Jones, he is likely to think that you are rubbing in the fact of his relative senescence.

The complement of that problem, which I fear more than anything except rattlesnakes and détente, is trying to be One of the Boys. "Just call me Bill," to the roommate of your son at college, is in my judgment an odious effort to efface a chronological interval as palpable as the wrinkles on my face, and the maturity of my judgments. On the other hand, one has to struggle to avoid stuffiness: so I arrived, for a while, at the understanding that I was Mister to everyone under the age of 21, or thereabouts, and only then, cautiously, Bill. It is a subproblem how to break the habit. Here I made a subrule: that I would invite younger people to call me "Bill" exactly one time. If thereafter they persisted in using the surname, well that was up to them: a second, redundant gesture on my part could be interpreted as pleading with them to accept me as a biological equal.

My bias, on the whole, continued in the direction of a tendency to formality, so in the last few years I made a determined effort to overcome it, wherein I came across my most recent humiliation. Mrs. Margaret Thatcher was my guest on

"Firing Line." Rather to my surprise, the English being more naturally formal than we are, halfway through the program she suddenly referred to me, once, as "Bill." I declined to break my "Firing Line" rule, and so persisted with "Mrs. Thatcher." However, the next day when we met again at a semi-social function, I braced myself on leaving and said, "Good-bye, Margaret." And a week later, writing her a note congratulating her on her performance, I addressed it: "Dear Margaret."

Today I have from her a most pleasant reply, about this and that. But it is addressed, in her own hand (as is the British habit: only the text is typed): "Dear Mr. Buckley." Shocked, I looked at the transcript—only to discover that, on the program, she was talking about a "Bill" that lay before the House of Commons. The trauma has set me back by years, and I may even find myself addressing "Mr. Carson" next time around. I suppose, though, that at fifty, the problem becomes easier in respect of the twenty-five-year-olds. At seventy it will be easier still. Well before then, I hope to be able to address Margaret, I mean Mrs. Thatcher, as Madam Prime Minister.

Reflections on gift-giving

December 23, 1976

GUESS WHAT Shirley Temple is doing right now? As chief of protocol, she has to decide whether William Simon should be permitted to buy from the United States Government some of the gifts he was given while Secretary of the Treasury, or whether that would be opposed to the "spirit" of the law. The gifts Mr. Simon desires to hang on to are those that "mean something special" to him, namely, A Russian shotgun, a cigarette box from Saudi Arabia, two silver-colored necklaces from Israel, a set of matched pistols from Argentina, a wristwatch from Leonid Brezhnev with Brezhnev's name engraved on it, and a porcelain sculpture from Spain. The law says that any gifts from foreign officials worth more than $50 must be turned over to the United States Government. What then happens to them, if you were President of the United States, is that they end up decorating those shrines ex-Presidents and their friends build to preserve their sacred memory; or, if you were a lesser light, they are quietly auctioned off a few years down the line by the General Services Administration.

Mr. Simon is a gun collector, which explains in part why he wants to hang on to the shotgun and to the pistols. The silver necklaces apparently have sentimental value (they alone are valued at less than $50, so there is no problem there). The porcelain sculpture from Spain presumably has nostalgic as well as artistic value. It isn't plain why he wants to hang on to the watch. The only gift I would accept from Brezhnev is an urn containing the ashes of the Brezhnev Doctrine. On the other hand, if every time you look at your watch you see Brezhnev's name, that's not a bad idea either, since it is good to remind ourselves that life is nasty, brutish, and short, thanks substantially to Brezhnev. Furthermore, William Simon being one of the world's exemplary libertarians, there are no grounds for suspecting any alienation of affection. If Mr. Simon goes back to Wall Street, he will no doubt want to be the only guy in the board room who tells the time by looking at Brezhnev's watch.

When I was a little boy, though not so little I shouldn't have known better, a lady at a souvenir shop in Stratford-on-Avon gave me, after my sisters and I had loaded up on Shakespeareana, a miniature *Hamlet*—the whole play, reduced to a book the size of a passport photograph. I was delighted, and fished out of my grubby pocket a shilling, which I, in turn, insisted on giving the lady. With us was an old friend who taught me piano, but has had no other recorded failure during her lifetime, and later she told me I must learn gracefully to accept gifts; that any methodical attempt to requite a gift has the effect of squirting cold water on acts of spontaneous generosity.

One supposes that the law binding William Simon was written on the assumption that foreign officials are not engaged in acts of spontaneous generosity, but rather in formalities, or even cynicism. The exchange of gifts between heads of state is a ritual that began with the beginning of history. The question arises whether it is possible for a foreign leader to make a spontaneous gift. Sadat, for instance, is clearly attached to Henry Kissinger, not to the Secretary of State. Will he wait until Mr. Kissinger is out of office, and then make him a gift? Not To Be Opened Until After Your Resignation?

It is one of the uglier aspects of public service that such spontaneities are forbidden because they are presumptively suspect. The next man who takes you to lunch may turn out to be the Korean ambassador. The late Democratic Senator Paul Douglas once wrote on the subject, laying down the law that $7 was the maximum value for an acceptable gift to an elected official, $7 being, in those days, the price of the most expensive book. A few Democratic Congresses later, you need to pay twice $7 to buy even a socialist primer to give to your local congressman.

I hope Mr. Simon gets to keep his presents, and if he doesn't, I'm going to send him two silver-colored necklaces, and pretend they came from Israel.

Pity Harry Reems?

December 21, 1976

BOYS WILL be boys, but to judge from the proliferation of committees to defend Harry Reems, grown men are determined to be boys. I know, having joined, and indeed helped to found, the ABCDEF Committee, as a schoolboy aged fifteen: to wit, the American Boys Club for the Defense of Errol Flynn, who a generation ago was charged with siring a child via a teen-aged girl. Harry Reems is endeavoring to persuade the community that if his conviction is upheld, lights will go out all over the world. Not quite, the situation being as follows:

Harry Reems, one day in 1972, gave himself over to a movie studio and for the sum of $100 performed sex for the benefit of the lewdest camera in town. The movie went out as *Deep Throat* and became the *Gone with the Wind* of the smut circuit, for reasons nobody quite understands. Somewhere along the line the Federal Government decided to move.

It did so by taking a dozen of the persons principally involved in the venture and charging them with conspiracy to violate the law that prohibits interstate commerce in obscene materials. As we all know, the jurisdiction of the Federal Government is everywhere: so the prosecutor decided on Memphis as the place to try Reems. In the choice of that city, the defense finds dark cynicism. The implication is that only in Rubesville would a jury find *Deep Throat* to be obscene. This is difficult to follow. *Deep Throat* would be found obscene if shown in Sodom and Gomorrah.

The so-called Memphis argument goes on to say that if the conviction of Reems is upheld, the Federal Government would have at its disposal the means of setting obscenity standards for the whole nation by the simple act of finding the chastest corner of the Republic, and prosecuting a film or book there, gaining a conviction and then driving the product out of the projection rooms and bookstores of the more cosmopolitan, raunchier parts of the country. Moreover, they warn us, if the government is allowed to succeed with *Deep Throat*, where will the government stop? Will it go back and find *Ulysses* was obscene after all, reversing a generation of progress since Judge Woolsey made his liberating decision?

Then—the defense goes on—there is the *ex post facto* problem. In 1972, when Harry Reems made the movie, the courts were being guided by the Roth standard. That decision, handed down by Justice Brennan in 1957, held that something was obscene if it appealed exclusively to the prurient interest and had no "redeeming social importance" whatever. It wasn't until 1973 that the Supreme Court revised that definition, doing away with the social importance clause and leaving the definition of obscenity to be if the "average person, applying contemporary community standards, would find that the work, taken as a whole, appeals to the prurient interest." That means that in 1976, Reems was tried by 1973 standards for doing something he did in 1972.

Where are we left?

In a way, *Deep Throat* is the perfect target precisely because those who defend it cannot, however resourceful their reserves of sophism, maintain that it is anything less than what Harry Reems was paid $100 to do: make obscenity. All other positions on the film are not worth listening to.

The two questions that survive are: Is the government legitimately concerned with obscenity? If so, then it must be legitimately concerned with *Deep Throat*. The argument that if the government is permitted to move against *Deep Throat*, tomorrow it will move against the Song of Solomon, is the old argument of give him an inch and he'll take a mile. It is not without merit. The government that was given the right to tax income by a Congress that spoke as if 10 percent was higher than the government would ever reach out for, in a generation or so was happily taxing at a 90 percent rate. Still, a self-governing people has primarily itself to consult when setting standards. The history of capital punishment suggests that the government can retreat from the exercise of a drastic sanction, rather than the necessity that it will (adapting the obscenity logic) move in the direction of electrocuting double-parkers.

The second question has to do with the authority of the community, and with the question whether Memphis can "set standards" for San Francisco and New York. Well, as a libertarian the whole business makes one uneasy. But isn't it a fact that standards are in fact being set by San Francisco and New York for Memphis?

Even little gulls do it

November 29, 1977

IN A RECENT period spent mostly aboard airplanes, my wife, at the end of a long leg of the trip, threw down a book and said, "*That* is the worst *and* the most disgusting book I've ever read." That was a challenge, so I picked it up and, a day or so later, arrived at pretty much the identical conclusion. The book in question is the latest by Harold Robbins, who is an American industry specializing in sex & power books.

The minor difference between the incumbent Robbins and the one I had read a decade ago is that scant attention is given to a plausible plot. The major difference is that a third of the sex scenes are explicitly homosexual.

Robbins is one thing, John Cheever is something quite other. Cheever is a marvelously gifted writer who made his reputation by chronicling the decline of the aristocratic Wapshot family of Massachusetts over the course of two books in which is recorded with splendid imagination the attrition of gentility by creeping poverty, sexual promiscuity, booze, and a social tempo at odds with traditional concepts of life and leisure. The latest Cheever novel, *Falconer*, continues on the general theme of social and personal disintegration, but it ups the ante, so that we have degradation rather than mere disintegration; and a number of the metaphors used, and the descriptive tissue of the book, are—quite suddenly, for Cheever—homosexual. What's going on?

That was on a Saturday I read *Falconer*.

On Sunday I read the account of the tergiversation of Betty Friedan at Houston. It came, appropriately enough from every point of view, with tears in her eyes. You see, Betty Friedan was really the founder of the modern feminist movement in the

United States, and a couple of years ago she dug in her heels. No lesbian stuff for her, she said. This greatly outraged the left wing of the feminist movement, which considers lesbianism the highest form of emancipation from male sexism, or however you want to put it.

Betty Friedan had said all along that there was nothing whatever in the women's movement that argued against the cohesiveness of the family unit. But she was beginning to lose her popularity, and last weekend, in Houston, she capitulated. In an emotional statement, she said to her sisters that, really, she had been wrong. Woman must be free to love woman. The ineluctable laws of nature require us to conclude that there is nothing then left of the family to *be* cohesive. Although perhaps Bishop Moore of New York will, while he is at it, go beyond the redefinition of marriage to redefine a family as consisting of two girls. Or, of course, two boys.

It was a rough week, and then on Wednesday, the headline in the New York *Times:* "EXTENSIVE HOMOSEXUALITY/IS FOUND AMONG SEAGULLS/OFF COAST OF CALIFORNIA." One would like to think that the Seagulls/Off New England would not engage in such a thing, but resignation is in the saddle, and one must suppose that It goes on everywhere.

Now it is one thing to shrink from the excesses of Anita Bryant, who, it is rumored, is toying with the idea of making homosexuality illegal. While she is at it, she might go on and make lust illegal. But it is alarming when a Harold Robbins, for reasons purely commercial, and a John Cheever, for reasons poetic, find that homosexuality has wide appeal.

Such homosexuality as went into the popular play, *The Boys in the Band*, was intended to amuse (I say intended, because even some of us who are not Victorians did not find it amusing). But it was not designed to arouse. And clearly the passages in the Robbins book *are* designed to arouse. In that sense, Robbins's experiment is more significant than Cheever's. Because Cheever is a serious man, and it must be presumed that he intends to probe something or other when he goes on about homosexuality in a prison. Robbins has done one of two things. Either he has discovered that the gay readership is now large enough to make it lucrative explicitly to pander to it; or else he is experimenting with the notion that male homosexual sex is erotic for the woman reader. Or—most extraordinary—he is probing the notion that homosexual sex in general is arousing to the heterosexual.

This last thesis one can only suppose Mr. Robbins will find wrong. There is something perversely interesting in perversion. The most normal people in the world will have read one or perhaps two books by de Sade. But for magazine-rack reading, the thought that current novels with their OSS ("obligatory sex scene"—V. Nabokov, 1975) will have to go on to obligatory gay sex scenes, to appease the movement, makes one think, suddenly, lustful thoughts about Anita Bryant.

Do you know Barney's?

July 16, 1977

FEW THINGS better dispose a man to smile upon the world of getting and spending than an imminent vacation. It is, to be sure, a scandalous act of irresponsibility to suspend this column for a period of an entire week: rather as if the Magnetic North Pole were to take off a week to recharge its batteries. What will people do for orientation? It would be appropriate for Congress to adjourn for one week, and for President Carter to put all business in abeyance. . . . But before I go, I must reply to Barney's.

I have written on the uncrystallized ethic of product-endorsement. The general attitude on the subject is lackadaisical. People do not dislike Joe DiMaggio for puffing a bank whose policies he probably knows less about than the bank's advertising manager knows about batting averages. Everyone knows that, like professional wrestling, it is phony; and nobody appears to care. Laurence Olivier can move from playing Coriolanus, and disdaining the imperfections of human nature, to shilling for Polaroid: so what? Politicians read the lines someone writes for them, poets laureate can be got to praise a monarch notwithstanding their private opinions of him. Art is for hire.

Still, I have come recently across a category of people known in the trade as "virgins." They are public figures who decline to endorse a commercial product, period. I saw a list of prominent virgins recently, but recall only the name of James Stewart. I believe the definition is over-severe. One should be permitted to endorse a commercial product provided there is no remuneration involved. It is an overly antiseptic world in which one cannot say publicly: I had a marvelous experience on——Airlines the other day.

Now stratagems for deflorating virgins are wonderfully varied. For instance, I have here this most engaging letter.

"Dear Mr. Buckley: Would you be interested in appearing in a print ad for Barney's Men's Clothing Store? The ad would say: 'I'd like to commend Barney's for its incredible selection of conservative clothes.'

"I realize your answer will be predicated on a) whether you'd like to commend Barney's for its incredible selection of conservative clothes (there being the possibility you've never been to, heard of, or cared about Barney's or conservative clothes), and b) whether you care to do any endorsements whatsoever. At any rate, if you're interested, please get in touch with me at your earliest possible convenience."

There is a fine gentility in that letter. "[Advise] whether you care to do any endorsements whatsoever" suggests resignedly that there are still some of us who are stubbornly devoted to spinsterhood, but also leaves open the possibility that we are playing the role of the coy mistress—maybe we just wanna be coaxed. Another nice touch: "There being the possibility you've never been to, heard of, or cared about Barney's or conservative clothes." That possibility is, by the rhetorical construction of the sentence, held up as sheer hypothetical contingency: as if to say, "Of course, it's always possible you have never *heard* of Abraham Lincoln . . ." And the closing phrase is a subtle blandishment. As if to say, ". . . and it's always possible you don't *care* about Abraham Lincoln."

The virgin blushes, and, to defend her intellectual rectitude, comes close to sacrificing her chastity.

It is the soft sell, the cool sell: more English than American, but becoming modish over here. Is it a coincidence that that which is becoming rhetorically modish should declare itself enthusiastic over "conservative" clothes? Would Barney's launch a national campaign for funky clothes? If so, whom would they approach to advertise them? The Led Zeppelin?

The only appropriate answer to the author of so beguiling a letter is: I *do* care about conservative clothes. If I knew Barney's, I'm sure I would love Barney's. But I intend to remain a virgin until the time comes when no one will any longer care to seduce me.

The selling of your own books: a bill of rights

July 1976

YEARS AGO, A COG in the man-eating machine having malfunctioned, I found myself in midsummer in the deserted deep-South residence of my parents (they summered in New England) with ten days to wait before my induction into the United States Infantry. I had come south expecting merely an overnight stay at the ghostly residence, only to learn that the date on the induction notice was incorrect. During that period I spent happy evening hours cultivating the friendship of a middle-aged lawyer of aristocratic attitudes, huge and cosmopolitan erudition, and gentle manner, a bachelor crippled in his kindergarten days by polio who managed nevertheless to drive a specially built car and to fly an Ercoupe, which required no pedal motion, the ailerons having been synchronized with the wheel. At eighteen it never occurred to me to wonder why he consented to spend almost every evening with me at the local chicken and steak joint; now I know that he sensed the loneliness, and fright, of a boy from a large family experiencing an unscheduled hiatus before the ghastly procrusteanization ahead and no doubt felt that the war, inasmuch as it had to be fought by men of sounder limb than his, could at least benefit from whatever kindness he was in a position to pay to a prospective young soldier.

We became very good friends, and much of what he spoke about I remember. But I suppose I remember most vividly what he told me casually in one conversation, because it so much offended my sensibilities, which at that time suffered from not having been coarsened by experience. He spoke about a rendezvous a few weeks before with an attractive young lady from our town, who agreed to drive with him for a weekend at Myrtle Beach, which is the Gold Coast of South Carolina. They arrived, checked in at the hotel, puttered about the beach, had an extensive and vinous dinner, after which she declined to accompany my friend back to his little suite. His greatest strength was his irony, and, concentrating his energy to appear judicious, the effect was arresting. "Bill, that woman is a cheat. She broke an implicit contract."

I tended, under the impulse of congeniality, to agree with him whenever he asseverated about this or that, which was not all that often. But now I said nothing. My reasoning quickly became obvious to him. I was clearly having trouble associating the ethics of contract law with the ethics of seduction. Perhaps the lady had thought all along that the gambol at Myrtle Beach was to be entirely chaste. Perhaps, on discovering otherwise, she maneuvered as best she could without calling the police. Still, if my friend's accounting was correct, one had to take sides: either in favor of sin being committed or a contract being broken. Which was the greater offense?

It occurs to me, after much experience with the same dilemma in another form, that worldly authors of worldly books are, paradoxically, the most regularly cheated class of people on earth. We are always taking them to Myrtle Beach—Barbara Walters, Johnny Carson, Merv Griffin, Dick Cavett, Dinah Shore, Mike Douglas—time after time after time, and when the moment comes, what do they do? They talk about New York municipal bonds. What the profession needs is a code of fair practices, toward a formulation of which these words are dedicated.

Let us begin by laying down a few distinctions. Some authors are willing to appear on television and radio for the fun of it. It is, after all, a form of entertainment and, as such, something of an act of self-discipline. It requires a kind of straitjacketed geniality that is good for people inclined to sourpussery. George C. Scott was recently on the circuit to promote his movie, and one could detect the awful burden the medium imposed on him, straining a nature so clearly inclined to misanthropy, toward that ingratiation required to effect his seductions. Some people—believe me, this is true—find it enjoyable. Some, because they are born evangelists and are happiest instructing others, whether on how to conduct foreign policy or how to make tomato soup. Some, because they find it stimulating. Some, because they find it gratifying to the ego to appear before an audience.

I think, however, that it is safe to say about most authors that we do *not* enjoy working the talk shows. Here, too, there are good and bad reasons. Perhaps because we are a little lazy. Perhaps because we are too fastidious, too used to the luxury of editing our remarks; horrified at the licentious results of extemporaneity. Vladimir Nabokov, who has this problem, solved it pretty much the way General de Gaulle solved it. General de Gaulle hated press conferences, so he all but abolished them. He conducted about two a year. And he pre-stipulated the questions and memorized the answers to them. Nabokov does about two television appearances a decade. And he memorizes every single thing he permits himself to say, wisecracks and all.

Others dislike the talk show because they feel that necessarily it will trivialize any subject under discussion. Still others lack confidence in their capacity for small talk and are afraid of sounding either simple-minded or arrogant.

Even so, most authors will consent to do almost anything to promote their books. Doing *anything* to promote one's book I define as appearing on the David Susskind show. Doing *almost* anything, I define as appearing on the other shows. John Kenneth Galbraith lives by the rule, "I write 'em, you [he is addressing Houghton Mifflin] sell 'em." But even JKG will appear on the "Today" show to promote his books. And when he does, there is an air of no-nonsense. He is not there, at seven-thirty in the morning at Rockefeller Center, to give free advice on public policy. He is there to talk about his new book. It happened once, riding in the car with him to a joint appearance on the "Today" show, that I complained to him about his cupidity, even as a co-beneficiary of it. "Because your agent insisted we get paid so much money for our appearance this morning," I explained, "it was made discreetly clear to me through an intermediary that they are *not* going to mention my new book." His legs stretched out in the car and he tilted his head, looking and sounding more Scottish than Annie Laurie, and with wry delight suggested a formula. "When *you* say whatever nonsense you are bound to say in defense of poverty and ill health and atom bombs, *I'll* say, 'Bill, that reminds me of your new book, *Execution Eve*, which I believe is published by Putnam's and is in any case available at any bookstore.' And then when *I* am defending the poor and the sick and advocating peace in the world, *you* break in and say, 'Well, Ken, you do take those positions very persuasively and eloquently in your book on *Money*—was it Houghton Mifflin?'" We giggled like schoolgirls and of course didn't. We are pros. We were getting paid not to talk about our books. But when you aren't getting paid (and by being paid, I don't mean scale), the other guys should act like pros.

I am among those authors who agree to appear publicly to promote their books; to do almost anything to promote them, as I have put it, though I set a limit of approximately one week and eight appearances. I am not a Stakhanovite book promoter on the order of, say, Jacqueline Susann, one of whose tours consumed three months, or Joe McGinniss, who wrote charmingly on *The Making of a Best-Seller*. Still, like so many authors, I recognize that there is no easy way to make excuses for not making a few public appearances. There are two important reasons for this. The first is that to refuse to put in the dozen hours necessary to appear on the top five or six shows in order to bring to the public's attention a book on which you spent a dozen hundred hours is not quite logical. The second is that it is difficult to prod a publisher to promote a publication at great cost to himself which you decline to promote at very little cost to yourself.

Now, when I say at little cost to the author, once again we need to pause to consider the snares. One of them is being made to become, so to speak, a member of the Beverly Hillbillies. Usually I have contrived to appear and depart, resisting that commingling that can transform an appearance on a talk show into a prolonged nightmare. During my youth, promoting my books on the old Dave Garroway "Today" show, I once found myself thinking of J. Fred Muggs as probably my closest friend. Nowadays, I gently, but firmly, insist on in-and-out, even if this means I am placed at the tail end of the program.

My worst tumble, snarewise, occurred in connection with the Dinah Shore show. I can only say in self-defense, have *you* ever tried to defend yourself against Dinah Shore? I found it, after her third letter, impossible.

It wasn't only that she wanted me to appear on her show. It was that... she wanted me to play something on the harpsichord on her show. This was several years ago, when her formula was fairly rigid. She would give the audience the recipe and there and then cook a particular dish, her guest acting as straight man, passing her the salt and the onions and so forth. Bad enough. But there is worse to come. The guest must perform at his hobby. I must play the harpsichord for her. One of the difficulties with the harpischord is that it cannot be made to sound, at the hands of an amateur, endearing—like Jack Benny's violin. It just sounds like amateur night.

I tried and for two years succeeded in putting her off. But that third letter—in which she said she had learned I would be in Los Angeles to appear on the Johnny Carson show—wasn't that wonderful—because now I could appear that same afternoon on her show as I had promised one day I would. . . .

It was Appear or Break with her. There was no Middle Way.

But then I thought of something that suddenly gave me great comfort. In my entire life, I had never met anyone who had ever seen the Dinah Shore show. I say that this thought crossed my mind with no intention of slighting the most attractive woman in the entire world. But, after all, it is another . . . set . . . of people who watch daytime television shows; so I felt that I could safely make a fool of myself playing the harpsichord on the Dinah Shore show. I felt as secure from detection as if I had contracted with the CIA for the loan of a safe house wherein to play the harpsichord, the kind of place in which I ought to play the harpischord. And—who knows—perhaps the mention of my book might effect a sale or two. A week later, I had forgotten it all, save the wonderful persona of Dinah Shore.

Two weeks after that, I landed in a small private airplane with a friend from Mississippi who was taking me to meet, and lunch with, my hero. My hero is Walker Percy, the novelist. We pulled up to the terminal of the little airstrip east of New Orleans and a tall lanky man in Levi's approached the airplane and, as I emerged from it, shot out his hand. "I'm Walker Percy, Mr. Buckley. I feel I know you. Just saw you on the Dinah Shore show." (Providence was looking after me, as it happened. Before lunch, mint julep in hand, I was dictating my column over the telephone to New York. Halfway through, the operator in my office interrupted to say that Dr. Kissinger was on the line, which he was; he told me, apropos of this or that, that the terms had finally been arrived at for the Paris accord on Vietnam. Accordingly, when I returned to the porch I managed to say to Walker Percy, as theatrically as possible, "I bring you peace in our time." Just in case he got the impression that all I do in life is play the harpischord that way.)

I forget which book it was, but I remember that Miss Shore—excuse me, Dinah—lived quite scrupulously up to her implicit part of the bargain. She mentioned the book several times, asked me a couple of questions about it, and flashed the jacket on the screen. That was her *quid pro quo*. In return for that, she got me playing the harpischord; *she* could have got me doing anything, though now I know that her show isn't run on closed-circuit TV.

The first thing, then, is to watch out for the snares. And then to make it unmistakably clear to the prospective host (best done through an intermediary) that the purpose of the visit is *to talk about the book*. Thought should be given to what it is about the book that is of general interest. It is obviously easier for Jacqueline Susann than, say, Alfred North Whitehead. Joe

McGinniss was somewhere in between, but he had it pretty easy. He had a story to tell (narrative); it took a while to tell it (making it impossible to interrupt him without killing the narrative); and the victim of the story, Richard Nixon, was very much in the public mind (he was President). McGinniss had no problem at all. His book occupied center stage in all his appearances.

As all authors know, the safest assumption in the trade is that the host of a talk show has not read your book. (The notable exceptions in New York are Arlene Francis and Barry Farber, whose industry is both exemplary and astonishing; and, of course, Robert Cromie.) There is no point in taking offense on the score. It is simply impossible to do a program five times a week, of which the author will occupy perhaps only 10 percent of the time, and prepare for him by reading his entire book. What not every author knows is that *some* talk-show hosts haven't even read the one- or two-page digest of the book prepared by the publisher. Mary Ellen Chase, of Smith College, once asked at the bookstore for a new volume by a colleague in the history department, *The Gateway to the Middle Ages*, and was offered in its place, by the salesgirl, *Life Begins at Forty*. That salesgirl was borrowed from the talk shows. It appears to make no difference at all that the major talk shows dispatch a conscientious lieutenant either to visit with you personally or to speak with you over the telephone about areas of interest in your book, the better to brief the host. Generally the host is slimly informed about your book; sometimes he is *entirely* ignorant of it.

Now, collections are especially hard to handle. I have attempted to promote five and cannot remember a single successful network talk-show encounter. A year ago, I published *Execution Eve*, subtitled *And Other Contemporary Ballads*. The difficulty was that there is virtually no subject the book neglects to impinge upon.

"... So let's have a big hand for Mr. William F. Buckley, Jr....

"Bill, why did you call your book *Execution Eve*?"

"Well, you know, you've got to call a book *something*. And

I got a telegram from my publisher and he said: SEND TITLE FOR YOUR NEW BOOK BY NOON MONDAY. So, I thought maybe that some of the essays in the book are pretty pessimistic, so, you know . . ."

"Pessimistic? Tell me, Bill, are you pessimistic about the future of New York City?—Mr. Buckley here, some of you will remember, ran for mayor of New York back in, in . . . when was that, Bill?"

"1965."

"1965. That's right. Against John Lindsay. And when they asked him what would he do if he won, he said . . . tell 'em what you said, Bill."

"Uh, can I tell a story?"

"Of course. But hang on just a minute for a station break."

"Now, where were we? Oh, yes. New York. Do you believe the Federal Government should help out New York City with more or less aid than it sends to Afghanistan?"

Since I didn't get to tell my story, I must unburden myself of it, even though the lights are off now and the house is empty. It has to do with Rachmaninoff, and the occasion was his seventieth birthday. His friends (it is said) organized a big celebration for him at Carnegie Hall.

Arthur Rubinstein was now at center stage, sitting in front of a concert grand. Rachmaninoff was sitting onstage in the place of honor and did not know what was coming. Silence. Rubinstein's hands descend on the piano and the majestic opening octaves—POM, POM, POM (this story is easier to tell than to write)—are sounded. Rachmaninoff, hearing them, lurches forward, pale: but then, unaccountably, the music goes off in an entirely unfamiliar direction. (Rubinstein premieres a prelude, specially composed by a chic composer in honor of Rachmaninoff.) Rachmaninoff leans back, visibly relieved. The crowd howls with delighted laughter.

It is an inside joke. You see, Rachmaninoff was nineteen when he composed the C-sharp Minor Prelude. He has not succeeded in playing a single recital since then without having to play the goddamn prelude as an encore. It is his *Clair de*

Lune. He has become so sick of it, it turns his stomach. When he heard those telltale notes, he actually thought he was going to have to *sit and listen to somebody else play his C-sharp Minor Prelude*—on his seventieth birthday! Some birthday .... You see, Johnny, that's how *I* feel when I am introduced as the man who, on being asked what he would do if he won the election, replied, "Demand a recount."

Pretty rococo stuff for a talk show. Anyway, the story wouldn't have been a conduit back to *Execution Eve*. But it will appear in my next collection. [And welcome!—W.F.B.]

So: when you have a collection, or a tricky novel, you need more cooperation from the host than when you are dealing with books easier to talk about. Dan Wakefield complained, in an article in the New York *Times*, that people on talk shows tend to resist *any* discussion of novels, and he gave as an example, coincidentally, my brother Reid, interviewed on the "Today" show on the publication of his novel, *Servants and Their Masters*. He was introduced as the author and within forty-five seconds was being asked to comment on Nixon's trip to China. He did as bidden—we all do—and his novel never saw the light of day again.

This last time around, I thought that, finally, I had the problem licked. I had written a novel. My first, as it happened. But see, this is no *Naked Lunch* or *Giles Goat Boy*. The hero of my novel works for the CIA. In the course of pursuing his quarry in England, in 1951, he s-c-r-e-w-s the queen. No, no, not the incumbent—a fictitious queen. Then he fights a duel, ostensibly a demonstration at an air show—actually, the *real* thing!—and, and, well....

"Mr. Buckley has written a novel, *Saving the Queen* [a book jacket is shown on the screen. Unhappily, it is the jacket of a book I didn't write and have never heard of]. It is a novel about the CIA"—that much the host could have gotten by reading just the jacket.

"Mr. Buckley, you were yourself in the CIA, weren't you?"

"Yes, I was—in 1951 and 1952, for eight months."

"Tell me, do you believe the CIA has the right to assassinate people?"

"Well, I think that is a complicated question. I don't think the CIA has the 'right' to assassinate people, but I can think of things that are worse than a CIA assassination—a world war, for instance. It's hard to answer categorically. In *Saving the Queen*..."

"Well, take the case of Patrice Lumumba, did the CIA..."

What's going on, I wondered? This was publication day. *Surely* the interviewer will get plenty of mileage—from the *interviewer's* point of view let alone the author's—out of such a question as, "Mr. Buckley, in your novel, the CIA agent has an affair with the Queen of England. Would you say that was in the line of duty?"

So help me, the two interviewers did not even know that that was, so to speak, the climax of the book we were all supposed to be talking about. I had the feeling, after going out of the studio, that if I had revealed in my book that it was I, not Alger Hiss, who gave Whittaker Chambers the Pumpkin Papers, we would still have spent our twelve minutes talking about yesterday's accusations by the Church committee. If you can't find a way to interest a general audience in a book in which the Queen of England does it with a CIA agent, what are you going to do with *Execution Eve*?

That was the first of the eight days allotted to promotion. Another day, the producer having faithfully promised that my book would be the only subject for discussion, I found waiting for me on the set in Philadelphia Jack Anderson. Now I like Jack Anderson, and I don't mind discussing the CIA with him—*another time*. My book occupied exactly thirty seconds of that half-hour. My final experience, on the eighth day, was on a network show. The entire hour would be given to my book. I was brought in to visit briefly with the host in his makeup room. He reached out and shook my hand, then warmed me with the following words. "Just got back from a week's vacation in Nassau. Took your book with me but couldn't get past the first six pages." I was affronted—but only for a very little while. After the first six minutes on the air with him, it became clear to me that he had never got past the first six pages of any book. You will assume that we devoted the hour to a general discussion of CIA; and you will be correct.

I have just completed a new book, and, a few months from now, I shall face the question all authors face so agonizingly: Shall I do it again? Must I? There is no way to be tougher than the publisher's agents, and my Miss Bronson, have been. They have gotten, from representatives of the big shows, everything short of tattooed promises to keep to the subject of the book. But when you are on the air, though you can attempt, for a little bit, a King Charles's head approach to your book ("What do I think of Jimmy Carter's chances? It's a funny thing about Jimmy Carter. He looks just like the father of the protagonist in my novel—Blackford Oakes, the guy who, you know, has this secret mission in London which ends up him sharing state secrets—and, ho ho ho, other secrets—with the Queen of England"), the trouble with that approach is that it makes you feel exactly as you should feel using it. Vulgar. It is better to be angry with the talk-show host than with yourself.

What is needed is a formula: AUTHOR AND HOST: BOOK AND NON-BOOK—SEPARATE AND EQUAL.

It is based on these propositions:

1. The desire of an author to bring attention to his book is entirely normal. Perhaps the author's interest is only commercial. Even if that is the case, so what? Actually, most authors write books for reasons not exclusively commercial. Agatha Christie, it is somewhere recorded, once said that she would write books even if they were read only by her husband. Most books can be legitimately advertised by their authors as meaning something to them not completely transcribed in their royalty statements. Obviously this is so in respect of books that are forthrightly evangelistic. But it is also so about books that are merely ventures in entertainment. Jimmy Durante, Bing Crosby and Bob Hope performed, in part, because they wanted to perform or felt the need to perform. Under the circumstances, the attendant hypocrisy in authors' appearances on talk shows is really unnecessary.

2. If an author is invited to make an appearance on a talk show, it is generally true that the producer has judged the author to be interesting or else newsworthy; and, of course, possibly he is both. In any event, extremely dull authors of even very popular books do not get invited to talk shows, so that the mere

appearance of a guest is a presumption that he can hold the interest of an audience. That presumption should be carried forward to the presumption that he can be interesting in discussing his own book.

3. Even though that is the case, it is true that a particular author may be more interesting to the audience curious about other matters than those the author discusses in the book. A novel by Spiro Agnew is a case in point. When he completes his novel, and if he consents to publicize it, it cannot reasonably be expected that, appearing on the "Today" show, questions would be limited to the content of the novel.

4. Under the circumstances, producers and authors should agree that where this is the case there will be a rough division of time. Part of it spent on the book, part of it on other matters.

The question of how to *deal* with a book is, I think, less difficult to answer if a formula is agreed upon rather than day-by-day improvisation. The obvious springboard is the reviews.

"Mr. Buckley, the reviewer from the San Francisco *Chronicle* says that the experiences of your hero are obviously autobiographical."

"Yes, he did say that, Johnny. But then the reviewer for the Kansas City *Star* said that since the hero is irresistibly handsome and charming, at least the reader can take satisfaction from knowing it is not autobiographical."

"Several of the reviews make reference to the extraordinary wit, charm, and good looks of the hero. Did you have any design in mind in making him so?"

"Yes, as a matter of fact. One thing I was doing intentionally, the second, I realized I was doing only when the book was well along. As you know, I have had no experience in fiction. Or, rather, my experience was limited to one session with two editors at Doubleday and one reading of John Braine's book, *Writing a Novel*. One of the editors told me that a novel tends to succeed if, early on, the reader forms an attachment to the protagonist and comes really to care about his future. So I tried to make my hero appealing. Beyond that, I found myself resisting, as I went along, the craze for the anti-hero—so much so that I permitted something of Billy Budd to enter into my portrait."

"Billy Budd? Who is he?"

* * *

And so on.

The host of the talk show would, of course, be furnished with provocative excerpts from reviews of the book. (These, limited to one page, he would *have to read.*) This becomes easier as the season advances. The "Today" show tends to want to weigh in on publication date, which would require that the interviewers be satisfied with the *Publishers Weekly* review and Virginia Kirkus—and the two or three reviews that, inevitably, break the publication date. Even so, there is always plenty to talk about, and my guess is that the interviewers would find themselves emancipated by the candor of the format. Consider the difference in the introductions:

A. "Mr. William F. Buckley, Jr., whose recent book, *Saving the Queen*, is just published, is a man with many views on many subjects, almost always controversial. There's a lot to be controversial about these days, so let's hear from Mr. William F. Buckley, Jr."

B. "Mr. William F. Buckley, Jr. is here to talk about his new book, *Saving the Queen*. After we have discussed that book, we'll turn to other matters about which—you can depend on it!—Mr. Buckley is bound to have some controversial things to say."

I should think that the formula would be appealing not only to authors but also to the hosts. And certainly to the audience which, intuiting the real reason for the author's appearance on the program, resents the conventional obliquity of the references to his new book; or—depending on where his sympathies or interests lie—feels cheated by the victimization of the author, who is suddenly being made to talk about New York municipal bonds; or grateful to the host who conned the author by getting his book out of the way with such dispatch. And the host can't help experiencing relief at the crystallization of an implicit contract which relieves him, in the eyes of the audience, of any alternative other than spending a few minutes on the book. They might even find that the audience likes it that way. At least they should feel better. And if they do not institute such a reform, they should be made to feel worse. Authors of the world, unite! We have nothing to lose but our publicity.

v. *Crime and Punishment*

Chicago Is Not the Worst

November 25, 1976

ONE WONDERS why he is so obstinately good-natured, but some people—not enough, alas—are simply born that way. His beat, in Chicago, comprehends an area near the University of Chicago distinguished by the highest homicide rate in the United States. He is thirty years old, was married at nineteen, has two children, and you would think his beat was the Garden of Eden. He does, however, tell you that the system is simply not working. In Chicago, as in so many other places, crime is something of a licensed activity.

At the moment, he is involved in a case involving three boys, aged fourteen, fifteen, and sixteen. They have had a merry old time during the past season. Their specialty was breaking silently into a small house, or apartment, immobilizing the mother at gunpoint, bringing down the children and the father, tying them up, and ceremonially raping the mother in their presence. Then they would pick up the portable artifacts—color television sets were specially prized—and, with exemplary filial devotion, give these to their mothers, who, when questioned about the appearance of their homes, which had begun to look like Macy's bargain basement, informed the police that they assumed their sons were profitably engaged, which is certainly true, crime being extremely profitable in Chicago. What, the visitor asked, would the boys receive in the way of prison sentences, now that they were finally apprehended? "Two years, maximum," the policeman said.

How did they get their guns?

Nothing, it appears, could be easier. There is a gun-registration law in Chicago, indeed in Illinois. The effect of it, said the policeman, is to make it more difficult for people who are straight (his word) to arm themselves. Others have no problem at all—guns abound. And get this. There is one outfit, apparently known to just about everyone, which rents you guns. The rental is very simple: 10 percent of the money that gun helps you to rob. Besides, Indiana is only twenty miles away, and there are no effective registration laws there.

But what if you get caught with a gun on your person, without a permit? What happens then, said the policeman, smiling, is—nothing. What do you mean, "nothing"? Well, the policeman takes you before a judge, and the judge says, "Case dismissed." *"That's* what I mean by nothing."

Why are things so bad? Well, the cop says, there is one obvious reason why. The prisons are full, and there isn't any room for extra people. So when anybody who has done anything less than torture his grandmother to death comes before the judge, the judge tends just to shove the case to one side, grant continuance after continuance, and, eventually, the case, if not formally dismissed, sort of dies from attrition.

"Isn't that pretty demoralizing for the police?" "Yes," he said, beaming.

Then there is the problem of getting people to testify. If there are ten witnesses to a felony, you are lucky if you can persuade one, or at most two, to testify. There are reasons: the general solidarity of a culture resigned to living on the other side of the law. Fear of reprisal. But above all, a sense of uselessness. It isn't as though you were a party to collaring a rabid dog, and removing him from the playground, so that your children could ever after be safe. These rabid dogs are simply sent to the pound for a day or two, or a week, perhaps a month, and they are back. And in any case, the density of the dog population does not visibly diminish.

It is as useless as swatting the legendary mosquito on your arm when traveling up the Amazon. Why bother yourself? The judges don't care. The lawyers will make you out a liar. The legislature won't vote the money for the prisons. The politicians don't even bother anymore to run for office calling for law and order. And indeed it is significant that the most prestigious civil rights organization in the country (in the world?) has given more attention during this period to the right of a Utah killer not to get killed even though he wants to be killed, than to a half-million people in Chicago who, every day, are deprived of their life, liberty, and property by a criminal class that enjoys permanent predatory rights to mug, rape, and kill.

"But believe me," the cop said happily. "Chicago isn't the worst. Not by any means."

Death for Gilmore?

November 23, 1976

IN THE MATTER of Gary Mark Gilmore, we note the strange behavior, as so often is the case, of the American Civil Liberties Union, which has entered the case in opposition to Gilmore's plea to the state of Utah to get on with its capital sentence.

The reasoning of the ACLU is roughly as follows: Capital punishment is evil. Therefore, if you cannot persuade a state to repeal its capital-punishment law, and if you cannot persuade the Supreme Court to declare such a law, if passed by a state, unconstitutional: then use whatever devices you can to stand in the way of the execution of such a law. Never mind that the condemned man asks the state to proceed. All that man is doing is saying that he would rather be shot than live a lifetime in prison. His wish should not prevail, for the simple reason that an individual's opting for an end the state ought never to have authorized does not have the effect of baptizing that end. If—let us say—a prisoner offered to permit his hands to be amputated, preferring that punishment over a ten-year sentence for theft, the state ought not to comply with the prisoner's choice. That which is barbaric remains so irrespective of an individual's preferences.

The logic, so far as it goes, is good. Although it is at odds with the overarching commitment of the ACLU to the notion of sovereignty over one's own body. Let us examine one or two variations of the argument:

1. Does an individual have the right to submit to sadistic treatment? To judge from the flotsam that silts up in the magazine racks, there is a considerable appetite for this sort of thing. Let us hypothesize an off-Broadway show, featuring an S/M production in which the heroine is flailed—real whips, real woman, real blood—for the delectation of the depraved. One assumes that the ACLU would defend the right of the producers to get on with it, trotting out the argument that no one has the right to interfere with the means by which others take their pleasure. The opposing argument is that the community has the right right to define, then to suppress, depravity. Moreover, the community legitimately concerns itself over the coarsening effect of depravity.

2. Does the individual's right over his own body extend to suicide? Most states have laws against suicide, notwithstanding that of all unenforceable laws, this is probably the most conspicuously unenforceable. Still, the policeman who at great risk to himself succeeds in aborting a suicide by climbing up to the window of the skyscraper in which the woman hovers, and grabbing her before she jumps, more often than not aborts an impulse permanently. The figures show that the inclination to suicide is more often than not permanently choked off, if only the suicide is prevented. Moreover, the theological argument is profoundly relevant. That which is vouchsafed to the human being by providence, he must not dispossess himself of. It is the right to life. Gilmore has greatly confused matters by attempting suicide. Strangely, there are few voices to be heard saying that the prison authorities were wrong in using

a stomach pump to revive Gilmore. No doubt the judiciary in Utah would have taken quiet satisfaction if Gilmore, by successfully ending his own life, had relieved the state of the necessity of coping with the difficult questions he has raised.

3. Assuming that there were no capital punishment, what would be the position of the ACLU toward a prisoner who, having been sentenced to life in jail, presented himself before the authorities and asked for drugs sufficient to end his own life? Here the state would not be executing the prisoner, merely making available to the prisoner the means by which the prisoner could legislate an alternative for himself. Or are there people around who believe that the state should be permitted to prescribe the exact nature of the punishment? We saw that impulse at work in Nuremberg when Hermann Goering managed to swallow poison on the eve of his scheduled hanging. (The memorable lead on United Press Radio on that occasion was: "Hermann Goering cheated death today by committing suicide.") There was general consternation, stomach pumps working overtime, because it was decided that Goering undergo the ritual execution. The condemned man is not free to mull over the known means of extinguishing human life, and then express his preference.

The arguments are complex, and Gilmore, perhaps inadvertently, has confronted the community with them by his bizarre request. In theatrical terms, after ten years without capital punishment, his request is something of a bridge between total abstinence and systematic resumption of capital punishment. Moreover, he has made it plain for all to see that capital punishment is cruel and unusual insofar as it is eccentrically meted out. The state has the right to take life, when the right to life is forfeited. The torture is the result of indecision.

The Electric Chair and the Mayoral Campaign

September 15, 1977

THE RACE in New York, barring a welcome upset by the candidate of the Conservative Party Mr. Barry Farber, is between Edward Koch and Mario Cuomo, and you will never guess what Mr. Cuomo is spending his time on. Edward Koch's qualified endorsement of capital punishment.

One must assume that this is viewed as a shrewd maneuver by somebody, else presumably it would not happen. As things now stand Representative Edward Koch, whose credentials are impeccably liberal, but who appeals to a great many independents precisely because of the independence of his mind and his inquisitive disposition, has the slight edge. He has the advantages and disadvantages of being Jewish, even as Mr. Cuomo has the advantages and disadvantages of being Italian in an ethnic-oriented community (the melting pot was buried about fifteen years ago by Nathan Glazer and Patrick Moynihan in a slender book appropriately called *Beyond the Melting Pot*). Call it a draw.

Mr. Koch has the advantage of five terms in Congress during which he gradually crystallized as an institutional municipal fixture as solid as Grand Central Station. Cuomo has the advantage of backing from Albany, backing from the Liberal Party, and a certain mysterious freshness that wafts in from the image of the Italian-intellectual-romancer. As so often is the case, the two men facing each other during the run-off don't quite know how to go about disparaging each other, and therefore Mr. Cuomo elected to highlight his opponent's endorsement of the return of capital punishment.

Here exactly is what Representative Koch had said: "Society has the right to show its sense of moral outrage in particularly heinous crimes by providing that the death penalty be an option available to a judge and jury."

To judge from Cuomo's reaction, Koch was sounding the tocsin for the nuclear obliteration of our crime centers. Addressing a congregation of worshipers, mostly black, at a local church, Mr. Cuomo retorted, "*The electric chair cannot produce jobs for the poor.*"

That statement can only be met by a retort of equivalent intellectual profundity. If I had been there, I swear I'd have risen and said, "B-b-but Mr. Cuomo, wouldn't it provide jobs for executioners?"

Cuomo went on: "*The electric chair cannot balance the budget.*"

One possible comment on that would be: "Well, it could *help* balance the budget. Convicted murderers cost the state $30,000 a year to keep alive." Would Cuomo have thought this a niggling economy? One could have answered that piggy-bank savings add up to balanced budgets.

Did Cuomo finally stop there? Not at all. "*The electric chair cannot educate our children.*" No no no no no, I'd have said. *Surely* it would help to educate those of our children who are considering a life of violent crime? Surely if the prospect of a hairbrush, at the margin, can help to educate some children (if Cuomo had demurred here, Koch, citing the Old Testament sanction for the use of the rod, could have denounced Cuomo as anti-Semitic), the prospect of an electric chair might deter an eighteen-year-old from ice-picking an old lady to death?

Was he through *yet*? Oh no/Never Cuomo. "*The electric chair cannot give us a sound economy or save us from bankruptcy or even save my seventy-seven-year-old mother from muggers.*" Why stop there? He might have added that the electric chair cannot give us rainbows in the sky, or chocolate malted milk shakes, or skating rinks.

It is interesting that Mr. Cuomo should choose to elevate one part of Mr. Koch's program as the most conspicuous and presumably the most vulnerable. The attitude of the majority of New Yorkers is that something needs to be done about crime beyond that which is now being done about crime, and there is the intuitive feeling about the return of capital punishment that it may have *something* to do with incidence of murder. To deduce that Congressman Koch (or any other American politician) proposes capital punishment as a panacea is to play the old logical trick of *ignoratio elenchi*. The voters will probably see through that. And having seen it, they may be reminded to vote for Koch because, besides everything else, he believes in the use of capital punishment under certain circumstances. The electric chair cannot elect Cuomo mayor.

Thinking about Crime

August 11, 1977

THE CONVENTIONAL wisdom is that one needs to spend one's time in probing the *causes* of our social maladies. A few very bright men (e.g., James Q. Wilson, Ernest van den Haag) have been trying to tell us, particularly in the field of penology, that it would be splendid if we were to discover the causes of crime, or the techniques of rehabilitation, but it is our absorption with these pursuits that distracts us from coping with crime. Weeks after the anarchic outburst in New York City, the talk still tends to dwell on the causes of it. But what should be *done*?

Herewith a few propositions:

1. More people than are now in jail ought to be in jail.

2. The objection that there are not enough jails is an insufficient one. There are two ways of dealing with the problem.

The first would be to build more jails. The second would be to release from jail prisoners who have been sent there as punishment for committing non-violent crimes. In federal institutions, only 25 percent of the inmates are there for having murdered, kidnapped, raped, or mugged. In New York State prisons, 30 percent of the inhabitants are not guilty of violent crimes. These people could be punished in different ways, outside jail.

3. There being no way to make parents responsible for the behavior of their children when there are no parents (it is estimated that more than 50 percent of black teenagers in New York City live without one or both of their parents), legal distinctions between children and adults should be abolished where there are no parents; and where there are parents, these distinctions should be abolished after repeated offenses.

4. Judges or parole boards who release, before he is twenty-five years old, a prisoner of whatever age who has been convicted three times of a Class A misdemeanor, or twice of a Class E felony, should be subject to impeachment proceedings.

5. The community should acknowledge responsibility for failure to grant adequate protection to a member of that community. Victims of violent crimes should be compensated; so also should victims of theft, under reasonable regulations.

Now none of this suggests thought should cease to be given to the causes of every kind of misbehavior. If the future holds for us some thaumaturgical medication that will transform the Son of Sam into St. Francis of Assisi, we should by all means do our best to get it past the Federal Drug Administration. But the methodological breakthrough is overdue: we must reason from the particular back toward the general, rather than the other way around. It is nice to see old Spencer Tracy movies with Father Flanagan saying such things as: "There's no such thing as a bad boy." But the broken arm, the ravished girl, the tortured old man, are the concrete realities. It does not preclude any kind of inventive ministrations to bad boys to rule that these should be given inside prison walls. Going after the symptom of the disease (a cognate cliché) is unreasonable only when it is known how to treat the disease. Since we do not know how to treat the disease, lacking—for instance—the authority to require people to procreate children only in wedlock, then we must ask whether dealing with the symptom isn't to be preferred to doing nothing at all.

The answer should be plain. But of course it isn't; and that is why no reform movement has grown out of the awful events of the past weeks, and years.

The Return of Edgar Smith

November 20, 1976

I AM BEHIND the curtain of the auditorium at the University of Alabama in Huntsville, and my host now slips through to the podium. Presently he will introduce me; I am to follow in his footsteps, and begin my speech. Just then a student puffs in, having taken the steps three at a time. Before I go on—he stammers out—I am to telephone Bodino Rodino at the *Bergen Record*, re: Edgar Smith. I stuff the message in my pocket, a bottomless pit by now for messages from people who wish to speak to me about Edgar Smith.

Now it is a television studio, a live show, coast to coast, "Good Morning, America." I am there to discuss a new book I have written on a subject far removed from the world of getting and spending and killing: sailing boats. The props—

enticing pictures, taken at sea—are all in place, and the star of the show opens up: "First, Mr. Buckley, I'd like to ask you about Edgar Smith . . ."

Very well, I surrender.

1. Edgar Smith was tried and convicted in 1957 of murdering a fifteen-year-old girl. In 1964, we began a correspondence. Over the ensuing seven years, he wrote me 2,900 pages of letters (he counted them). I became convinced that he had not been fairly tried, and that he could not have committed the murder in the time and under the circumstances alleged.

Two gifted attorneys, for the most part volunteering their services, persuaded a very bright judge that Edgar Smith had not been fairly tried. Rather than re-try him for first-degree murder, the New Jersey court bargained with him. If he would say that he killed the girl, the prosecution would reduce the charge to second-degree murder. Counting "good" time, his release would be effective one hour after he stood up in open court pleading guilty. One hour later, he emerged from Trenton State Prison into my waiting car and drove to New York City where, before the cameras, he retracted his confession, which he attributed to the requirements of "court theater." He had been in the death house longer than anyone in American history. The judge who let him out was profoundly convinced that Smith had in fact, as a seedy, shiftless twenty-three-year-old, killed the girl. But, said the judge, if he had ever seen a rehabilitated man, here he was. Edgar Smith, member of Mensa, author of two best-selling books.

2. Just short of five years later, one of the attorneys telephones. He had received a report that Edgar Smith is wanted in San Diego, California, for "atrocious assault," kidnapping, and attempted murder. A young woman, her week's forlorn salary in her handbag, is dragged into a car by a man who announces that he wants her money. She resists and he plunges a six-inch knife into her, narrowly missing vital organs. She is a tiger, thrusts her two feet through the windshield, lunges against the wheel of the car, which lurches now off to the side of the road.

Desperately she maneuvers to open the door, and spills out in sight of a half-dozen pedestrians who take the number of the license plate of the car that careens screechingly off. The car is registered in the name of Mrs. Edgar Smith. The woman recovers in the hospital, is shown a picture, and identifies her assailant as: Edgar Smith.

3. The telephone rings in my office, and my secretary, Miss Bronson, answers—like all of us around the shop, an old enthusiast in the Smith cause. It is Edgar Smith, calling from Las Vegas, "Is Bill there?" He had been hiding in and around New York for a week, not disclosing his whereabouts to anyone. He had promised his mother he would fly directly to San Diego, give himself up. Now, he tells Miss Bronson, he has been mugged, and has lost all his money; would I call him? She telephones me in Albuquerque, and I telephone the FBI. Within fifteen minutes Edgar Smith, napping in his hotel room, is picked up. My next two calls are to his mother and his wife, to tell them what I did.

4. What are my "comments"? Why, I believe now that he was guilty of the first crime. There is no mechanism as yet perfected that will establish beyond question a person's guilt or innocence. There will be guilty people freed this year and every year. But for those who believe that the case of Edgar Smith warrants a vow to accept the ruling of a court as always definitive, it is only necessary to remind ourselves that, this year and every year, an innocent man will be convicted. Edgar Smith has done enough damage in his lifetime without underwriting the doctrine that the verdict of a court is infallible.

VI. *At Home*

The House

February 1976

WE WANTED something by the sea, which excluded my native green and beautiful Sharon, Connecticut, and within commuting distance of New York, which also excluded Sharon. My wife set out every day, at about the time I would go off to the office. We tried leaving the apartment at staggered hours, on the assumption that, that way, one of us would one day bump into our fellow-tenant Marilyn Monroe in the elevator; but we never did lay eyes on her, and about a month and thirty or forty houses later my wife approached me with some excitement. She had found it. "It" meant reasonably priced, on the water, and not further than an hour from Grand Central.

We came to it on a spring day—I remember Adlai Stevenson had announced that morning that the future of the Republic required him, after all, to accept the Democratic Presidential nomination if proffered. It was wet and cold, and the owner was not there to let us in; so I broke a tiny window, unlatched the kitchen-door bolt, and left a pleasant note of explanation.

We wandered through a house at once startlingly ugly and entirely captivating. Its immediate background was romantic. Chérie—as we refer to her—had recently been phased out, and her benefactor gave her nothing less than this squat, stolid, fifteen-room house—built sixty years earlier in an unsuccessful flight from Victorian excess—surrounded by beautiful trees, three acres of lawn, a four-car garage with upstairs apartment that, rented, would bring in the tax. The furnishings were startling. I remember mostly chairs, and pink plastic orchids on black wallpaper, and a total of six books—all of them *Reader's Digest* condensations. There was a bar full of shimmering mirrors and neon lights. There must have been chairs there to seat everyone in the county who voted for Adlai Stevenson.

Few things hit me instinctively; and I was deeply rooted, along with my nine brothers and sisters, practically all of whom settled in or near Sharon. But I knew that I would never want to live anywhere else; and so it was with my wife, who was now three thousand miles away from her family home in Vancouver, Canada.

I called my father, who authorized me to liquidate capital; and in two weeks we had the closing—after the bankers had poked the furnace, and had found nothing flimsy in the old stucco walls, and a check for $65,000 had passed hands; and a little while later I got a $25,000 mortgage from an insurance company, at the eyebrow-raising interest rate of 4⅜ percent—twice the highest rate recommended by Lord Keynes, whose dicta on such subjects my classmates at Yale had received as revelation, poor darlings.

There was a transformation. Several, in fact. One watches, and says very little, when the lady of the house is pursuing a vision. There was a fairly orthodox phase, consummated in splendid taste; and I was happy. But soon she began to stir again; and, during the cultural revolution of the Sixties, our haven was not unaffected. One day she presented me the new room—tactfully executed during my prolonged absence from the country. It is much better to be presented with a *fait accompli*. The mind reeled. I thought of the Château at Blois, with its eclectic styles, and the one room—some famous Frenchman (as usual, the wrong one) was murdered there—full of colored spangles and dark and wine-colored bric-a-brac and ornate parquetry. It was the dining room, and its appeal had the at-onceness that Clement Greenberg celebrates as the unique attribute of art.

There was no stopping her. The sun-room soon became the bordello the Shah couldn't afford. Then the living room, a kind of Haitian concentrate. Self-respect required me, at one point a couple of years ago, to insist on a room of my own—a music room, featuring a beautiful harpsichord and the worst keyboard artist since Harry Truman. I got as far as the windows and the paintings (they are all by the fine Raymond de Botton); but She took over, which is why the room—framing the garden, a slender treetrunk trained like a geisha girl from childhood to give pleasure; the largest wild apple tree *our* treeman has ever seen; and, out there, Long Island Sound, with as many moods as those ersatz fountains the big hotels are constructing, with the Teamster Aeolus who will blow you up a storm, or whisper the sea into kittenlike placidity by turning the pressure gauges—is correspondingly beautiful on the inside. There, in the winter, the fireplace alight, a proper musician performing live or on record, you can see what the pilgrims saw, as if under glass, and understand the compulsion to Thanksgiving.

The neighborhood is wonderful. There has been, to be sure, a touch of Peyton Place in the seven or eight houses that occupy the point; but, although everyone is friendly, no one is importunate. In twenty-four years, we have been out to dinner not more than three times. That is true hospitality. Life is totally informal, though some of that will now have to go. A week or so after acquiring the house, we lost the keys to it; but it didn't seem to matter since nobody had ever heard of a burglar in the area. Until two weeks ago. A couple of them (by the evidence) found their way in, and helped themselves to three generations of silver, two apples, and one box of peanut brittle, which they pried out of a postal package—thus Federalizing their little transgression. If, after they are caught, convicted, and sentenced, they should choose to come back for another course, they will find a house as penetrable as a jewelry store at midnight.

I understand the territorial imperative. I have been (roughly) everywhere. Here is where I find, increasingly, I want to be. With Her. God knows what She will come up with next, maybe (but I don't believe it) a Warhol room. But ingenious though she is, she could never succeed in defacing that house. She has only made it more desirable, and anybody who tries to take it from me should be warned that, in addition to a mad wife, I have three mad dogs, and lots and lotsa ammunition.

The Cook

November 10, 1976

SHORTLY AFTER I was snatched from the arms of my mother to go fight in the world war to liberate Poland, I found myself doing duty in the mess hall at Camp Wheeler, Georgia, when the company commander, accompanied by sycophantic aides with polished gold bars, paid a state visit to the chef to report the findings of the Inspector General, on what it is that affects the morale of America's fighting men. In order, (1) The food he eats. (2) Mail from home. (3) Periodic furloughs.

I was very surprised. I lived for those letters from home, and had not yet tasted the joys of a furlough. But food? My attention had simply never turned to the subject. I remembered dimly that the food at school in England was bad, at home good, at prep school in Millbrook, New York, tolerable, in the

Army about what one would expect which, if served with ketchup, which it always was, was also tolerable. This, then, was my intellectual introduction to the importance of good food. I was an opsimath. Others come to an appreciation of food early.

Much later I heard about the suicide at a boys' school in England, in the Twenties. At the inquest convened by a flustered headmaster, he addressed the student body: "Did anyone present," he asked, "have any idea what might have been the tragic cause of Jones's suicide?" Lord Harlech, then eight years old, raised his hand. "Could it have been the food, sir?" *He* knew that food was a matter of life and death. Even at that age.

When I married, it was to a beautiful young woman who knew as much about cooking as Congress knows about husbandry. But she craved good food, and was entirely instrumental in her approach to the problem of her ignorance. Chesterton was asked what single volume would he take with him to a desert island. He replied, "Dobson's Guide to Shipbuilding." Of course. And, in the little house in Hamden, Connecticut, while I marshaled the case of God and man against Yale, Pat sat on a high stool, turning the pages of cookbooks.

I had two functions during that era. The first was to turn off the pressure cooker when the sound rang out, while Pat would hide under the staircase, assuming a fetal position, resignedly awaiting the explosion, and, as resignedly, her impending widowhood. The second was to taste what she ate. Taste it no matter what. A dear friend, dining with us one evening, made the mistake of taking her chocolate mousse to his lips and also swallowing it. He noticed that I brought it to my lips, only to set it, surreptitiously, down again—like Nixon handling the strong stuff in Moscow. "Bill," my friend said, "you're not pulling your oar."

It was hard, but not for very long. In a matter of months, her art flowered. And, little by little, her friends acclaimed her kitchen as a joy-stop.

Her inclination is French. Pure French. Other cuisines she tolerates, now and again even celebrates, the Chinese a mysterious exception. Here are her hard biases. There must be a first course, and it must not be routine. Not fair simply to serve melon, or a canned soup. The only first course she will serve pristine is smoked salmon or caviar, lightly embellished. She has ten or fifteen openers. My favorite is (I am unskilled at describing these things) a red caviar, mixed in onion, and sour cream, and herbs, in inscrutable, symbiotic combinations: served on fried toast, with, say, a Gewurztraminer. Another I remember is a greenish pea soup, cold, with lots of seasoning and (so help me) apple slices. On this course several years ago Daniel Patrick Moynihan became almost speechless (unhappily, not entirely so: he was in town to sell me and my colleagues on the virtues of the Family Assistance Plan) with pleasure, demanding the recipe. This my Pat forgot to furnish him, and one week later my conscience woke me, so I got it from Pat, and telegraphed it to Patrick at the White House, where—I have ever since assumed—it reposes with a cryptographer in the special prosecutor's office, as the putative marching orders for Watergate, rendered, however, in apparently impenetrable code.

Then comes fish—served very, very plain, like gold. Or (with a nod to Italy) a risotto: I do not know why it tastes as it tastes. What is it that brings on the knowledge of the animating ingredient? I know an eccentric and hugely talented painter who inclines to blue and was asked at his gallery by Helen Hokinson: "Sir, why do you use so much blue paint?" He rose up on his toes, and gave the only appropriate answer. "Madam, blue paint is *cheaper*!" I wonder, is butter cheaper? It is certainly critical.

Or, there is veal (important, cut down on the butter; sear it, as the British said to the executioners at Rouen). About the vegetables, the most important point (how nobly our omniscient friend Nika Hazelton has dwelled on the point in her articles and books)—they must be fresh. Then, depending on the species, the appropriate sauce. My Michelangelo has not, incredibly, yet mastered a plain French salad dressing—I suspect it is her thralldom to lemon. She advised the cook on my schooner to stock the boat with lemon for a week's cruise for six people, and he produced a dozen lemons. The boat was stopped as abruptly as if we had sighted Niagara Falls 100 feet ahead, and she sent my son Christopher out on the dinghy for 100 more.

Lamb, beef, chicken, moussaka . . . with the fish and the meat, always potatoes. She doesn't like fried potatoes, so she makes them listlessly. Not so the other varieties, which appear permeated with something or other that makes even self-consciously thin men ask for more. To go, at our house it is the rule, with a non-pricey red wine. (To buy very good wine nowadays requires only money. To serve it to your guests is a sign of fatigue. Vintage wine should be bought only as presents *for* your friends, and drunk, in private, only as presents *from* your friends.)

And for dessert—always fruit and cheese, more or less there, like finger-bowls, even if only to be seen, and not experienced. But usually a creation, pears, say, with one of those bittersweet yellow sauces. Or chocolate mousse (no longer is it necessary to pull one's oar). Baklava (beware the Greeks bearing gifts). Pecan pie (with a light, liqueured cream). A strawberry tarte (with crème fraîche). And, after the meal, the antiseptic restorative; superstrong coffee. If it is evening, she offers liqueurs. Did you ever have Willième, with bittersweet chocolate, or ginger? Try it on your next furlough when, after all, you do not need any letters from home, so that all those pleasures decocted by the Inspector General are subsumed in that meal, the deprivation of which, in the opinion of a precocious future diplomat in Her Majesty's Service, drove a little boy to fatal despair. Indeed we do not live by bread alone. But the defeat of Manichaeanism deserves celebrating. Once, even twice a day. My Patsy will never cease to pull her oar.

The American Look

April 1978

WHEN, HAVING no idea where I was going, I sat down to write my first novel, it suddenly occurred to me that it would need a protagonist. The alternative of trying to persuade Doubleday that I might create a new art form and write a novel about *nobody* struck me as unprofitable; and so, by the end of the day, I had created Blackford Oakes. And lo, there have been those, the feature editor of this journal included, who have denominated him distinctively American; and the editor asks now that I should say a few words about "the American look." I do so only on the understanding that I reject the very notion of quintessentiality. It is a concept that runs into itself, like F. P. Adams's remark that the average American is a little above average. The reason you cannot have the quintessential American is the very same reason you cannot have a quintessential apple pie, or indeed anything composed of ingredients. In composites, there has got to be an arrangement of attributes and no such arrangement can project one quality to the point of distorting others. This is true even in the matter of physical beauty. An absolutely perfect nose has the effect of satellizing the other features of a human face, and a beautiful face is a comprehensive achievement.

So anyway, Blackford Oakes is not the quintessential American, but I fancy he *is* distinctively American, and the first feature of the distinctively American male is, I think, spontaneity. A kind of freshness born of curiosity and enterprise and wit. Would you believe that three days after meeting her, Blackford Oakes was in bed with the Queen of England? (Not, I hasten to elucidate, the incumbent: Blackford Oakes, as the distinctive American, is a young man of taste, who sleeps only with fictitious queens, thereby avoiding international incidents.) There is something wonderfully American, it struck me, about bedding down a British queen: a kind of arrant but lovable presumption. But always on the understanding that it is done decorously, and that there is no aftertaste of the gigolo in the encounter. I remember, even now with some trepidation, when my first novel, *Saving the Queen,* came out in the British edition. The first questioner at the press conference in London was, no less, the editor of *The Economist*, and he said with, I thought, a quite un-British lack of circumspection: "Mr. Buckley, would you like to sleep with the Queen?" Now, such a question poses quite awful responsibilities. There being a most conspicuous incumbent, one could hardly wrinkle up one's nose as if the question evoked the vision of an evening with Queen Victoria on her Diamond Jubilee. The American with taste has to guard against a lack of gallantry, so that the first order of business becomes the assertion of an emancipating perspective which leads Queen Elizabeth II gently out of the room before she is embarrassed. This was accomplished by saying, just a little sleepily, as Blackford Oakes would have done, "Which queen?"—and then quickly, before the interrogator could lug his monarch back into the smoker—"Judging from historical experience, I would need to consult my lawyer before risking an affair with just *any* British queen." The

American male must be tactful, and tact consists mostly in changing the subject without its appearing that you have done so as a rebuke.

Blackford Oakes appears at age twenty-three, so I stuck him in Yale, which gave me the advantage of being able to write about a familiar few acres and, I suppose, Blackford Oakes emerged with a few characteristics associated in the literature, with Yale men. Like what? Principally, I think, self-confidence; a certain worldliness that is neither bookish nor in any sense of the word anti-intellectual. Blackford Oakes is an engineer by training, and his non-royal girl friend is studying for her Ph.D. and doing her doctorate on Jane Austen. *She* is not expected to show any curiosity about how to build bridges. The American look wears offhandedly its special proficiencies: If one is a lawyer, one does not go about sounding like Oliver Wendell Holmes, any more than Charles Lindbergh went about sounding like Charles Lindbergh. But Blackford quite rightly shows a certain curiosity about Jane Austen, and probably has read (actually, reread: one never *reads* Jane Austen, one *rereads* her) *Pride and Prejudice*.

Blackford Oakes is physically handsome. Here, I took something of a chance. I decided not only to make him routinely good-looking but to make him startlingly so. I don't mean startling in the sense that, let us say, Elizabeth Taylor is startlingly beautiful. It is hard to imagine a male counterpart for pulchritude. An extremely handsome man is not the *equivalent* of an extremely beautiful woman, he is the *complement*; and that is very important to bear in mind in probing the American look which is not, for example, the same as the Italian look. So that when I decided that Blackford Oakes should be startlingly handsome, it was required that he be that in a distinctively American way, and what does that mean? Well, it doesn't mean you look like Mickey Rooney, obviously. But it doesn't mean you look like Tyrone Power, either.

I think the startlingly handsome American male is made so not by the regularity of his features, however necessary that regularity may be, but by the special quality of his expression. It has to be for this reason that, flipping past the male models exhibited in the advertising sections of the New York *Times* or *Esquire*, one never finds oneself pausing to think: that man is startlingly handsome. But such an impression is taken away, from time to time, from a personal encounter, or even from a candid photo. And the American look, in the startlingly handsome man, requires: animation, tempered by a certain shyness, a reserve.

I thought of Billy Budd. I have long since forgotten how Melville actually described him, but he communicated that Budd was startlingly handsome. Looks aside, Budd's distinctiveness was not that of Blackford Oakes. Billy Budd is practically an eponym for innocence, purity. Oakes, though far removed from jadedness, is worldly.

Billy Budd, alas, is humorless. Correction: not *alas*. "Do not go about as a demagogue, encouraging triangles to break out of the prison of their three sides," G. K. Chesterton warned us, because if you succeed, ". . . its life comes to a lamentable end." Give Billy Budd a sense of humor and he shatters in front of you into thousands of little pieces. Blackford Oakes doesn't go about like Wilfred Sheed's protagonist in *Transatlantic Blues* or John Gregory Dunne's in *True Confessions* being hilariously mordant. The American look here is a leavened sarcasm.

Escalate sarcasm and you break through the clouds into the ice-cold of nihilism, and that is my last word on the American look. The American must—*believe*. However discreetly. Blackford Oakes believes. He tends to divulge his beliefs in a kind of slouchy, oblique way. But, at the margin, he is, well—an American with American predilections and he knows, as with the clothes he wears so casually, that he is snug as such; that, like his easygoing sweater and trousers, they . . . fit him. As do the ideals, and even most of the practices, of his country.

VII. *Education*

God and Man at Yale: Twenty-five Years Later

1977

I WAS STILL familiar with the arguments of *God and Man at Yale* when Henry Regnery, its original publisher, asked whether I would furnish a fresh introduction to a re-issue of it. But I had not seen the book since I finally closed its covers, six months after its publication in the fall of 1951. It had caused a most fearful row and required me over a period of several months to spend considerable time re-reading what I had written, sometimes to check what I remembered having said against a reviewer's rendition of it; sometimes to reassure myself on one or another point. The prospect of rereading it a quarter-century later, in order to write this introduction, was uninviting.

Granted, my reluctance was mostly for stylistic reasons. I was twenty-four when I wrote the book, freshly married, living in a suburb of New Haven and teaching a course in beginning Spanish at Yale University. I had help, notably from Frank Chodorov, the gentle, elderly anarchist, friend and disciple of Albert Jay Nock, pamphleteer, editor, founder of the Intercollegiate Society of Individualists, a fine essayist whose thought turned on a single spit: all the reasons why one should be distrustful of state activity, round and round, and round again. And help, also, from Willmoore Kendall, at that time a tenured associate professor of political science at Yale, on leave of absence in Washington, where he worked for an army think tank ("Every time I ask Yale for a leave of absence," he once remarked, "I find it insultingly cooperative").

Kendall had greatly influenced me as an undergraduate. He was a conservative all right, but invariably he gave the impression that he was being a conservative because he was surrounded by liberals; that he'd have been a revolutionist if that had been required in order to be socially disruptive. Those were the days when the Hiss-Chambers case broke, when Senator McCarthy was first heard from, when the leaders of the Communist Party were prosecuted at Foley Square and sentenced to jail for violating the Smith Act. That conviction greatly incensed Kendall's colleagues, and a meeting of the faculty was called for the special purpose of discussing this outrage on civil liberties and framing appropriate articles of indignation. Kendall listened for two hours and then raised his hand to recite an exchange he had had that morning with the colored janitor who cleaned the fellows' suites at Pierson College.

"Is it true, professor"—Kendall, with his Oklahoma drawl, idiosyncratically Oxfordized while he studied as a Rhodes scholar in England, imitated the janitor—"Is it true, professor, dat dere's people in New York City who want to . . . destroy the guvamint of the United States?"

"Yes, Oliver, that is true," Willmoore had replied.

"Well, why don't we lock 'em up?"

That insight, Kendall informed his colleagues, reflected more political wisdom than he had heard from the entire faculty of Yale's political science department since the meeting began. Thus did Kendall make his way through Yale, endearing himself on all occasions.

Kendall was a genius of sorts, and his posthumous reputation continues to grow; but not very long after this book was published he proposed to Yale that the matter of their mutual incompatibility be settled by Yale's buying up his contract, which Yale elatedly agreed to do, paying more than forty thousand dollars to relieve itself of his alien presence. Willmoore Kendall went over the manuscript of *God and Man at Yale* and, as a matter of fact, was responsible for the provocative arrangement of a pair of sentences that got me into more trouble than any others in the book. Since any collusion or suspected collusion in this book was deemed a form of high treason at Yale, I have always believed that the inhospitable treatment of Kendall (after all, there were other eccentrics at Yale who survived) may in part have traced to his suspected association with it and to his very public friendship with me (he became a founding senior editor of *National Review* while still at Yale).

You see, the rumors that the book was being written had got around. They caused considerable consternation at Woodbridge Hall, which is Yale's White House. Yale had a brand new president, A. Whitney Griswold, and he had not yet acquired the savoir faire of high office (when the controversy raged, Dwight Macdonald would comment that Yale's authorities "reacted with all the grace and agility of an elephant cornered by a mouse"—but more on that later). I remember, while doing the research, making an appointment with a professor of economics who privately deplored the hot collectivist turn taken by the economics faculty after the war. At Yale—at least this was so when I was there—the relation between faculty and students (properly speaking I was no longer a student, having graduated in the spring) is wonderfully genial, though (again, this is how it *was*) there was no confusing who was the professor, who the student. I told him I was there to collect information about the left turn taken in the instruction of economics, and he reacted as a Soviet bureaucrat might have when questioned by a young KGB investigator on the putative heterodoxy of Josef Stalin. He told me, maintaining civility by his fingernails, that he would simply *not* discuss the subject with me in any way.

It was not so, however, in the research dealing with the treatment of religion at Yale, perhaps because I ambushed my Protestant friends. I asked the then president of Dwight Hall, the Protestant student organization, if he would bring together the chaplain and the half-dozen persons, staff and undergraduate, centrally concerned with religion to hear one afternoon my chapter on religion at Yale. Everyone came. I read them the chapter that appears in this book—save only the paragraph concerning Yale's chaplain, the Reverend Sidney Lovett. (I did not want to express even the tenderest criticism of him in his presence.) Three or four suggestions of a minor kind were made by members of the audience, and these corrections I entered. I wish I had recorded the episode in the book, because a great deal was made of the alleged singularity of my criticisms and of the distinctiveness of my position as a Roman Catholic. All that could have been difficult for the critics to say if they had known that the chapter had been read out verbatim to the half-dozen Protestant officials most intimately informed about the religious life of Yale, all of whom had acknowledged the validity of my findings, while dissociating themselves from my prescriptions.

I sent the completed manuscript to Henry Regnery in Chicago in April, and he instantly accepted it for publication. I had waited until then formally to apprise the president, Mr. Griswold, of the forthcoming event. We had crossed paths, never swords, several times while I was undergraduate chairman of the *Yale Daily News*. The conversation on the telephone was reserved, but not heated. He thanked me for the civility of a formal notification, told me he knew that I was at work on such a book, that he respected my right to make my views known. I was grateful that he did not ask to see a copy of the manuscript, as I knew there would be eternal wrangling on this point or the other.

But a week or so later I had a telephone call from an elderly tycoon with a huge opinion of himself. William Rogers Coe is mentioned in the book. He advised me that he knew about the manuscript and had splendid tidings for me: namely, I could safely withdraw the book because he, Mr. Coe, had got the private assurance of President Griswold that great reforms at Yale were under way and that conservative principles were in the ascendancy: so why bother to publish a book that would merely stir things up? I gasped at the blend of naïveté and effrontery. But although I had observed the phenomenon I was not yet as conversant as I would quickly become with the ease with which rich and vain men are manipulated by skillful educators. As a matter of fact, men who are not particularly rich or vain are pretty easy to manipulate also.

I did attempt to make one point in a correspondence with Mr. Coe that especially bears repeating. It is this, that a very recent graduate is not only supremely qualified, but uniquely qualified, to write about the ideological impact of an education he has experienced. I was asked recently whether I would "update" this book, to which the answer was very easy: this book cannot be updated, at least not by me. I could only undertake this if I were suddenly thirty years younger, slipped past the Admissions Committee of Yale University in a red wig, enrolled in the courses that serve as ideological pressure points; if I listened to the conversation of students and faculty, participated in the debates, read the college paper every day, read the textbooks, heard the classroom inflections, compared notes with other students in other courses. For years and years after this book came out I would receive letters from Yale alumni asking for an authoritative account of "how the situation at Yale is now." After about three or four years I wrote that I was incompetent to give such an account. I am as incompetent to judge Yale education today as most of the critics who reviewed this book were incompetent to correct me when I judged it twenty-five years ago. Only the man who makes the voyage can speak truly about it. I knew that most of my own classmates would disagree with me on any number of matters, most especially on my prescriptions. But at another level I'd have been surprised to find disagreement. Dwight Macdonald was among the few who spotted the point, though I don't think in his piece for the *Reporter* on the controversy he gave it quite the emphasis it deserved. But he did say, ". . . Nor does Buckley claim any sizable following among the undergraduates. They have discussed his book intensively—and critically. Richard Coulson ('52) notes in the *Yale Alumni* Magazine that 'it is a greater topic of serious and casual conversation than any philosophical or educational question that has been debated in quite a few years. . . .' In contrast to many of their elders the majority has not been blinded with surprise or carried away with rage at either Buckley or the Corporation by his claim that individualism, religion and capitalism are not being propounded strongly both in and out of the classroom. The undergraduate feels that this particular observation is correct."

Well then, if this is so, why republish *God and Man at Yale* in 1977, if it tells the story of Yale in 1950? The question is fair. I suppose a sufficient reason for republishing it is that the publisher has experienced a demand for it. Not, obviously, from people who desire to know the current ideological complexion at Yale—they will have to probe for an answer to that question elsewhere—but by whoever it is who is curious to know how one student, a Christian conservative, experienced and reacted to a postwar education at Yale University, and wants to read the document that caused such a huge fuss; and those who are curious—the purpose of this introduction, I suppose—about what, a quarter-century later, the author might have to say (if anything) about his original contentions, and the reaction to them. I do have some thoughts about the arguments of this book (which I have reread with great embarrassment at the immaturity of my expression—I wish Messrs. Chodorov and Kendall had used more blue pencil) and about the sociology of the educational controversy. It is extremely interesting how people react to the telling of the truth. We all know that, but should not tire of learning even more about it. But the problems raised by *God and Man at Yale* are most definitely with us yet. Some of the predictions made in it have already been realized. Some of the questions are still open. Some of the arguments appear antiquarian; others fresh, even urgent.

First, something on the matter of definitions. Several critics, notably McGeorge Bundy (whose scathing article-length review in the *Atlantic Monthly* was adopted unofficially by Yale as its showcase defense), objected to the looseness of the terms on which I relied. Throughout the book I used a term briefly fashionable after the war, commonplace at the turn of the century, which however now has ebbed out of most polemical intercourse. It is "individualism." I have mentioned Chodorov's Intercollegiate Society of Individualists. Well, about ten years ago even that society changed its name (to Intercollegiate Studies Institute). The term *individualism* was once used as the antonym of "collectivism." Today the preference is for more individuated terms. We hear now about the *private sector*. About *free market* solutions, or approaches. "Individualism" has moved toward its philosophic home—it always had a metaphysical usage. One would expect to hear the word nowadays from disciples of Ayn Rand, or Murray Rothbard; Neo-Spenserians. In any case, if I were rewriting the book I would in most cases reject it in preference for a broader (e.g., "conservative") or narrower term (e.g., "monetarist"). Even so, though it is unfashionable, "individualism" is not, I think, misleading as it here appears.

Now it was very widely alleged, in the course of criticizing the book's terminology, that the position of the authors of the economics texts cited here was misrepresented. For instance, Frank Ashburn, reviewing *Gamay* (the publisher's useful abbreviation in office correspondence) in the *Saturday Review*, wrote: "One economist took the trouble to extract quotations out of context from the same volumes Mr. Buckley used so freely, with the result that the texts seemed the last testaments of the robber barons." That statement puzzles me as much today as when I first read it. After all, on page 49 I had written, "All of these textbook authors take some pains to assure the student that they have in mind the 'strengthening' of the free enterprise system. Not one of them, I am certain, would call himself a socialist or even a confirmed collectivist. Witness, for example, [Theodore] Morgan's eulogy: [in *Income and Employment*]." I went on to quote Morgan:

> It is our general assumption that government should not do anything which individuals or voluntary associations can more efficiently do for themselves (page 184) . . . capitalist, or dominantly free-enterprise economies, have succeeded very well in the Western World in raising tremendously the volume of production (page 176). . . . Obviously, the American public does not want a nationalized economy or a totalitarian unity. We want to give up no segment of our area of freedom unless there is clear justification (page 177) . . . there are both economic and noneconomic reasons

for preserving a dominantly wide area of free enterprise (page 193)....

It is hard to understand how any critic, laboring the point that I had suppressed professions of allegiance to the free enterprise system by the authors under scrutiny, could do so persuasively in the face of the plain language quoted above. The technique of associating oneself for institutional convenience with a general position but disparaging it wherever it is engaged in wars or skirmishes along its frontiers is as old as the wisecrack about the man and woman who got on so splendidly during their married life, having arrived at a covenant that she would settle minor disagreements, he major: "We have never had a major disagreement," the husband ruminates. In this textbook Mr. Morgan, having professed his devotion to the private sector, went on to call for "diminishing the inequality of income and wealth," specifically for a tax of 75 to 99 percent on incomes over one hundred thousand dollars; the elimination of the exemption for capital gains; confiscatory taxes on inheritance "aimed at the goal of ending transmissions of hereditary fortunes"; the nationalization of monopolies, the universalization of social security coverage; family allowances from the government; and government guarantee of full employment. The preferences of this economist would even in 1977 be viewed as left of center. In 1950 they were very far to the left of anything the Democratic Party was calling for. To suggest, as Mr. Ashburn and others did, that there was distortion in representing such as Morgan as "collectivist" is, simply, astonishing; but at another level it is consistent with the public perceptions. Frank Ashburn was a trustee of Yale when he wrote. Yale University was thought of (and still is, though to a lesser extent) as a "citadel of conservatism" (*Time* magazine's phrase). Therefore what emerges to the myth-preserver as principally relevant is less the left-salients in a book like Morgan's, than the obeisances to orthodoxy. Very well. But who's misleading whom?

Now other reviewers graduated their criticism from misrepresentation to misunderstanding. These would stress that economics is a scientific discipline; that Keynes (for instance) could no more be called a left-wing economist than Buckminster Fuller could be called a collectivist architect.

Philip Kurland, writing in the *Northwestern Law Review*, was emphatic on the point. He quotes with some relish a statement by the author of another book reviewed in *Gamay*, Professor Lorie Tarshis. "A word must be said, before we begin our analysis, about the political implications of the Keynesian theory. This is necessary because there is so much misinformation on the subject. The truth is simple. The Keynesian theory no more supports the New Deal stand or the Republican stand than do the newest data on atomic fission. This does not mean that the Keynesian theory cannot be used by supporters of either political party; for it can be, and if it is properly used, it should be. The theory of employment we are going to study is simply an attempt to account for variations in the level of employment in a capitalist economy. It is possible, as we shall see later, to frame either the Republican or the Democratic economic dogma in terms of the theory."

This point, variously stated, was not infrequently made by reviewers. But, in fact, by the end of the 1940s the analysis of John Maynard Keynes was the enthusiastic ideological engine of the New Economics. There is documented evidence that Keynes himself was unhappy about the lengths to which "Keynesians" were going, presumably under his scientific auspices. Kurland, via Tarshis, was telling us in 1951 that Keynes was all technician. As a matter of fact even that is in dispute. It is not disputed that Keynes formulated an analytical vocabulary for addressing certain kinds of economic problems, and the universalization of his vocabulary is as much a fait accompli as the universalization of Freud. But there is continuing dispute over what it is to be "a Keynesian." A long series was published in the Sixties in *Encounter* magazine under the title, "Are We All Keynesians Now?" One contributor to that series—to demonstrate the confusion—maintained that one could not properly qualify as a "Keynesian" unless one believed that the apparatus of the government should be used to maintain low interest rates. Others argued that Keynes had higher—indeed much higher—priorities. Richard Nixon, early in his second term, made the statement, "We are all Keynesians now." Even in 1973 that statement shocked the orthodox. For a Republican to have said such a thing in 1950 is inconceivable—as inconceivable, to quote Professor John Kenneth Galbraith, as to have said "We are all Marxists." Whatever a Keynesian was, at least he was the archenemy of the balanced budget, the watermark of conservative economic thought.

It is especially significant that anti-Keynesian analyses of some gravity had been published at the time the class of 1950 graduated from Yale University. These were both technical and political. But the work of Robbins, Mises, Hutt, Anderson, Röpke—to mention a few—was not called to the attention of students of economics. The operative assumption was that the business cycle was the result of an organic deficiency in the market system and that interventionism was the only cure. We know now that the factor of the money supply looms larger in causing contraction and expansion than anyone surmised at the time. The texts reviewed in *Gamway* were, I am saying, heavily ideological, and "Keynesian" was the correct idiomatic word to use to describe economists who inclined to interventionist solutions for economic problems and, while at it, social problems as well.

I do not mean to give the impression that critics were united in their disdain of my analysis of economic education at Yale. Max Eastman, who had himself written books on socialist theory, was amusingly impatient, in his obstinate atheism, with the chapter on religion ("For my part, I fail to see why God cannot take care of Himself at Yale, or even for that matter at Harvard. To me it is ridiculous to see little, two-legged fanatics running around the earth fighting and arguing in behalf of a Deity whom they profess to consider omnipotent"). But he was forthrightly enthusiastic about the economics section: "His second chapter, Individualism at Yale, is by contrast entirely mature. And it is devastating." There were others, schooled in economics, who applauded the chapter, e.g., Felix Morley, Henry Hazlitt, John Davenport, Garret Garrett, and C. P. Ives.

Max Eastman's dichotomization brings up the heated reaction to a book that professes concurrently a concern over the ascendancy of religious skepticism and political statism. I spoke earlier about a set of sentences that many critics found especially galling. When I saw the suggested formulation, written out on the margin of my manuscript in Willmoore Kendall's bold green script, I suspected it would cause difficulty. But there was a nice rhetorical resonance and an intrinsic, almost nonchalant suggestion of an exciting symbiosis, so I let pass: *"I believe that the duel between Christianity and atheism is the most important in the world. I further believe that the struggle between individualism and collectivism is the same struggle reproduced on another level."* The words "the same struggle reproduced on another level" were not originally my own. In the prolonged defense of the book I did not renounce them, in part out of loyalty to my mentor, in part, no doubt, because it would have proved embarrassing to disavow a formulation published over one's signature, never mind its provenance. But in part also because I was tickled by the audacity of the sally and not unamused by the sputtering outrage of its critics.

They were, no doubt, particularly spurred on to lambaste the suggested nexus by their knowledge of its popularity in certain Christian-conservative circles, my favorite of them being the American Council of Christian Laymen in Madison, Wisconsin, which quoted the two sentences in its publication and then sighed, "No Solomon or Confucius or other wise man of the ages ever spoke or wrote truer words than the sentence just quoted." It was the very first time I had been compared to Solomon *or* Confucius.

The widespread objection was not only on the point that to suggest an affinity between the eschatological prospects of heaven and hell and the correct role of the state in achieving full employment was something on the order of blasphemy. It was fueled by the ideological conviction of many Christian modernists that the road to Christianity on earth lies through the Federal Government. Although these criticisms flowed in copiously from Protestant quarters, they were on the whole most bitter in the fashionable Catholic journals; and indeed my being a Catholic itself became something of an issue.

McGeorge Bundy, in his main-event review in the *Atlantic*, wrote directly on the point:

"Most remarkable of all, Mr. Buckley, who urges a return to what he considers to be Yale's true religious tradition, at no point says one word of the fact that he himself is an ardent Roman Catholic. In view of the pronounced and well-recognized difference between Protestant and Catholic views on education in America, and in view of Yale's Protestant history, it seems strange for any Roman Catholic to undertake to speak for the Yale religious tradition. . . . It is stranger still for Mr. Buckley to venture his prescription with no word or hint to show his special allegiance."

On this point Dwight Macdonald commented: "Buckley is indeed a Catholic, and an ardent one. But, oddly enough, this fact is irrelevant, since his book defines Christianity in Protestant terms, and his economics are Calvinist rather than Catholic. One of the wryest twists in the whole comedy is that the Catholic press has almost unanimously damned Buckley's economic views."

Macdonald exaggerated, but not entirely. "He quite unwittingly succeeds in contravening Catholic moral doctrine as applied to economics and politics on almost every topic he takes up," the Jesuits' *America* had editorialized, concluding, "Mr. Buckley's own social philosophy is almost as obnoxious to a well-instructed Catholic as the assaults on religion he rightly condemns." (Who is flirting with the nexus now?) *Commonweal*, the Catholic layman's journal of opinion, was right in there. "The nature of Mr. Buckley's heresies were pointed out again in the Catholic press, but apparently the young man remains unmoved. He continues to peddle his anti-papal economics without any noticeable changes often under the auspices of Catholics. . . ." Father Higgins, the labor priest, objected heatedly to my "attempt to identify the heresy of economic individualism with Catholic or Christian doctrine."

I am obliged to concede, at this distance, that, the attacks from the Catholics quite apart, it is probably true that there was a pretty distinct anti-Catholic animus in some of the criticism of this book. The Reverend Henry Sloane Coffin, former head of the Union Theological Seminary, former chairman of the Educational Policy Committee of Yale, former trustee of the Corporation, chairman of a committee commissioned by the Yale Corporation to investigate my charges about Yale education without ever acknowledging them (see below), was so incautious as to write to an alumnus who had questioned Coffin about my book, "Mr. Buckley's book is really a misrepresentation and [is] distorted by his Roman Catholic point of view. Yale is a Puritan and Protestant institution by its heritage and he should have attended Fordham or some similar institution."

Now there are three strands to the Catholic point. The first has to do with the allegedly distinctive Catholic definition of Christianity; the second with the allegedly distinctive Catholic understanding of the role of the university; and the third, most simply stated, was ad hominem, i.e., an attempt to suggest that by "concealing" my Catholicism I told the discerning reader a great deal about my deficient character and, derivatively, about the invalidity of my criticisms and arguments.

Taking the third point first, a semantic advantage was instantly achieved by those who spoke of my having "concealed" my Catholicism. By not advertising it—so ran the planted axiom—I was concealing it. Inasmuch as, on writing the book, I saw nothing in the least distinctively Catholic about the points I made, I had thought it irrelevant to advert to my Catholicism. Even as I was criticized for "concealing" my Catholicism, I could have been criticized had I identified myself as a Catholic on the grounds that I had "dragged in" my Catholicism as if it were relevant.

But see, for instance, Professor Fred Rodell (of the Yale Law School) writing in the *Progressive*, probably (though there are close runners-up—Arthur Schlesinger in the New York *Post*, Vern Countryman in the *Yale Law Journal*, Herman Liebert in the St. Louis *Post Dispatch*, Theodore Greene in the *Yale Daily News*, Frank Ashburn in the *Saturday Review*) the most acidulous review of the lot. ". . . most Catholics would resent both the un-Christian arrogance of his presentation and, particularly, his deliberate concealment—throughout the entire foreword, text, and appendices of a highly personalized book—of his very relevant church affiliation." Ah, the sweet uses of rhetoric. "No mention" of Catholicism elides to "concealment" of Catholicism elides to "deliberate concealment" (a tautology, by the way). That my affiliation was "very relevant" spared Mr. Rodell the pains of having to explain its relevance. By the same token would it have been relevant for a reviewer of a book by Fred Rodell on the *Supreme Court and Freedom of Religion* to accuse the author of "deliberate concealment" of the "very relevant" fact that his name used to be Fred Rodelheim, and that his interpretation of the Freedom Clause was tainted in virtue of his lifetime's concealment of his having been born Jewish? That would have gone down—quite properly—as anti-Semitism.

If one pauses to think about it, it is difficult to be at once an "ardent" Catholic, as everyone kept saying I was, and to "conceal" one's Catholicism (unless one worships furiously and furtively). The only place in the book in which I might unobtrusively have said that I am a Catholic is on page 31 where I mention an Inter-Faith Conference held in the spring of 1949 sponsored by Dwight Hall (Protestant), St. Thomas More (Catholic), and the Hillel Foundation (Jewish). I was the Catholic co-chairman of that conference, which is hardly the way to go about concealing one's affiliation. But even to have mentioned in this book that I had been co-chairman would have been irrelevant, perhaps even vainglorious. Should I have mentioned that I was the son of a wealthy father, in order to explain a prejudice in favor of capitalism?

With respect to the second point, I accepted as the operative definition of "Christianity" (see page 8) that of the World Council of Churches, supplemented by a definition of Dr. Reinhold Niebuhr—an organization, and an individual, never accused of being closet Catholics.

As to the remaining point, namely the purpose of education, it is hard to know what the Reverend Henry Sloane Coffin had in mind when he suggested that Yale's "Puritan and Protestant heritage" was responsible for a "distortion" that grew inevitably out of my Roman Catholicism, or McGeorge Bundy when he referred to the well-recognized difference between Protestant and Catholic views on education in America. I am aware of no difference, celebrated or obscure, with reference to the purpose of a *secular college*, about which I was writing. Yale was indeed founded as a Protestant institution, but the bearing of that datum on this book underscores rather than subverts its thesis. The man who was president of Yale while I was there said in his inaugural address, "I call on all members of the faculty, as members of a thinking body, freely to recognize the tremendous validity and power of the teachings of Christ in our life-and-death struggle against the force of selfish materialism." That wasn't Pope Pius IX talking. And, later, President Charles Seymour said, "Yale was dedicated to the training of spiritual leaders. We betray our trust if we fail to explore the various ways in which the youth who come to us may learn to appreciate spiritual values, whether by the example of our own lives or through the cogency of our philosophical arguments. The simple and direct way is through the maintenance and upbuilding of the Christian religion as a vital part of university life." Maybe Charles Seymour should have been made president of Fordham.

I have mentioned that the reaction to the publication of *Gamay* was quite startling. Louis Filler wrote in the *New England Quarterly*: "This book is a phenomenon of our time. It could hardly have been written ten years ago, at least for general circulation." He meant by that that no one ten years earlier a) was particularly alarmed by, or interested in, ideological trends in higher education; and that therefore b) nobody would have bothered to read a book that examined those themes, let alone one that focused on a single college.

So that the book's success as an attention-getter first surprised, then amazed. It was infuriating to the hostile critics that a man as eminent as John Chamberlain should have consented to write the introduction to it, and indeed Fred Rodell held him personally responsible for the notoriety of the book. ("It was doubtless the fact of a John Chamberlain introduction that lent the book, from the start, the aura of importance and respectability. . . .") But it was too late to ignore it. *Life* magazine did an editorial (cautious interest in the book's theme), *Time* and *Newsweek* ran news stories; the *Saturday Review*, a double review; and after a while there were reviews and news stories about the reviews and news stories. The critic Selden Rodman, although he disagreed with the book and its conclusions, had said of it in the *Saturday Review*, "[Mr. Buckley] writes with clarity, a sobriety, and an intellectual honesty that would be noteworthy if it came from a college president." (Compare Herman Liebert, from the staff of the Yale Library, writing for the St. Louis *Post Dispatch*: ". . . the book is a series of fanatically emotional attacks on a few professors who dare to approach religion and politics objectively." Note that collectivist economics and agnostic philosophy suddenly became the "objective" approaches. That they were so considered at Yale was of course the gravamen of the book which this critic, in his fustian, was witless to recognize.) Oh, yes, Fred Rodell: "I deem it irresponsible in a scholar like Selden Rodman to dignify the book as 'important' and 'thought-provoking.'" Max Eastman had written, in the *American Mercury*, "He names names, and quotes quotes, and conducts himself, in general, with a disrespect for his teachers that is charming and stimulating in a high degree.... This perhaps is the best feature of his book, certainly the most American in the old style—its arrant intellectual courage." (From the encephalophonic Mr. Rodell, his voice hoarse: "...I deem it irresponsible, in a scholar like Max Eastman, to shower the book with adulatory adjectives....")

And so on, for months and months. Official Yale took no official position but was very busy at every level. The *Yale Daily News* ran analyses of the book by six professors, only one of whom (William Wimsatt) found anything remotely commendable about the book. The series was introduced by an editorial of which a specimen sentence was "When the Buckley book has succeeded in turning the stomachs of its readers and lining up Yale men categorically on the side of that great 'hoax' academic freedom, Bill Buckley will, as Professor Greene suggests, have performed a great service to Yale."

In the *Yale Alumni* Magazine the book was treated with caution, but I was offhandedly coupled with a notorious and wealthy old crank called George Gundelfinger, a gentleman who had gone off his rocker a generation earlier and periodically drowned the campus with nervous exhalations of his arcane philosophy, which heralded as the key to the full life a kind of platonic masturbation ("sublimate pumping" he called it). Copies of McGeorge Bundy's review were sent out to questioning alumni. Meanwhile, in the trustees' room, a plan had been devised to commission an inquiry by a committee of eight alumni into "the intellectual and spiritual welfare of the university, the students, and its faculty." The chairman, as mentioned, was Henry Sloane Coffin. And among its members was Irving Olds, then chairman of the board of United States Steel Corporation, thus effecting representation for God and man. The committee was surreptitously set up during the summer, in anticipation of *Gamay*'s appearance in the fall, but its clear function of unsaying what this book said was acknowledged even in the news stories.

Yale didn't have an easy time of it. Too many people knew instinctively that the central charges of the book were correct, whatever the inflections distinctive to Yale. Felix Morley, formerly president of Haverford College, had written in *Barrons*, "[Buckley's] arguments must be taken seriously. As he suggests, and as this reviewer from personal knowledge of scores of American colleges can confirm, the indictment is equally applicable to many of our privately endowed institutions of higher learning. Mr. Buckley, says John Chamberlain in the latter's foreword, is incontestably right about the educational drift of modern times." It is confirmation of Morley's generalization that, twenty-five years later, references to religion and politics that were then eyebrow-raising seem utterly bland: almost conservative, in a way. What is unthinkable in the current scene isn't that an economics teacher should come out for a 100 percent excess profits tax, or that a teacher of sociology should mock religion. What is unthinkable today is an inaugural address by a president of a major university containing such passages as I have quoted from Charles Seymour.

So that Yale had that problem—that most people suspected that heterodoxy was rampant—and an additional problem which it needed to handle most deftly (and, on the whole, did). I made the suggestion in this book that the alumni of Yale play a greater role in directing the course of Yale education. That they proceed to govern the university, through their representatives, even as the people govern the country through theirs. This suggestion had a most startling effect. Yale's challenge has alwaye been to flatter its alumni while making certain they should continue impotent.

The purpose of a Yale education, never mind the strictures of this book, can hardly be to turn out a race of idiots. But one would have thought that was what Yale precisely engages in. Walking out of the Huntington Hotel in Pasadena during the hottest days of the controversy, I espied the Reverend Henry Sloane Coffin walking in. I introduced myself. He greeted me stiffly, and then said, as he resumed his way into the hotel, "Why do you want to turn Yale education over to a bunch of boobs?" Since Mr. Coffin had been chairman of the Educational Policy Committee of the Corporation, it struck me that if indeed the alumni were boobs he bore a considerable procreative responsibility. Certainly his contempt for Yale's demonstrated failure was far greater than my alarm at its potential failure.

He was not alone.

Bruce Barton, the anti-New Dealer at whose partial expense President Roosevelt had composed the rollicking taunt, "Martin, Barton and Fish," saw the need for reform. But by *alumni*? "As for Mr. Buckley's cure—letting the alumni dictate the teaching—what could be more terrifying? Are these noisy, perennial sophomores, who dress up in silly costumes and get drunk at reunions, who spend their thousands of dollars buying halfbacks and quarterbacks, and following the Big Blue Team—are they to be the nation's mental mentors?" I really had had no idea the contempt in which "alumni" qua alumni were so generally held.

My notion, as elaborated in the book, was that alumni would concern themselves with the purpose of a university; that, if mind and conscience led them to the conclusion, they would not only be free, but compelled, to decide that certain values should be encouraged, others discouraged. That, necessarily, this would give them, through their representatives, the right to judicious hiring and firing, precisely with the end in mind of furthering broad philosophical objectives and cultivating certain ideas—through the exposure of the undergraduate body to (President Seymour's phrase) cogent philosophical arguments.

There are many grounds for disapproving the proposal of alumni control. But the description, by some critics, of the state of affairs I sought led me to question my own sanity and then, finding it in good order, to question that of my critics. Consider the near-terminal pain of Frank Ashburn as he closed his long piece for the *Saturday Review*:

"The book is one which has the glow and appeal of a fiery cross on a hillside at night. There will undoubtedly be robed figures who gather to it, but the hoods will not be academic. They will cover the face."

Gee whiz. Now it is important to remember that Frank Ashburn is a very nice man. He is, moreover, quite intelligent. He founded a successful boys' preparatory school, Brooks School, and, years later, in his capacity as headmaster, he invited me to address the student body, proffering the customary fee. And I did, arriving without my hood; and, to the extent it is possible to do so under less than clinical conditions, I probed about a bit, and Frank Ashburn was to all appearances entirely normal. But that's the kind of thing *Gamay* did to people, especially people close to Yale. I did mention that Frank Ashburn was a trustee?

I must not let the point go, because one *has* to ask oneself *why* it is that supervision of the general direction of undergraduate instruction is so instinctively repugnant to nonjuveniles. I do not know whether Robert Hatch, who wrote for the *New Republic*, is a Yale graduate, but in terms of horror registered he might as well have been. He took pains, in his review, to try to explain what, in fact, I was *really* up to with my bizarre proposals. "It is astonishing," he wrote, "on the assumption that Buckley is well-meaning, that he has not realized that the methods he proposes for his alma mater are precisely those employed in Italy, Germany, and Russia. An elite shall establish the truth by ukase and no basic disagreement shall be tolerated."

It really wasn't all that astonishing that I did not spot the similarities in the methods I proposed and those of the Fascists, Nazis, and Communists, because there are no similarities. My book made it plain that alumni direction could be tolerated only over the college of which they were uniquely the constituents; that alumni of institutions that sought different ends should be equally free to pursue them. Moreover, the ideals I sought to serve were those that no authoritarian society would regard as other than seditious, namely, the ideals of a minimalist state, and deference to a transcendent order.

But the notion that the proposals were subversive was jubilantly contagious. Four months after the publication of *Gamay*, Chad Walsh was writing in the *Saturday Review*: "What Mr. Buckley really proposes is that the alumni of Yale should turn themselves into a politburo, and control the campus exactly as the Kremlin controls the intellectual life of Russia." "Exactly," in the sense used here, can only be understood to mean "analogously." Obviously there are no "exact" parallels between a state directing all education and enforcing a political orthodoxy and the constituency of discrete educational institutions, within a free and pluralist society, directing the education of its own educational enterprise. Indeed, so obviously is it inexact to draw the parallel, the heretical thought suggests itself that conventional limitations on alumni are closer to the authoritarian model. A free association, within a free society, shaping an educational institution toward its own purpose, is practicing a freedom which totalitarian societies would never permit it to do. An obvious example would be a German university under Hitler which prescribed that its faculty, in the relevant disciplines, should preach racial toleration and racial equality; or, in the Bolshevik model, a constituency backing a university that, athwart the political orthodoxy, insisted on preaching the ideals of freedom and pluralism.

I find it painful, at this remove, to make points so obvious. But if *Gamay* is to republished, it must surely be in part for the purpose of allowing us to examine specimens, however wilted, of the political literature of yesteryear; and to wonder what was the madness that seized so many people of such considerable reputation; and to wonder further that such profound misinterpretations were not more widely disavowed. Were these people lefties?—shrewdly protecting their positions by theoretical incantations? Yes, one supposes, in some cases. But surely not in others: Frank Ashburn was an Establishment figure, in lockstep with the Zeitgeist, who probably shed a wistful tear or two in private over some of the departed virtues at Yale. *They* are the enigma. The left was of course especially scornful. When, fifteen years later, a number of our colleges and universities were given over to the thousand blooms of the youth revolution, which demanded that colleges be "relevant"—i.e., that they become arms depots for the anti-Vietnam war—many of the same people who sharpened their teeth on *Gamay* were preternaturally silent.

Michael Harrington was in those days a socialist and a Christian. He would in due course repeal the laws of progress by reaffirming the one faith and renouncing the second. He wrote his review for Dorothy Day's *Catholic Worker*: "The frightening thing is that Mr. Buckley is not yet realistic enough for fascism. Mr. Buckley's aims can only be secured by fascist methods—coercion in favor of capitalists—a realistic conclusion which Mr. Buckley's five years in New Haven did not educate him to make." Neither five years' education in New Haven nor twenty-five years' education outside New Haven. The case for capitalism is stronger in 1977 than in 1950, having profited in the interim from the empirical failures of socialism, as from the scholarly accreditation of the presumptions of the free market. Besides which, the word "fascism" loses its pungency when it is used to mean, pure and simple, the exercise of authority. Mr. Harrington, even then, was flirting with heresy, which would become his succubus.

Authority is licitly and illicitly acquired by the democratic canon; and, once acquired, is then licitly and illicitly exercised. The "authority" to apprehend, try, and punish a lawbreaker is licitly acquired in the democratic circumstances of a society which, after popular consultation, makes its own laws, prescribes its own judicial procedures, and stipulates its own punishments—all subject to the rule of law. The line between licit and illicit authority in a secular society is, however, elusive, though it is generally acknowledged in the Judeo-Christian world that there is such a line, most resonantly affirmed by Christ's distinction between Caesar and God. It is an unusual experience for a libertarian to be catechized by a socialist on the theme of the dangers of coercion. Harrington's oxymoronic formulation—"coercion in favor of capitalists"—reminds us of the fashionable jargon in the commodity markets of the left (alas, not greatly changed). His sentence is on the order of "coercive freedom," or "the slavery of the bill of rights." Unless a "fascist method" can be distinguished from a plain old "method" by which the will of the entrepreneurial unit prevails over the will of the individual resolved subversively to gainsay that will, then paradoxically you are left without the freedom of the collectivity. The interdiction of that modest freedom on the grand piano Mr. Harrington is used to thumping in his full-throated crusade for state socialism is not only inconsistent, it is positively unseemly.

It is worth pursuing the matter yet one step further, I think, in order to notice the review by T. M. Greene. Professor Greene was a considerable character on the Yale campus. I think he was the most quintessentially liberal man I ever came upon, outside the pages of Randall Jarrell's *Pictures from an Institution*. As master of the largest residential college at Yale

(Silliman), he one day issued an order, in the interest of decorum, requiring students who ate dinner in the dining room to wear coats and ties. He was dismayed by the trickle of criticism, and very soon indignantly repealed his own order, apologizing for his lapse into dirigisme. He taught, as an explicit Christian, a course in the philosophy of religion which was widely attended; but I remarked that in the opinion of his students he was engaged, really, in reteaching ethics, not religion. (There's nothing against teaching ethics, but of course it isn't exactly the same thing.)

His reaction to *Gamay*, as published in the *Yale Daily News*, fairly took one's breath away. He fondled the word "fascist" as though he had come up with a Dead Sea Scroll vouchsafing the key word to the understanding of *God and Man at Yale*. In a few sentences he used the term thrice. "Mr. Buckley has done Yale a great service" (how I would tire of this pedestrian rhetorical device), "and he may well do the cause of liberal education in America an even greater service, by stating the fascist alternative to liberalism. This fascist thesis. . . . This . . . pure fascism. . . . What more could Hitler, Mussolini, or Stalin ask for . . . ? (They asked for, and got, a great deal more.)

What survives, from such stuff as this, is ne-plus-ultra relativism, idiot nihilism. "What is required," Professor Greene spoke, "is more, not less tolerance—not the tolerance of indifference, but the tolerance of honest respect for divergent convictions and the determination of all that such divergent opinions be heard without administrative censorship. I try my best in the classroom to expound and defend my faith, when it is relevant, as honestly and persuasively as I can. But I can do so only because many of my colleagues are expounding and defending their contrasting faiths, or skepticisms, as openly and honestly as I am mine."

A professor of *philosophy!* Question: What is the (1) ethical, (2) pragmatic or (3) epistemological argument for *requiring* continued tolerance of ideas whose discrediting it is the purpose of education to effect? What ethical code (in the Bible? in Plato? Kant? Hume?) requires "honest respect" for any divergent conviction? Even John Stuart Mill did not ask more than that a question be not considered as closed so long as any one man adhered to it; he did not require that that man, flourishing the map of a flat world, be seated in a chair of science at Yale. And this is to say nothing about the flamboyant contrast between Professor Greene's call to toleration in all circumstances and the toleration *he* showed to the book he was reviewing. An honest respect by him for my divergent conviction would have been an arresting application at once of his theoretical and charitable convictions.

The sleeper, in that issue of the *Yale Daily News*, was William Wimsatt. The late Professor Wimsatt, the renowned critic and teacher, was . . . a Catholic! Not an uppity Catholic. He was, simply, known by the cognoscenti to be one, and his friends found that charming. But under the circumstances, the pressure on Professor Wimsatt to Tom must have been very nearly unbearable, and his conciliatory motions must be weighted charitably under the circumstances. He denounced *Gamay* as "impudent," inasmuch as its author "used the entree and confidential advantage of a student and alumnus to publicize so widely both embarrassing personalities and problems of policy which are internal to the relation between administrative officers and alumni." A so-so point which, it happens, I dealt with in the book itself, in my discussion of the emasculating hold the Yale administration exercises over its alumni; but, in a sense, also a point gainsaid by the universal interest provoked by the book, which interest focused not on its gossip value involving any one or more professors (only three of the hundred reviews I have reread bother even to mention by name any individual professor named in the book).

Protected by such rhetorical cover, Professor Wimsatt went on to say some very interesting things. He began, for instance, by suavely blowing the whole Coffin-Bundy-Dwight Hall-Yale position about religion at Yale. "The prevailing secularism of the university is palpable," wrote Professor Wimsatt matter-of-factly. That's what I said. But lest that should shock, he added, What-else-is-new? "What else did Mr. Buckley expect when he elected to come here?" He went on to say, in effect, that a "modern" university cannot orient itself other than to fashion. "What would he expect of any modern American university large enough to be the representative of the culture in which he has lived all his life?"

Mr. Wimsatt is here carefully avoiding the point. Obviously

a modern, acquiescent, college will tend not to buck the Zeitgeist. This begs the question whether under certain circumstances it might do so; and certainly begs the question whether idealistically active alumni are entitled to apply pressure on it to do so.

But, despite himself, Professor Wimsatt was getting hotter and hotter. "It is more fundamental to ask . . . what is actually right, and how far any individual may in good conscience tolerate or assist the teaching of what he firmly believes wrong. If I knew that a professor were teaching the Baconian heresy about Shakespeare, I should think it a pity. If I knew that a professor were preaching genocide, I should think it a duty, if I were able, to prevent him—even though his views were being adequately refuted in the next classroom." That buzz saw ran right through the analysis of Professor Greene, adjacent on the page, leaving it bobbing and weaving in death agony. But nobody noticed. "As Mr. Buckley so earnestly pleads, it is indeed very far from being a fact that the truth, in such matters of value, is bound 'to emerge victorious'. It would be easy to name several doctrines, not only genocide but the less violent forms of racism, for instance, or an ethics of pre-marital sexual experiment—which the present administration of no university in this country would tolerate." (From the 25th Reunion Yearbook of the Yale Class of 1950, published in 1975, Questionnaire #13: "Are you in favor of or opposed to: . . . People living together out of wedlock? Oppose, 42%. Favor, 43%.") Although Professor Wimsatt was hardly quotable as an endorser of *Gamay*, the passages here reproduced take you exactly as far as I go in every theoretical point. Everything else he said was in the nature of social shock absorption.

It is worth it, before making a final comment on the grander points involved, to climb out of the polemical fever swamps and look with a little detachment on the purely economic question. When I wrote this book, there were reviewers who defended the factual generalities, indeed went so far as to say the points I made were obvious. Yale's teachings were distinct from Yale's preachings—"this rudimentary fact of life," Dwight Macdonald commented, "Buckley is rude enough to dwell on for 240 pages." On the other hand, very few reviewers (certainly not Macdonald) were prepared to associate themselves with my prescriptions—though some of them acknowledged nervously that any way you look at it there was a paradox in the circumstance of alumni agitatedly supporting the cultivation of values different from their own. I think it safe to say that no fully integrated member of the intellectual community associated himself with my position on academic freedom. In March of this year Irving Kristol, a professor, editor, author, philosopher of unassailable academic and intellectual standing, included in a casual essay in his regular series for the *Wall Street Journal* (which space he shares with such other scholars as Robert Nisbet and Arthur Schlesinger, Jr.) the comment:

"Business men or corporations do not have any obligation to give money to institutions whose views or attitudes they disapprove of. It's absurd to insist otherwise—yet this absurdity is consistently set forth in the name of 'academic freedom.'" The prose is an improvement on my own in *God and Man at Yale*, but the point is identical. Yet no one rose to say of Professor Kristol that he should be wearing a hood and that he was introducing fascism to American education.

Indeed the educational establishment, although it rose to smite my book hip and thigh, has since then tended to find it more useful to take the advice of that generic class of prudent lawyers who counsel their clients to say "No comment." Even now I rub my eyes in amazement at the silence given to events—historical, sociological, and even judicial—that tend to confirm and reconfirm the factual claims of my book, and to give support to its theoretical arguments. There was, for instance, the A. P. Smith case of 1953 (*A. P. Smith Manufacturing Company* v. *Barlow*). I should like to be able to refer to it as the "celebrated A. P. Smith case." But it is not celebrated at all. It is unknown.

What happened was that a New Jersey manufacturer of valves and hydrants made a gift of $1,500 to Princeton University, and a group of minority stockholders sued, saying in effect, What does Princeton University have to do with the fortunes of the A. P. Smith Company? The case was tried and most vigorously defended, with star witnesses moving in and out of the witness stand. Not because of the $1,500, obviously, but because the precedent was deemed very important.

Well, Princeton and the management of the A. P. Smith Company won. Two courts, the superior court of New Jersey and the Supreme Court of that state on appeal, affirmed the corporate validity of the gift. Why then is the case not more greatly celebrated?

Because the price of victory was academic freedom as commonly understood. The A. P. Smith Company, in its defense brief, took the position that by giving money to Princeton it was advancing its corporate purposes strictly defined. The defense brief said: "The Smith Company turned to philanthropy not for the sake of philanthropy but for the sake of selling more valves and hydrants." *How's that again?*

But there was no recorded objection from representatives of Princeton University. Expert witnesses were called. One of them was: Irving Olds. Our old friend! Chairman of the board of United States Steel! Mr. Olds testified soberly on the stand that "our American institutions of higher learning can and do perform a service of tremendous importance to the corporations of this and other states, through acquainting their students with the facts about different economic theories and ideologies. With the good educational facilities provided by these institutions, the courses of instruction will and do lead the student body to recognize the virtues and achievements of our well-proven economic system; and, on the other hand, to discover the faults and weaknesses of an arbitrary, government-directed and controlled system of production and distribution."

That testimony by Mr. Olds was given approximately on the first anniversary of the release of the report of the Yale committee to investigate the charges leveled in this book, and Mr. Olds had then put his signature on a document that said:

"A university does not take sides in the questions that are discussed in its halls. The business of a university is to educate, not to indoctrinate its students. In the ideal university all sides of any issue are presented as impartially and as forcefully as possible. This is Yale's policy." Now the only course in comparative economic systems being taught at Yale at that time is described in this book. The professor who taught it proclaimed himself an ardent socialist in the British tradition, and defended the socialist alternative to the free market system, which one would suppose is not the system that, in the understanding of

A. P. Smith, the lower court, the higher court, and Irving Olds, promotes the "selling of more valves and hydrants."

The worst was yet to be. The lower court, in authorizing the gift, ruled: "It is the youth of today which also furnishes tomorrow's leaders in economics and in government, thereby erecting a strong breastwork against any onslaught from hostile forces which would change our way of life either in respect of private enterprise or democratic self-government. The proofs before me are abundant that Princeton emphasizes by precept and indoctrination [*precept and indoctrination!*] the principles which are very vital to the preservation of our democratic system of business and government. . . . I cannot conceive of any greater benefit to corporations in this country than to build, and continue to build, respect for and adherence to a system of free enterprise and democratic government, the serious impairment of either of which may well spell the destruction of all corporate enterprise." I cannot think of a more excruciatingly embarrassing victory in Princeton's history.

Dumb judge? I invite you to find a denunciation of him by an official of Princeton University. The decision was appealed and went on to the Supreme Court of New Jersey where *another* dumb judge affirmed the lower court's decision, and made it all worse. Because *he* reminded the "objecting stockholders" that they had "not disputed any of the foregoing testimony" asserting the service Princeton is performing in behalf of free market economy; and the court reminded them, paternalistically, that "more and more they [private corporations] have come to recognize that their salvation rests upon a sound economic and social environment which in turn rests in no insignificant part upon free and vigorous non-governmental institutions of learning." Princeton didn't take its $1,500 and go hang itself, but one can imagine the gloom in the paneled office where they all met to open that judicial valentine.

·

The educators were saying, in response to this book, that college is a cultural sanctuary from the commerce of life. That such concessions as periodically were made by university officials were purely rhetorical—President Seymour, enjoining the faculty to cultivate the doctrines of Christ at inaugural ceremonies; Princeton deans, nodding their heads acquiescently when the court upholds a financial award on the ground that Princeton is "by precept and indoctrination" committed to spreading the gospel of free enterprise. Actually, they were saying, no interference is possible. All ideas must start out equal. (All ideas *are* equal!) To make demands on a college is totalitarian, fascist, communist, condemned by all men of understanding, reaching back to Thomas Jefferson. How widely he was used during the controversy! "Subject opinion to coercion," Philip Kurland quoted him; "whom will you make your inquisitors? Fallible men; men governed by bad passions, by private as well as public reasons. And why subject it to coercion? To produce uniformity. But is uniformity of opinion desirable? No more than of face and stature... difference of opinion is advantageous." And, of course, who would disagree that men are fallible? But does that mean we can rely, at the margin, other than on men? On whom was Jefferson relying for remedies when in 1821 he wrote to General Breckinridge to complain of "seminaries [where] our sons [are] imbibing opinions and principles in discord with those of their own country." Did Jefferson wish to do something about it? Or was he describing only a situation which could not be corrected, because men are fallible, dominated by passion. No. Jefferson continued, "This canker is eating on the vitals of our existence, and if not arrested at once, will be beyond remedy." If not arrested by whom? Surely not the state. We would all agree on this? Not quite all. The state would prove to have its uses. President Seymour warned urgently and repeatedly against accepting federal aid to education on the grounds that it would bring federal interference. President Seymour retired in 1950. In the succeeding generation major private universities became totally dependent on federal funds. Remove the federal subsidy to Yale (35 percent), or to Harvard (25 percent), or to MIT (65 percent) and what would happen to them? The notion of mere trustees influencing the choice of textbooks was—and is—thought scandalous: by the same people who, calling such interference fascism, backed, or were indifferent to, legislation which twenty-five years later would permit the attorney general of the United States (ironically, a former college president, in a Republican administration, executing laws passed by a Democratic Congress) to pry out of a thoroughly private association—the American Institute of Real Estate Appraisers—the promise to destroy a textbook called *The Appraisal of Real Estate*, in which appraisers are advised that the ethnic composition of a neighborhood in fact influences the value of real estate. Under the proposed consent decree, the Institute agrees to strike from the present (sixth) edition of its textbook all the improper language. Specific textbook revisions have been prepared. These changes "will be included in the seventh edition of the text" not later than September 5, 1978. Sixty days after the decree is entered, the Institute "will commence a review of all booklets, manuals, monographs, guides, lexicons, and... other instructional material published under its auspices" to assure that they too conform with the text revisions. And they called fascistic a summons to free citizens freely associated, exercising no judicial or legislative power, to communicate their ideals at a private college through the appropriate selection of texts and teachers.

"Unless the great concepts which have been traditional to the Western world are rooted in a reasoned view of the universe and man's place in it, and unless this reasoned view contains in its orbit a place for the spirit, man is left in our day with archaic weapons unsuited for the problems of the present." I don't know who wrote that sentence, which appeared in an editorial in the Boston *Pilot*, but I know I wish I had written it because with great economy of expression it says, really, everything my book sought to say. It leaves unsaid only this. Is there a role for the non-academician in formulating that "reasoned view"? Or if not that, in catalyzing that "reasoned view"? Or if not that, in providing genial ground in which to cultivate that "reasoned view"? It is on this point that I declare myself, a generation after the event, on the side of the university with a mission.

In recent months I have been asked by representatives of Yale University to make a public declaration urging contributions to the university's capital fund. I dealt with the first such communication most tactfully, uttering an evasion, stuttering off like a member of the Drones Club. It did not work. A second request came in. I had, this time, to say No, but I begged off giving the reasons why. A third request came in, and there was then nothing to do—I was backed up against the wall: my correspondent had never learned Machiavelli's axiom that you should not cut off the enemy's line of retreat.

I have always held in high esteem the genial tradition, and I hope it is something other than sentimentality that inclines me to believe that one of the reasons I was so happy at Yale was that that geniality is—forget, and forgive, the intemperances necessarily recorded here—as natural to Yale as laughter is to Dublin, song to Milan, or angst to the *New York Review of Books*. Mostly I prefer nowadays to contend with the slogan, rather than with the man who hoists it. But sometimes there are no alternatives (in particular as the anthropomorphization of public life proceeds—you do not talk about the Democratic Party, you talk about Kennedy, Johnson, Carter). So, in my third communication, I answered directly.

"In the ideal university all sides of any issue are presented as impartially and as forcefully as possible." This was Official Yale's answer to *Gamay*. In a world governed by compromise, in which opportunism can be virtuous—such a world as our own—I am obliged to confess: I would probably settle for such an arrangement. A truly balanced curriculum, in which as much time, by professors as talented as their counterparts, in courses as critical as the others, were given to demonstrating the cogency of the arguments for God and man. This book establishes that nothing like that balance obtained twenty-five years ago. But the allocation of ideological and philosophical commitments aside, I cannot come to terms with a university that accepts the philosophical proposition that it is there for the purpose of presenting "all sides" of "any issue" as impartially and as forcefully as possible. That will not do, for the reasons Professor Wimsatt gave.

And so I was driven to write, in what I swore until I was seduced to write this essay would be my last exchange on the Yale question. And what I said was:

"What's the problem? Why doesn't Yale donate itself to the State of Connecticut?"

The mechanical problem, as it happens, is virtually nonexistent. There is a thing called the Yale Corporation. It literally "owns" Yale. If the trustees of Yale were to vote tomorrow to give "Yale" to the State of Connecticut, there would be lots of amazement and thunderstorms of indignation—and no recourse. Obviously the State of Connecticut would accept the gift. We are talking about several hundred million dollars of real property, and half-billion or so in endowments.

What then would happen?

To tell the truth, I don't know that anything much would happen. Obviously there would be changes at the corporate level. Instead of fourteen trustees, eight of them elected by their predecessors the balance by the alumni, there would, presumably, be fourteen (or more, or less) trustees named by the Governor of Connecticut (who is already *ex officio* a trustee), and confirmed by the state legistlature. Would these be a scurvy lot? That is hard to say. If you look at the board of trustees of the University of California you would not find a significant difference in the profile of its membership and that of Yale today. The University of California, particularly in recent days, has its share of flower children; but, lo, so does Yale.

What else would be different? Standards of admission?

Why? The University of California at Berkeley is as hard to get into as Yale. A state university can be "elitist" and get away with it provided there are other universities within the system that will accept the less gifted students.

The curriculum would be less varied?

I don't think that would necessarily follow. There is a luxurious offering at Yale of courses in the recondite byways of human knowledge, wonderful to behold. But—that is also true of the University of California.

Excellence of faculty? But the University of California has the highest concentration of Nobel Prize winners in the country. It is simply no longer true that the most gifted scholars insist on joining the faculties of privately run universities. As for the maintenance of a Yale tradition within the faculty, the incidence of Yale-educated members continues to decline, consistent with the de-traditionalization of Yale.

What about the quality of undergraduate instruction?

There are a lot of complaints about the mega-university, large lecture courses, graduate-student instruction. But these complaints are also increasingly lodged against Yale and Harvard as well as Berkeley, and as the economic noose tightens, economizing at the expense of the student is likelier at private colleges, whose resources are limited, than at the public universities, whose resources are less limited.

The quality of undergraduate life? Why should it be affected? Yale has insisted it can show no genealogical preferences—neither would the State of Connecticut; neither, of course, does Berkeley. Would state ownership interfere with undergraduate social life? How? There is only a single fraternity surviving in Yale; there are dozens in many state colleges. Yale's senior societies are unique, but they are privately owned; and, in any case, their survival (so heatedly opposed, for instance, by the recent chaplain of Yale, among others) would hardly be the pivotal justification for withholding the gift of Yale to the State of Connecticut.

And consider the advantages! Yale's painful annual deficit is a mere added calorie in the paunch of Connecticut's deficit. Those who desire to contribute to Yale to promote specific activities within Yale could continue to do so, even as there are private endowments at Berkeley.

And—the most interesting point of all, I think—what, in the absence of specific objections, are the philosophical objections? The sense of the swingers in the social science faculty even twenty-five years ago was to prefer the public sector over the private sector. I cannot think what arguments most of the distinguished teachers mentioned in this book would use to oppose in principle turning Yale over to the public sector.

Now, having said all that, let me say that I know why Yale shouldn't be turned over to the state. Because there are great historical presumptions that from time to time the interests of the state and those of civilization will bifurcate, and unless there is independence, the cause of civilization is neglected. Individual professors can raise their fists and cry out against the howling of the storm; but professors so inclined are resident alike at Berkeley, as at New Haven. The critical difference is the corporate sense of mission. At Berkeley that sense of mission is as diffuse and inchoate—and unspecified and unspecifiable—as the resolute pluralism of California society. At the private college, the sense of mission is distinguishing. It is, however, strangled by what goes under the presumptuous designation of academic freedom. It is a terrible loss, the loss of the sense of mission. It makes the private university, sad to say, incoherent; and that is what I was trying to say when, two months out of Yale, I sat down to write this book.

VIII. *Sport*

We Learned to Ski

November 9, 1975

"EFFICIENT SKIING requires us to stand flat on both skis and to be able to roll over each ski (edge it) to the same angle. To do that most of us need to some varying degree to have wedges of plastic or metal between boot and ski to compensate for our natural stance."

If you do not ski, or aspire to, this passage is as arresting as a resolution of the General Assembly of the United Nations. If you do ski, it is quite simply electrifying. It is as if you picked up a tax aid book somewhere that had in it the casual comment: "If on completing your income tax return you will remember to add the number 2X 37 08 after your name, you may, by the working of an obscure provision of the law, cut your income tax in half."

I exaggerate? I have skied every winter for twenty-one winters, in every country except maybe Guatemala. I take lessons these days from the grandchildren of those who first taught me. *And I never heard of wedges before*. Apparently this is not a coincidence, either of a conspiracy by my teachers to keep the goose unsteady on his feet the better to lay more eggs; or of an eccentric tone-deafness on the matter of the wedges. "Most resorts have barely heard of wedges, and they are almost universally ignored in textbooks on skiing."

What is also ignored in textbooks on skiing is usable material on how to ski. I leafed through a number of them years ago, and can report that, in twenty years, no skier has said to me: "*There* is a book on skiing you must read." The reason is that the textbooks are almost universally the product of expert skiers who, while trying to demonstrate their knowledge of skiing, succeed only in demonstrating their incapacity to communicate that knowledge. Commonly, their faults are either a jargon that quickly leaves the reader with the feeling that he has stumbled into a graduate school seminar conducted in German; or else a complex of instructions that leaves the reader feeling entirely helpless.

"Remember, while holding out your hip uphill, to exert downhill pressure with your ankles, forward pressure on the balls of your feet, while maintaining a slightly oblique inclination, pointing roughly at 10:30 o'clock (Amundsen and Clark, concededly, would say 11 o'clock, though we respectfully disagree) along the axis of your shoulders, making certain that your seat is parallel to your skis, notwithstanding any hip motion, or the necessity to keep your downhill arm balanced relaxedly at right angles (Masterson and Leif would, concededly, prefer an angle of 100 degrees) to the fall line." Whether such instructions are delivered in writing by ski teachers or orally by them, those are the moments—more so by far than any physical misadventure—when the mind turns to beach life. Messrs. Evans, Jackman and Ottaway have now given us an alternative, and I am not surprised to learn that it is a best-seller in Great Britain.

The temptation always in pedagogy is to communicate everything you know. The instinct is born of a combination of vanity and magnanimity. I do not know whether the authors in fact know more than they tell us about the morphology of skiing, but if they do, I most heartily congratulate them on their restraint in keeping to themselves material entirely unnecessary to the attainment of the skill to which so many of us aspire: how to ski competently, safely and gracefully. They satisfy only the normal curiosity, and in doing so they take care first to provoke that curiosity. "The secret of the turning ski is the 'side' cut of the ski." The secret! Everybody loves a secret. They then tell you something easily graspable by non-mechanical minds, but stop well short of the frontier of physics—again, whether out of ignorance or editorial instinct one knows not, being content to express either gratitude, or admiration, as called for.

The book is full of fascinating information, neatly and readably brought together. They even think, toward the end, to remind us to have a look at the mountains while skiing. And, at the beginning, to console ourselves with the extraordinary statistic that the average skier needs medical help after 200 days of skiing, and 400 days of not skiing—it is only twice as dangerous to slide down the mountain on two narrow planks of wood, as to walk your dog in Scarsdale. The concern by the authors for safety leads them to implore us, at one point in the book describing how we should test our safety bindings, to "Please do that." They succeed, moreover, in giving the impression that they and we are learning jointly, and develop an almost confessional intimacy as we move along. "This was our commonest fault," they tell us in the chapter on how to handle a mogul. You are tempted to call them up to recite your particular problems. Stylistic lapses are so rare as to make one suspect they are the responsibility of a wayward editor. (I decline to believe that Messrs. Evans, Jackman and Ottaway were responsible for the subhead, "Is your traverse a travesty?")

The authors are not ski teachers. Indeed, Mr. Evans did not begin to ski until he was forty. He is the editor of *The Sunday Times* of London. The other two gentlemen, also late starters as skiers, are his associates, as are the illustrators, who, in a perfectly spliced volume, make vivid what the authors are talking about through the use of photographs, sketches and red ink. It is a masterful job of pedagogy, and St. Martin's is hereby congratulated on bringing the book out at $12.95. It required that they reproduce photographically the English text, with the mildly annoying national idiosyncrasies ("ski-ing"). But, after all, the English invented not only the language but, for all intents and purposes, the sport; and they have certainly cornered the market now in an instructional manual that, although it will need to be brought up to date from time to time to keep pace with improvements in ski technology and hardware, is unlikely to be improved on in the lifetime of its authors.

Learning to Fly

September 1977

I HAD NO FEAR of flying when I matriculated at Yale but a very considerable fear of my father's learning that I had taken up a sport that, in 1946, he was unprepared to concede was anything more than rank technological presumption, fit only for daredevils. It turned out that several of my co-conspirators had fathers with similar prejudices, so that when our little syndicate was formed, we all agreed that communications to each other on the subject of our surreptitious hobby would go forward discreetly, lest they be intercepted. During the Christmas holidays, it was my duty to send out the accrued bills from the little grass-strip airport at Bethany where we lodged *Alexander's Horse* (as we called the little Ercoupe), and I realized, envelope in hand, I could not remember whether T. Leroy

Morgan, one of the six partners, was a junior. With a name like that, I felt he must surely be a junior—was there any other excuse? On the other hand, if I wrote "Jr." after this name and my friend was in fact the "III," then his father would open the letter. I assumed his father must be formidable, since who else would live at One Quincy Street, Chevy Chase, Maryland?

So, to play it safe, I addressed the letter to: "T. Leroy Morgan—the one who goes to Yale, One Quincy Street, Chevy Chase, Maryland." It happened that, at the breakfast table distributing the mail among the family, Mr. Morgan *père* displayed an imperious curiosity about the contents of a letter so manifestly intended to be seen only by his son.

I will contract the suspense and say that in no time at all, the word passed around a circle of fathers, reaching my own. Whenever my father was faced with rank transgression by any of his ten children, he replied to it in one of two ways, sometimes both. His first line of attack would be to announce that the child could not afford whatever it was my father disapproved. He tried that for an entire year in his running war against cigarettes, but the effect was ruined when we all saw *The Grapes of Wrath* and Henry Fonda, between heaves of hunger, kept smoking. His second line of attack would be to ignore the delinquency, pretending it simply did not exist. Thus one of my brothers, who hated to practice the piano, was relieved from ever having to play it again by the simple expedient of being held up by my father in public discussions of the matter as the most exemplary pianist in the family.

I received a brisk memorandum (his reproachful communications were normally rendered in that mode) advising me that he had "learned" that I was "flying an airplane" at college, and that the distractions to my academic career quite apart, I clearly could not afford such an extravagance. One didn't argue with Father, who in any case would never return to the subject except in a vague, sarcastic way. Three years later, he would write my prospective father-in-law, "You will find it very easy to entertain Bill when he visits you. You need only provide him with a horse, a yacht or an airplane."

And so for the few months of our joint venture, we continued to pass around the bills, like tablets in pre-Christian Rome. They were not, by current standards, frightening. Our capital was $1,800—$300 apiece. We paid that exactly for the secondhand airplane. We decided, after getting quotations from the insurance companies, to insure ourselves, subject to a $300 deductible payable by the offending partner. Anyone using the plane would pay his own gas, oil and instructor. All capital improvements would have to be approved unanimously. Anybody could sell his one-sixth interest to anyone at any time. Reservations to use the airplane would be filed with the secretary of the *Yale Daily News*. These, we satisfied ourselves, were surely the most informal articles of association in modern history, though I suppose it is appropriate to add that the association was one of the briefest in history.

I was off to a very bad start. My experience was akin to arriving at a casino for the first time at age twenty and winning a dozen straight passes at the crap table. When Bob Kraut, my instructor—a dour, hungry ex-army pilot, ex-mechanic, owner of the starveling little airport, who would sell you anything from a new airplane to a Milky Way—took me up for an hour's instruction, I could not believe how easy it all was. I remember it to this day: check the oil, check the gas, turn your wheel and check ailerons, pull and check elevator. Run your engine at 1,500 rpm, check one magneto, then the second, then back to both. Then gun her up to 2,250. Then exercise the knob that said "carburetor heat." Then head into the wind (or as close as possible at the single-strip field), push the throttle all the way forward, roll down the strip, when you reach sixty miles per hour ease the wheel back, and after the plane lifts off, push the wheel forward to level until you reach eighty mph. Then adjust your trim tab to maintain a speed of eighty mph. Rise to 600 feet on your course, then turn left until you get to 800 feet. Then do anything you want.

Landing? Go back to approximately where you were when you hit 800 feet and proceed downwind twice the length of the field while descending to 600 feet. Then turn left descending to 400 feet. (I forgot something: you should pull out your carburetor heat when you begin your descent.) Then turn in toward the field, reducing your throttle to idling speed, coast down, glance sideways—which helps perspective—don't let your speed fall under eighty mph till you are over the field, then keep easing the wheel back until your tires touch down, at which point *immediately* set your nosewheel right down; Ercoupes, you see, had no separate rudders, the wheel incorporating that function—a nice advantage except that you cannot cope easily with crosswind landings.

The first lesson consumed an hour, the second a half hour, and that very night I was speaking to a forlorn junior who had been a pilot during the war and grieved greatly that he could not be the following day at dinner with his inamorata in Boston. Why could he not? Because his car wasn't working, and no train would get him up in time, since he could not leave until after lunch. I found myself saying, as though I were P. G. Wodehouse himself, "Why my dear friend, grieve no more. I shall fly you to Boston."

It was all very well for my friend, who with 2,000 hours' flying, navigated us expertly to Boston, landed the airplane and waved me a happy good-bye. I was left at Boston Airport, headed back to Bethany, Connecticut, never having soloed and having flown a total of three times.

Well, the only thing to do was to proceed. I remembered that the plane came equipped with a radio of sorts and that my friend had exchanged arcane observations and sentiments with the tower coming in, so as I sashayed to the end of the runway, I flipped the switch—and found myself tuned in to an episode of "Life Can Be Beautiful." I truly didn't know how to account for this, and I remember even thinking fleetingly that when the traffic was light, perhaps the tower entertained area traffic by wiring it in to the controller's favorite program. This bizarre thought I managed to overcome, but it was too late to stop and fiddle with a radio I hadn't been instructed in the use of, so I went through my little motions, looked about to see that I wasn't in anybody's way, and zoomed off.

I was flying not exactly contentedly that bright autumn day. I felt a little lonely, and a little apprehensive, though I did not know exactly why. I was past Providence, Rhode Island, when suddenly my heart began to ice up as I recognized that either I was quickly going blind or the sun was going down. I looked at my watch. We should have another hour and a half of light! Ah so, except that I had neglected to account for the switch overnight away from daylight saving time. I had put forward my watch dutifully at about midnight, but today I thought in terms of light until about 7 P.M., same as yesterday. I looked at the air chart, so awfully cluttered and concentrated by comparison with those lovely, descriptive, onomatopoeic ocean charts you can read as easily as a comic book. I discerned that the New York, New Haven & Hartford railroad tracks passed within a few hundred yards of the airport at Groton. I descended, lower and lower, as the white began to fade, as from an overexposed negative soaking up developing solution. By the time I reached Groton, I was flying at 100 feet, and when I spotted the lights on the runway for the airfield, I was so grateful as if, coming up from the asphyxiative depths, I had reached oxygen.

I approached the field, did the ritual turns and landed without difficulty—my first, exhilarating solo landing; my first night landing; on the whole, the culmination of my most egregious stupidity. But there we were: plane and pilot, intact. I hitchhiked to the station, waited for a train, and by 10 o'clock was sitting at a bar in New Haven, chatting with my roommate about this and that. I never gave a thought to Mr. Kraut.

I have been awakened by angry voices, but by none to equal Robert Kraut's the following morning. While hauling the plane from the hangar, an assistant at the airfield had overheard me conversing excitedly with my friend on my impending solo flight from Boston to New York. In the internalizing tradition of New England, he had said nothing to me about my projected violation of the law. But he spoke to his boss about it later in the afternoon, who exploded with rage and apprehension. Kraut called the tower at Boston, which told of an Ercoupe having landed and then taken off at 4:07, without communication with the tower. Kraut calculated that I would arrive in the Bethany area in total darkness and thereupon began frantically collecting friends and passersby, who ringed the field with their headlights, providing a workmanlike illumination of a country strip. Then they waited. And waited. Finally, at about 10, Kraut knew I must be out of fuel and, therefore, on the ground somewhere other than at Bethany. Whether alive or dead, no one could say, but at least, Kraut growled into the telephone, he had the pleasure of *hoping* I was dead. *Why hadn't I called him?* I explained, lamely, that I did not know he even knew about my flight let alone that he thought to provide for my safe return. He consoled himself by itemizing lasciviously all the extra charges he intended to put on my bill for his exertions and those of his friends, which charges the executive committee of *Alexander's Horse* Associates voted unanimously and without extensive discussion would be paid exclusively by me.

I got my clearance to solo; and, twenty flying hours later, my license to fly other people. I am compelled to admit that I cheated a little in logging those twenty hours, giving the odd half-hour's flight in the benefit of the doubt, listing it at one hour, and I feel bad about this. But I did achieve a limited proficiency, and I would often go out to the field and take up a friend for a jaunty half-hour or so in my little silver monoplane, though I never felt confident enough to do any serious cross-country work, having no serviceable radio.

I remember two experiences before the final episode. In the early spring I invited aboard a classmate, a seasoned navy veteran pilot. We roared off the lumpy field under an overcast that the mechanic on duty assured us was 1,200 feet high. It wasn't. The Bethany airport is 700 feet above sea level, and at 1,000 feet, we were entirely enveloped in cloud. I had never experienced such a thing, and the sensation was terrifying, robbing you, in an instant, of all the relevant coordinates of normal life, including any sense of what is up and down. We would need, I calculated, to maintain altitude and fly south until we figured ourselves well over Long Island Sound. Then turn east and descend steadily, until we broke out unencumbered by New England foothills; then crawl over to the New Haven airport, which is at sea level. I willingly gave over the controls to my friend Ray, who assumed them with great competence as we began our maneuver. Then suddenly there was a hole in the clouds, and he dove for it, swooping into the Bethany strip, landing not more than three minutes after our departure. I stayed scared after that one and resolved never again to risk flying in overcast.

Then there was the bright spring day with the lazy-summer temperature. My exams, it happened, were banked during the first two days of a ten-day exam period. In between I did not sleep but did take Benzedrine. Walking out of the final exam at five the second afternoon, numb with fatigue and elation, I was wild with liberty, and I knew I must stretch my limbs in the sky. So I drove out to Bethany, pulled out *Alexander's Horse* and zoomed off by myself, heading toward downtown New Haven and climbing to 4,000 invigorating feet. There I fell asleep.

I have ever since understood what they mean when they write about the titanic intellectual-muscular energy required to keep one's eyes open when they are set on closing. What happened was that the drug had suddenly worn off, and the biological imperative was asserting itself with vindictive adamance. It was, curiously, only after I landed that I found it relatively easy to summon the adrenalin to stay awake for long enough to make it back to my bedroom. In the tortured fifteen minutes in the air, my eyes closed a dozen times between the moment I discovered myself asleep and the moment I landed. It is safer to learn these things about the human body aboard a sailboat than an airplane. Boats can be dangerous, but they don't often sink when you go to sleep at the wheel.

My final flight, like so many others, was propelled by a certain mental fog. My best friend at Yale became engaged to my favorite sister. All my siblings had met Brent, save my poor sister Maureen, cloistered at the Ethel Walker School, in Simsbury, Connecticut. I would instantly remedy that, and I wrote my sister, age fifteen, telling her to send a map of the huge lawn that rolls out from the school (which I had many times seen while attending various graduations of older sisters). It arrived by return mail—on all accounts the most nonchalant map in the history of cartography. At the east end, she had drawn vertical lines marked "trees." Running parallel from the top and bottom of that line to the west were two more lines, also marked "trees." At the extreme left end of the paper she had marked "main schoolhouse." Armed with that map and my future brother-in-law, I set out on a bright spring afternoon for Simsbury, which was about an hour's flight away.

I found the school and flew around it a couple of times with a creeping agitation. My sister having advised her classmates of my impending arrival, the entire school was out on the lawn, and, when they spotted us, their great cheer reached us through the roar of the little engine. The trees at the east side happened to be the tallest trees this side of the California redwoods. I buzzed them a time or two. Could they really be *that* tall? I estimated them at a couple hundred feet. That meant I would have to come over them, then drop very sharply, because a normal landing approach would have had me three-quarters down the length of the lawn before touch-down. "Well," I said to my stoical friend, "what do you say?" Fortunately, he knew nothing about flying.

I was terribly proud of the way I executed it all, and I wished Mr. Kraut had been there to admire the deftness with which I managed to sink down after skimming the treetops, touching down on the lawn as though it were an eggshell. I looked triumphantly over to Brent as our speed reduced to thirty mph. The very next glimpse I had of him was, so to speak, upside-downsideways. We hit a drainage ditch, unmarked by my sister, that traversed the lawn. The problem now was quite straightforward. The aircraft was nosed down absolutely vertical into the ditch, into which we had perfect visibility. We were held by our seat belts, without which our heads would be playing the role of our feet. We were there at least a full minute before the girls came. I am not sure I recall the conversation exactly, but it was on the order of:

"Are we alive?"

"I think so."

"What happened?"

"Ditch."

"Why did you run into it?"

"Very funny."

"Well, why didn't you fly over it?"

"We had landed. We were just braking down."

But the girls, with high good humor, giggles and exertion, managed to pry us out. We dusted ourselves off outside the vertical plane, attempted languidly to assert our dignity, and were greeted most politely by the headmistress, who said she had tea ready in anticipation of our arrival. We walked sedately up the lawn to her living room, accompanied by Maureen and two roommates. The talk was of spring, Yale, summer plans, the Attlee Government and General MacArthur, but Maureen and her friends would, every now and then, emit uncontainable giggles, which we manfully ignored. It all went moderately well under the circumstances until the knock on the door. An assistant to the headmistress arrived, to ask whether her guests had any use for—"this," and she held forth *Alexander's Horse*'s propeller or, rather, most of the propeller. I told her thank you very much, but broken propellers were not of any particular use to anyone, and she was free to discard it.

Eventually we left, having arranged by telephone with Mr. Kraut to come and fetch the corpse at his convenience. We returned to New Haven by bus. Brent, who had a good book along, did not seem terribly surprised, even after I assured him that most of my airplane rides out of Bethany were round trips.

Oh, the sadness of the ending. The plane was barely restored when, during a lesson, one of my partners was pleased by hearing his instructor say as they approached the strip for a landing, "You're hot!" My friend figured, in the idiom of the day, that this meant he was proceeding splendidly, so he nosed the ship on down, crashing it quite completely. As he later explained, what reason did he have to know that, in the jargon of the trade, to say you were "hot" meant, "You're going too fast"? He had a point. The estimate to repair *Alexander's Horse* was an uncanny $1,800—exactly what we had paid for it. Mournfully, we decided to let her rest, selling the carcass for $100. Father was right, as usual. I couldn't afford to fly.

At Sea

August 1976

I HAVE HAD the curious career of sailing since I was thirteen but having sailed only four times other than as captain of the vessel I was on. Except for reading about it, I am somewhat ignorant of how other captains and their crews behave. The first of the four exceptions was aboard my own boat, in my first ocean race, the Vineyard Race, from Stamford to the lightship off Martha's Vineyard and back—260 miles, over a three-day weekend in 1955. My experience had been only on lakes and, after buying *The Panic*—a forty-four-foot steel cutter, and my first ocean boat—a couple of weeks of poking about on Long Island Sound before signing on for the race. I asked a friend of vast experience to serve as skipper, and he agreed. He had raced at sea all his life, and during that weekend

I learned much about starting tactics, racing strategy, flag protocol, current and drift anticipation, and weight distribution; and about the importance to me of the skipper's having a relentless, if tough-minded, good humor.

The next spring, having resolved to make the glamorous Bermuda Race, I looked again for a skipper. I was still too inexperienced to be my own captain, and had not yet taught myself celestial navigation. A young banker was recommended, but he withdrew late in the spring after detecting an insuperable incompatibility between us. My friend of the Vineyard Race (he was himself committed to another vessel) suggested an old sailing partner from St. Louis, who turned out to be agreeable and competent, and I also brought on the phlegmatic, genial, super-competent Mike Mitchell, who was then my insurance agent and is now running the motel and yacht marina at Christmas Cove, Maine. And all went well, if that can be said about any ocean passage.

It was five years before I sailed under another skipper. This was at the invitation of Mike Mitchell, who was acting as first mate on a gorgeous thoroughbred in an afternoon race on Long Island Sound. The owner-skipper, altogether civil on shore, became the legendary tyrant on board, and yelled orders as though he were Ahab espying the whale at last. These orders came out in a complex, largely incoherent tangle, omnidirectionally beamed to his eight subjects—including one sixteen-year-old, whom he addressed only as "Boy!" All this commotion seemed especially incongruous in an afternoon of winds so lazy they nearly fell asleep in the sun. At one point, I walked over to the windward side to slacken a snagged genoa sheet, and the skipper exploded with imprecations to the effect that I had fatally unbalanced the boat. I looked sidewise at Mike Mitchell, who returned me a Yankee smile, part pain, part amusement, part cunning—Mike sold insurance to the old tyrant. It was worse that every time he spoke he proved he knew less about sailing than any of the eight of us. Less, even, than Boy! One leaves such people alone. Permanently.

Ten years after that, I was invited to sail in an overnight race with my hero. My hero was William Snaith, whose book *Across the Western Ocean* I had read with near-idolatrous pleasure. We knew each other only slightly, and when, expansively, he asked me at a friend's house one night if I would like to navigate for him the following weekend, I accepted, with trepidation. It was as if Toscanini had invited me to take the concertmaster's chair at his concert the following weekend. I would be sailing, for the first time, on a boat every member of whose crew could be expected to be a finished ocean racer. I recognized, when I was introduced to them, two of Snaith's sons and a regular sailing companion, described in Snaith's book. The mood struck at the outset was a kind of short, competent civility irradiating from the volatile, brilliant skipper. Before it was over, the rhetoric had developed into a surrealistic, sustained hostility, mostly between the skipper and his older son, spokesman for the crew, which I understood to be metaphorical in nature, but which once or twice flirted toward a stridency that froze my blood. Such rhetoric, I take it, is accepted as entirely routine aboard many happy vessels, but I was already too old to adapt to that kind of thing. Besides, even if I could succeed in breaking a lifetime habit and substituting billingsgate for my normal hearty command, laced only with a little genial sarcasm when its absence would clearly disappoint, perhaps even confuse, I would so surprise my companions that they would either walk off or send in their resignations on reaching home.

Your companions on board are a crucial consideration. For me, there is one no-further-questions-asked disqualifier: personal rudeness of any sort—and rudeness includes any sign of impatience. (The exception: the captain, or the helmsman, shouting out impatiently the need for a snatch block, a flashlight, a Scotch-and-soda.) I know of a yacht that raced across the Atlantic, everyone aboard a perfect gentleman but inexperienced in the absoluteness of the law of proper shipboard behavior. And so it happened that a few days out, A watch made a rather provocative entry in the log respecting the inferior achievements of B watch during the antecedent tour of duty. B watch fired back in its own entry four hours later. After twenty-two days, arriving at Santander, Spain, the four members of A watch and the four members of B watch got off the boat with their gear, and from that moment on no member of either watch ever addressed a single word to a member of the other, even when they were all cozily back in New York, or whatever.

Aboard a yacht, the resonance of bad humor shatters everything that the entire experience is designed to bring you—like an alarm clock going off in Carnegie Hall. I remember years ago resolving never again to invite to race with me one friend for the simple sin, on his day as breakfast cook, of responding to a request from the cockpit to pass the honey with "Can't you just wait a minute!" On board, the protocol is that anyone will do anything for anyone—the perfect crucible for the Golden Rule. "While you're below, would you bring me up some foul-weather gear [my sunglasses] [my book] [an aspirin]?" is the operative social convention aboard a sailing boat. It was pushed to its limit one day by a famous yacht designer when his eighteen-year-old son slipped down the companionway to visit the head, leaving the father and six companions at the wheel: "John? While you're below, would you cook dinner?"

I engaged once in a polemic with Norris Hoyt, a veteran seaman who taught English to fortunate students at St. George's School, in Newport, and is now retired. He took public issue with me over a complaint I had published against the creeping professionalization of sailing. In pointing out the mysterious inexactitude of specialized knowledge about a boat and its accessories, I gave as only one of many examples the demonstrated inadequacy of foul-weather gear advertised as competent to keep a man dry at sea. With great huff, Mr. Hoyt (whom I subsequently discovered to be a most engaging and undogmatic man) replied in a published article that he had made numerous transatlantic crossings in his life, and that he had not once—not *once*—been either cold or wet. Now, you must understand the gravity of this kind of boast in the amateur community I write of. It is—simply—*unbelievable*.

In his article, Mr. Hoyt gave a step-by-step account of just how he handles the problem of dressing for the cold and the wet. His methods remind me of my trip to the Antarctic, before which I submitted to a technician's lecture on how to keep warm. I walked away from the lecture with a trunk-load of clothes supplied by the United States Navy which, when I donned them, left me entirely comfortable in temperatures that brushed up against fifty below zero. But I must add that it could not have taken the Queen of England as long to dress for her Coronation as it took me to put on my costume in the mornings I was in the Antarctic; and it is a wonder that Mr. Hoyt has any time to devote to watch duty after preparing himself for it. But let us leave the point moot and agree to say modestly: You *can* keep warm on a boat, but the preparations necessary for doing so vitiate, substantially, the pleasure of the day's sail.

On the matter of keeping dry, I remain, perforce, a skeptic. My brother-in-law Austin Taylor, who is called Firpo, believes in attacking problems head on, and he designed his own foul-weather gear for our first race to Bermuda. It was the grandest and most elaborate piece of gear I have ever seen, not less imposing for its responsibility of keeping dry 250 pounds of human flesh. It had rubber gloves with shockcord belts, all-directional zippers, seamless balaclavas—everything except, perhaps, a catheter tube. The first hard wave that tore into *The Panic's* cockpit left Firpo totally drenched and, on top of that, facing twenty minutes of disassembly before he could dry his bare skin. A sailing companion who had observed with awe the design and engineering of the ultimate foul-weather suit comforted Firpo with a practical suggestion for the next trip: "You must go to a garage, strip, and have yourself vulcanized."

I have done a lot of racing—on a lake as a boy, and at sea on *The Panic* and its successor, *Suzy Wong*, a forty-foot yawl. Since 1972, my sailing has all been cruising, mostly aboard *Cyrano*, a sixty-foot schooner I bought in 1968, but I am not absolutely sure that if *Suzy* and I had developed into a highly successful racing combination I wouldn't be out there racing still. Though the estrangement from racing came gradually, I think I can trace the seeds of it to 1965. I disappeared surreptitiously from the campaign for mayor of New York in order to participate in the race from Marblehead, Massachusetts, to Halifax, Nova Scotia, which I had roughly the same chance of winning. Though it was a rough ride, my crew—Peter Starr, my (young) old friend, who began sailing with me twenty-one years ago, when he was thirteen; Reginald Stoops, my plastics-engineer buddy; Evan Galbraith, my classmate, lawyer, banker, and splendid companion; and two friends with whom I now raced more or less regularly—managed *Suzy* well. We made no significant errors in seamanship or navigation or strategy, but when we finally slipped across the finish line there was only a single boat that hadn't yet come in. (It was F. Lee Bailey's. He told me later that on learning I had beaten him he deserted ocean racing and bought a jet airplane. I comforted him by telling him that at least he had effected an economy.) By contrast, in the very first race to Bermuda on *The Panic,* we had done quite creditably, halfway in our class.

Suzy, although she was designed by Sparkman & Stephens, which is like saying about a violin that it was made by Stradivarius, could never live up to her theoretical rating—that is, her rating under something called the Rule. The first comprehensive Rule was formulated by the Cruising Club of America in the mid-1930's; there are now other Rules, formulated by other sailing organizations, but yachtsmen speak simply of "the Rule." The Rule is designed to make all vessels that compete in an ocean race theoretically equal in speed by imposing graduated handicaps. These are calculated by such compounded anfractuosities that nowadays only a half-dozen men even affect to understand the Rule, and no one can give you your rating without feeding all the relevant factors into a computer—not just any computer but a monster type bunkered somewhere on Long Island for the purpose of guiding missiles to Mars and giving yachtsmen their ratings. The original idea of the Rule was to keep ocean racing from being only a rich man's sport. It is still such a sport, substantially, but certainly not so much so as it would have been in the absence of the Rule. The first handicaps imposed under the rule were designed to discourage the idea that every yachtsman had to own two boats—one to race in, the other to be comfortable in. Fifty years ago, it was assumed that a very narrow-hulled boat would easily beat a boat with a beamy hull. Since narrow hulls make for uncomfortable living quarters, the very rich had begun the practice of racing in their sleek, thin boats, after which ordeal their second boats, tubby and comfortable, would rescue them from asceticism.

Other factors crept in as the Rule grew in complexity: for instance, the desirable balance between safety and speed. In order to support a mast on which you have run up a huge stretch of canvas whose purpose is to trap the wind and convert its force into forward motion, you must relieve it of unbearable strain. The cables that reach from the head of the mast fore and aft (they are called, respectively, the headstay and the backstay) present no problem. The angle going up from the bow and the stern will be sufficiently acute to give the mast fore and aft stability. But the two cables that go to the beams ends of a boat (they are called shrouds) are something else. Exaggerate the problem. Suppose your responsibility is to secure a thousand-foot-high radio tower. If you ran wires from the top of the tower to points not more than six feet away from the base, you would have shrouds that ran very nearly parallel to the tower itself, providing practically no additional support. Accordingly, the closer to the base of the tower the shrouds are fastened, the heavier they have to be. At the other extreme, if you were permitted to go out, say, 500 feet from the base on either side to rivet down the shrouds, you would end with an equilateral triangle of sorts, and the shrouds would head up from the ground to the top at a comfortable angle of sixty degrees, permitting relatively light cable. So it is on a boat. The wider the beam, the easier it is to provide stability for the mast, with a light cable. The slimmer the beam, conversely, the more difficult the matter of stability, and the greater the need for heavy cable; and, ultimately—since something has to give if you keep narrowing the beam—you will have to shorten the mast. The Rule penalizes masts according to their length.

Every two years or so, the Rule is changed, mostly to frustrate the loop-holer, the Rule-beater. One inventive yachtsman discovered that *his* handicap was decreased much more than his speed by his simply eliminating his mainsail. By a single modification in the Rule, a hundred million dollars of racing boat can be anachronized. Nowadays, a successful racing boat is a tangle of expensive mechanisms designed to beat the Rule. *Suzy*, with her noble teak, is probably too heavy to have profited even from radical surgery. We raced her in 1971, in the annual race from Stamford to Martha's Vineyard and back. Once again, boat and crew were in nearly perfect sync, and once again we trailed the fleet. So in due course I retired her from regular campaigning, though I would still race her, if I got around to it, for the fun of it, which was mostly why I raced her and *The Panic* all those years—my point being that an ocean race is really a test of yourself and your crew, that there are too many variables to permit one to conclude that this vessel or crew is superior to that other vessel or crew.

There are, of course, considerable differences between racing and cruising. Normally, a cruise is conceived as a daytime sail from one harbor to another. You arrive late in the afternoon, drop anchor, swim, hike, have a drink, cook and eat dinner, and then perhaps play cards, simply talk, or address yourself to an especially recalcitrant part of the boat's equipment which you neglected during the day. Everyone eventually turns in, sleeps soundly, wakes up rested. The whole of the ship's complement is up, and down, together.

So is it in the daytime race as well. It is when you sail over distances requiring shifts in crew that the nature of the experience radically changes. When you race, you need more men on watch: at least three (in a boat up to fifty feet long), and if you need to perform intricate work, such as jibing the spinnaker or reefing the mainsail, you generally wake up a fourth. When you cruise, you don't, in serene circumstances, need more than two men on watch. This means that in overnight cruising you are on duty less than half the time. To go on duty for four hours, then off duty for eight hours, is manifestly more relaxing than to go back on duty after only four hours off. Moreover, since under such arrangements you have roughly sixteen hours of leisure to deploy, there is more time to be gregarious, to read, to attend to miscellaneous projects.

That is one difference between cruising and racing—important, but not really the principal difference. During a race, when the wind is very light—two or three knots—you itch with frustration, and tread carefully as you go back and forth on deck lest you upset the delicately weighted list of the boat, calculated to expose the sails most seductively to the anemic wind. In gale force, you struggle to keep hoisted the maximum serviceable canvas, driving the boat through discomfort as fast as you can make it go without blowing out the sails or generating counterproductive nose dives into the sea or heeling over so far as to neutralize the top area of your sail. If you are working in the wind—that is, if you are zigzagging toward your objective, because it lies ahead of you in the same direction whence blows the wind—you strap in the sails ("close-hauled"), and the boat heels over, making its way over and under breaking waves, which periodically roar down the deck and inundate you, your sandwich, and, occasionally, your spirits. There is the single objective: to get there as fast as possible.

When you cruise and the wind roars, you reef, or even lower, a sail that is inimical to your special purposes. It does not matter to you that during that night you will travel seventy miles instead of seventy-five. And anyway, over the long haul—over stretches of sea in which all sorts of conditions are met—you will get where you are going as soon as the racer, because you will use engine power during the slack stretches. Although there is no reason to emasculate a sailing boat when cruising, and no way to assure comfort—in very heavy weather a boat racing and a boat cruising will behave almost identically—there are times when little concessions, made at the sacrifice of speed, give you a margin of comfort you are denied in a race: dousing your genoa jib (the largest) and putting up the No. 2 at midnight if it is getting rough; leaving off the fisherman in a schooner or the mizzen staysail in a yawl; leaving the reef tucked in for an extra hour when the wind lightens, instead of shaking it out the moment you think the boat is capable of taking the extra strain.

Mike Mitchell used to sail with an old friend, the owner of a racing boat, and the friend's freshly taken wife. The wife was unshakable in her belief that there was no reason at all for a sailboat to right itself after being knocked on its side, with the result that whenever the boat heeled over sharply she would don her life preserver, recite her prayers, and prepare to abandon ship—a comprehensively distracting performance in a Sunday afternoon's race. Mike's friend finally took his wife to a psychiatrist for help. The psychiatrist, himself a sailor, prescribed for her one of those roly-poly dolls that little children amuse themselves with. They knock it down, only to see it bounce up again. It is Wimpy-like in shape, with, instead of feet, a sealed bowl full of bird shot. Even if you tilt the head right down on the floor, the weight of the bird shot easily overcomes the light weight of the head, rolling the doll back on its feet. Thus, the doctor explained, a sailboat. If you have ten thousand pounds of lead (exactly what we had on *The Panic*) at the bottom of six feet of keel (the depth of ours), and the boat is pushed over on its (rounded) side, then you have 60,000 pounds of pressure agitating to right that boat. Meanwhile, since the boat's mast, in the hypothesis, is now parallel to the water, or almost parallel, the sails have obviously lost the air power that knocked the boat over. Accordingly, with 60,000 pounds insisting on rectitude vs. zero pounds insisting on distortion, the boat will right.

When the woman heard this explanation, she asked, "Why do some boats sink, then?"

"Other factors," her husband snapped.

This woman's opinion of sailboats was shared by my wife, Pat, but I was able to persuade Pat early in our cruising career (she resolutely refused to race), even without the roly-poly doll, that a sailboat *will* right itself. Nevertheless, the second day out on *The Panic* I noticed a two-inch section of that omnipresent plastic tape from which you punch out labels and the like. It was pegged to the circumference of the boat's inclinometer, a four-dollar piece of hardware you tack on the cockpit bulkhead. The inclinometer has a pendulum that indicates, on an arc, the angle of the boat's heel at any given moment. Opposite the twenty-five-degree point on the scale was the tape, reading "PATSY GETS OFF."

For *years*, I whispered in Pat's ear the safety features of oceangoing sailboats. I even told her that, in a sense, the *smaller* the boat, the *greater* the safety—as a cork bobbing on the water is indestructible, whereas a destroyer clearly isn't. That was a mistake; thereafter, she rejoiced at any opportunity to lavish on her friends my implied preference for riding out a storm on a cork instead of on the Queen Elizabeth. In my flying days, before we were married, and before I learned to say "I'm going to do it anyway," I tried telling her that gliders, which I had recently cultivated, were actually safer than airplanes with engines, because something could go wrong with an engine but the glider depended only on gravity and updrafts. That became another of her favorites, and she has several times suggested, with radiant scorn, and in disgustingly appreciative company, that I should communicate my insight to Pan American, which by doing away with its engines would increase its safety record and save a lot of money.

And, it is true, I have had a few unpleasant experiences at sea—one or two of them with her aboard.

My first misadventure happened in the spring of my second year at the Millbrook School. I was sixteen. Four years earlier, in 1938, my father had transported two of my sisters and me, much against our will, to boarding school in England for a year. I had detected a bargaining position, and asked my father if, on my return from England, he would give me a sailboat. He was better than his word, giving me not only a sailboat but a sailing instructor, who spent the summer with me. The boat was a seventeen-foot Barracuda-class sloop, and I kept it at Lake Wononskopomuc, about seven miles from our home in Sharon, Connecticut. The lake, which is also known as Lakeville Lake, is very beautiful, about one square mile, spring fed, surrounded by high, wooded hills. It then had two landmarks. At one end was the Hotchkiss School. At the other, Wanda Landowska.

All summer for three summers, we raced three days a week, twice each day, a ragtag fleet of six boats, each of different design. The dictator of the fleet was a retired martinet who had served in some nautical capacity during the First World War and never got over it. He rejoiced at any infraction of the rules, because it permitted him to schedule, at his lakeside cottage, a court-martial of sorts, which he conducted with great gravity, managing nearly full attendance by the primitively effective expedient of giving all the boat-owners a great deal of whiskey to drink, to help them endure the discipline of his ruling, which, after much exegesis, he would eventually divulge. The five other boat-owners ranged in age from twenty-five to fifty; I was thirteen that first summer, and I had never before (nor have I since) devoted myself so completely to any single enterprise. Seventy-five races a summer for three summers may strike some as a few races too many. It struck me as too few races by far, and I would go to bed Tuesday and Friday and Saturday nights in delirious anticipation of the next day's drama on the water, waking early to see how the wind was blowing. My boat, *Sweet Isolation* (I named it in honor of my father's political preferences in 1939), did very well in all but the lightest and the heaviest airs. Two of the three summers that I raced, I won the trophy for scoring the most points. The trophy had been donated by the Lakeville Community Chest—cost, retail, $12.50—and I still have it.

It was well before the racing season, a cold spring day early in May. I took out for an afternoon's sail my sister Patricia, her English tutor, Cecilia Reilly, and a classmate from Millbrook, David Cates. A sudden puff swept down from the surrounding hills, and we capsized. It was not unusual to capsize in the lake; it was more a nuisance than an event. A motorboat would tow you to shore, and you would bail out the boat and relaunch her. Though the water was cold, it wasn't paralyzingly cold. But after we had been clinging to the boat for a few minutes it dawned on us that a) there were no other boats in sight; b) we were exactly in mid-lake, and therefore were unlikely to be spotted; c) we had only two life preservers on board; and d) Miss Reilly did not know how to swim, and David Cates not at all well.

I decided to leave Patricia (Trish) in charge of the boat. She and David could stay afloat by hanging on to it. Miss Reilly must don one life preserver. I would set out with the other and swim the half-mile to the Hotchkiss School and get help. A hundred yards along the way, I abandoned the life preserver, which was slowing me down. A hundred yards farther, I abandoned my shoes, socks, and pants. When I finally reached shore, I was bitterly cold, and frightened about the condition of the crew. I rushed up the huge lawn that slopes up from the Hotchkiss boathouse, spotted a door in thc nearest building, and opened it, interrupting a full faculty meeting of the Hotchkiss School, presided over by a legendary and terrifying headmaster—learned, austere, caustic, and widely known for his impatience with schoolboyism. Shivering in my dripping shorts and T-shirt, I had trouble making sense, but the Duke, as they called the headmaster, calmly emitted a cluster of instructions, which resulted simultaneously in a motorboat's being dispatched to the middle of the lake, my being led off to the infirmary, and a telephone call's being placed to my parents. That night, it was all the subject of great excitement. As is almost always the case, the shock came a little later. David Cates, Trish told me—and he eventually admitted it—could not have held out much longer.

Five eventful years after that, I took *Sweet Isolation* on a trailer, with Trish, my sister Jane, and Richard O'Neill, who would be my roommate at Yale when we matriculated the following month, for a weekend of sailing off Edgartown. During those five years, I had graduated from prep school, done a half year at the National University of Mexico, undergone basic training in the infantry, attended officers training school, and served as platoon leader in infantry basic-training centers, while Richie, a resident of Lakeville, a graduate of the Hotchkiss School, and a boyhood friend, had fought in the war in Europe. We all felt terribly grownup until, the first evening, the waitress refused to serve the grizzled veterans a beer. Our driver's licenses betrayed us as being just short of twenty-one; only Jane, freshly graduated from Smith at twenty-two, could order from the bar. After dinner, we took a ride around the harbor in the Edgartown Yacht Club launch, which we boarded as though we were on our way to our own yacht. The New York Yacht Club fleet was in, and I had never before seen a fleet of oceangoing boats. I looked about me with admiration and envy: the trim, exquisitely maintained boats, ranging in size from thirty-five to seventy-two feet, with owners and crew comfortably aboard, chatting, drinking, washing the dinner dishes; the little anchor lights almost perfectly integrated with the stars above; the moon highlighting the crosscurrents of the harbor. I was still unhooked by the lure of blue-water sailing, but I sensed that night that sometime, years away—exactly nine years, it proved—I would be back in the harbor, boarding my own boat.

It was blowing hard the next day, and the Yacht Club had its own race going, out in the Sound. We boarded our launch, launched my little open boat, and set out downwind, along Chappaquiddick. A mile out, the mainmast suddenly lurched crookedly aft. The headstay had parted at the turnbuckle, and the foot of the mast, unsecured, slipped proportionately forward along the boat's bottom. The mainsail had to come down, and as I loosed the halyard, Trish reached for it, slipped, and fell into the sea. She was quickly separated from us as we went ineluctably downwind. I reached for a heavy prewar outboard motor and seated it with difficulty on the transom mount, and quickly threaded the starting cord. I pulled it once, twice, ten times. By now, Trish was barely visible astern. We could not tack our way back to her without rerigging the headstay, and that required straightening the mast. Richie tried starting the motor. My heart beat in an agony of frustration. Then, with great poise, a launch suddenly materialized, and a moment later we could see Trish being hauled out of the water. The launch then came to us, threw out a line, and towed us back into the harbor. Everyone was talking when we were reunited at the dock, and I was cursing the defective turnbuckle and the outboard motor. Exhausted, we trudged back to our hotel. Late in the afternoon, I returned alone to attend to the boat, which was sitting now in a boatyard; and, concealed behind its hull, I wept, hysterical at the thought of what had nearly happened. I had very nearly drowned my sister. It was, to use the word formally, a trauma. It haunted me into my twenties. I rehearsed a thousand times what I should have done. It was as simple as instantly—by reflex action—tossing out a life preserver. *The moment someone goes overboard*. It sounds axiomatic. But at sea in an emergency very little is axiomatic that you have not silently drilled yourself to do—like steering in the direction of a skid when you're driving in the snow. Man overboard is the greatest single menace of the sea.

It cannot exactly be classified as a misadventure of the perils-of-the-sea variety when your ship sinks and nobody is in it, but it is the kind of thing that creates apprehension in people like Pat, and even in people unlike Pat. Two months before my first Bermuda Race, in 1956, the switchboard operator at my office told me my boatyard, in Stamford, was calling. (I have, by the way, long since discovered how you get through on the telephone to yachtsmen who are otherwise unapproachable people. You simply tell the operator you are calling from the boatyard. No yachtsman in the history of the world has ever been too busy to talk to his boatyard.) It was Eva Swann, a secretary at the boatyard.

"Mr. Buckley, I'm afraid I have some bad news." She was clearly on edge.

"What is it, Miss Swann?"

"The Panic sank."

"Sank?"

It transpired that, going down to the dock that morning, the yardmen had seen in the space previously occupied by a forty-four-foot steel cutter only fifty feet of mast, rising straight—indeed, proudly, one supposes—out of the water. Everything stopped, and the whole force of the yard was mobilized to pump out the boat and bring her, slowly, to the surface. The damage was unspeakable. When the seawater reached the level of the batteries, the acid was drawn out. Since the hull was made of steel, the entire boat was converted into a huge galvanic field, so to speak, which corrosively began to gnaw away at the wiring, reducing it in a few hours to copper filigree.

Miss Swann having prepared me, she put me on to William Muzzio, the volatile, peppery, omnicompetent owner of the yard. We would need, he said, new wiring throughout, a rebuilt engine, a new generator, all new upholstery, a new radio direction finder, a new radiotelephone. He was sure the sails had survived—they had been quickly washed in fresh water. The gas and water tanks would survive, he thought. He did not know whether all that work could be completed in time for the Bermuda Race, but he would make every effort.

"What happened?" I managed to ask.

"I don't know," he said. "We checked all the sea cocks. They're O.K."

If Mr. Muzzio didn't know what happened, it was unlikely that anyone would know; but, even as the work began, I found it endlessly disconcerting that the boat, sitting jauntily at dock one night, three days after it had last been sailed, should simply . . . sink. There is something less than an unquenchable intellectual curiosity among professional boat people. The insurance company had to pay out $10,000 to put *The Panic* right, but the company's inspector would not engage in anything like an exhaustive discussion of what might have been the cause of it all, though Stamford does not lie within the perimeter of the Bermuda Triangle, where One Isn't Supposed to Ask What Happened. The reason there are so many mysteries at sea is that nobody bothers to try to solve them. This particular mystery was solved, quite accidentally, under circumstances more hectic than the sedentary, regal sinking in the womb of Muzzio Brothers Yacht Yard.

It happened more than a year after my family had rechristened my boat *The Ti-panic*, and we were racing from Annapolis to Newport. All night long, we had tacked against a relentless southerly, fighting our way down the Chesapeake. At ten in the morning, I was off duty and sound asleep, with Mike Mitchell at the wheel, when Reggie woke me. In his calm way, he told me to look down at the floorboards. They were underwater. I jumped up, tore up the floorboards, and saw a mass of water overflowing the bilges and rushing up into the lockers with every leeward roll of the ship. Reggie and I could feel no water coming into the boat from the engine water-cooling system or from the stuffing box. A quick investigation of the sea cocks showed them to be in good order. Two crew members were mobilized to work the big hand pump. Working steadily, they only just managed to keep pace with the leak. I raced back to the cockpit, and Reggie, Mike, and I conferred. The water is shallow in the Chesapeake, and in the southern section there are stretches of mud and sand at depths of two feet. We decided that the only thing to do was to head for a sand shoal and beach *The Panic* before she sank from under us. Moving to the wheel, I took a bearing, bore off the wind, and headed for shallow water about a mile away while Mike jumped into the bilges to have his own look. Seven or eight minutes later, he ambled up, a smile on his face and a beer in his hand. "Let's get back on course," he said. "I found the trouble."

The electric bilge pump, which Reggie had switched on before waking me, was, of course, the first mechanism I had checked, and it had been humming away industriously, though its capacity was insufficient to keep up with the flow of water coming into the boat. But Mike, unsatisfied, had unscrewed the hose from the pump, thinking that perhaps the rubber impeller had burned and that if he replaced it we might get some relief. He found that the pump was working fine, except that instead of drawing water from the boat into the sea it was drawing water from the sea into the boat. Astonished, he turned the switch off, then on again—and suddenly the flow of water was in the right direction. In a minute or two, he could see the water level receding.

Here was the mystery solved. An electric pump sucks water from the bilges and forces it up a hose, which becomes a copper pipe that rises above the water level outside the boat. The pipe elbows around, and the water falls by gravity down the pipe and out to sea through an open sea cock. We could now easily reconstruct what had happened. A piece of mud or sponge or whatever had been sucked up from the bilge and was rising under pressure up the pipe just at the moment, sometime during the night, when a crew member checked the bilges and, finding them dry, turned off the pump. There the foreign matter lodged, beneath sea level, like a cork, sustaining the weight of the water above it. In due course, the cork began to dissolve, and the dammed waterfall poured into the bilges—creating suction sufficient to bring a continuous flow of water up from the sea to the elbow. And now, by the law that specifies that water will seek its own level, Chesapeake Bay was happily filling up the cavity in the hull of *The Panic*. And, of course, the more water we took in, the lower the boat sank, guaranteeing a disparity in water level until our boat's decks were level with the sea. At that point, water would cease flowing into our bilges—a point of only academic comfort, since the boat would now sink like a full bathtub. When Reggie turned the electric pump on, the impeller was set in motion, but the pressure of the water flowing down redirected the innocent pump's energies, which now added mechanical pressure to the gravitational pressure bringing seawater into the boat. It was instantly clear what had caused *The Panic* to sink the year before. But on that occasion it had taken two and a half days for the clot in the pipe to disintegrate. It was simplicity itself to guard against a recurrence of the problem. We merely ripped out a tiny section from the pipe that moved down to the sea cock, so that if a reverse flow were started it would abort at that air hole.

End of problem. But there is always the scar left, causing

you to wonder: How many other causes are there, potentially, for boats suddenly to drown?

Three months after every Bermuda Race and every Annapolis-Newport Race, which are run in alternate years, comes the last of the season's major offshore races, the annual Vineyard Race, in which I made my debut in 1955. The next year, I was the skipper. We had rounded the lightship and were headed for the finish line at Stamford, 130 miles almost due west. Mike was at the tiller when I went below to sleep. The spinnaker was flying, under a stiff northeasterly, the fog was pearly thick, and we posted a member of the crew forward to listen hard, away from the distractions of cockpit talk and grinding winches, while every few minutes we sounded our own foghorn, and occasionally looked up at the radar reflector, designed to attract maximum attention on the radar screens of the big boats. I slept fitfully until I was summoned to relieve Mike, near midnight. Mike, always the competitor, was very excited. *"See over there?"* he said, pointing ahead. I could make out a few lights through the fog—a stern light, a masthead light, and perhaps a flashlight. "We're overhauling that poor bastard!" Mike exulted, handing me the tiller. He stepped up from the cockpit to experience from the deck the special pleasure of sliding by a competitor. Mike was right. We were getting closer and closer. I checked the compass—dead on the course I had stipulated. I eased the bow the slightest bit up, to make certain we would be comfortably to windward of the boat. Then came the screech, the ricocheting crunch of steel bouncing over rocks, and, in a moment, motionlessness. There is nothing to match the motionlessness of running solidly aground. It is as if concrete had suddenly hardened around you. Now that we were no longer moving downwind at eight knots, the wind on our backs was eight knots stronger. A hundred yards away was the boat we were pursuing, now plainly visible: two forlorn street lights, one mile north of Point Judith, Rhode Island. We were two miles off course.

I looked down at the compass in dismay. Even now, it pointed us in the direction I had charted. But there was urgent work to be done. Already, Reggie had the tide tables out. He told us that we were one hour and a half past low tide, and that the water would be high just before five in the morning. We called Peter Starr, who was fourteen years old and was asleep in the forecastle, but there was no rousing him. We pulled up a hundred yards of chain past his ear, and two hundred yards of line, and he heard nothing. The boat's steel hull ground away on the rocks, and he heard nothing. We eased our heaviest anchor into the dinghy, and rowed out a hundred yards astern. After attaching our nylon mooring line to the anchor, we dropped it into the water, rowed back, and attached the end of the line to a bridle that we rigged from one to the other of our heavy genoa winches, which were situated across from each other above the cockpit. Now we had a harness of sorts, allowing us to apply simultaneous pressure on both winches. Thus prepared, we began working the boat aft, using also the reverse power of the engine at full r.p.m. We succeeded in moving about five yards, but then we came on something like an underwater stone wall, over which, under the careening force of eight knots, *The Panic* had leaped. She was not about to leap back over, even at the urging of a couple of No. 4 winches. We finally stopped, and I cut the motor.

It was the moment to call the Coast Guard. To my astonishment, the Coast Guard Station at Point Judith, which was almost within hailing distance, acknowledged our distress call immediately. After a considerable conference at the other end, we were informed that we lay in waters so pockmarked with rocky shoals that no Coast Guard vessel could approach us to bring help without endangering itself. The officer recommended that we wait until the next day and get a barge from Newport to float us out. We were not in any personal danger, the Coast Guard reminded us—all we had to do to start life afresh would be to abandon ship and walk to the beach. And, of course, wake up Peter.

There was nothing to do except to make a massive effort at exactly high tide. To lighten the boat, we emptied our water tanks. (We had 120 gallons, which at about eight pounds per gallon is a lot of weight.) Then I noticed that the spotlight was weakening, and decided to put a fresh battery in it, to be ready for the big effort at four-thirty, but I couldn't find one in with the flashlight batteries. Mike poked around. "Here it is," he said, opening the binnacle box. I removed the battery. "Do that again," Reggie said, "and look at the compass." The battery removed, the compass changed its heading eleven degrees.

We made it, but it was close. If the wind had been from the southeast, we would not have had the protection of the peninsula opposite, and the waves during the night would have battered the boat to pieces. A wooden boat would probably not have survived. As it was, the damage to the keel and rudder was extensive.

I thought we could conceal this episode from our families without any problem at all, and it was agreed all the way around. There was theoretically no need to conceal it from Peter, who was entirely unaware of it, waking relaxed at about seven. I would simply say that we had withdrawn from the race because our spinnaker had blown out and there was no substitute. In the early afternoon, we stumbled into a marina in New London and docked. I went to the telephone and reached Pat, who was visiting her parents in Vancouver, three thousand miles away. Her first words were peremptory: "What time did you get off the rocks?" At least she said it before listening to a vivid narrative about the decomposition of the spinnaker.

I could not tease out of her the source of her intelligence until, home from her visit, she finally broke down, with great relish. She had been at a cocktail party while her father, at home, listened to the evening news on the radio. It must have been a very slow night, because the last item was to the effect that the Coast Guard in Boston had reported that the cutter *Panic*, owned by the writer William F. Buckley, Jr., was on the rocks off Point Judith, Rhode Island. My father-in-law was a heavy man, of decisive mien and habit. He dispatched the chauffeur for his daughter, authorizing him only to instruct her that she was to return instantly to the house. There, with much solemnity, he gave her the news, and soon the Royal Canadian Navy in Ottawa was on the telephone to the Coast Guard in Boston, which relayed back a conversation with the Coast Guard in Point Judith to the effect that nothing more had been heard from *The Panic* but there was no reason to fear for the safety of the crew. Mike's father had heard the same broadcast, and welcomed his son home with a new drink, "Point Judith Scotch" (on the rocks).

A misadventure. It taught me not only to inspect the compass area from time to time for magnetic distractions but never to rely on a compass alone, if there was an alternative to doing so, in a fog anywhere near land. The radio direction finder, trained on Point Judith, would have alerted us to a deteriorating situation. There were, of course, months and years ahead of us to improvise on Mike's calling enthusiastic attention to boats we were about to overtake.

The most illuminating experience I have had at sea was in October of 1958. Pat's brother Firpo and I (we were co-owners) resolved to cruise *The Panic* to Bermuda, leave it there during the winter, and charter it by the day in the spring to tourists who desired a cruise in Bermudian waters. We yanked Peter out of school and assembled a crew—fine fellows all, but undistinguished as seamen, through no fault of theirs. I picked the fifteenth of October to set out, because, on the one hand, we wanted weather as warm as possible, and, on the other hand, we wanted to be on the safe side of the hurricane period. The Defense Mapping Agency Hydrographic Center puts out a chart for every month of every year on which are tracked the major storms and the paths they traveled the same month during the preceding ten (or more) years. Our chart showed only one storm of hurricane strength in the general area after the fifteenth of October, and it had done its mischief comfortably to the east of Bermuda.

After three or four of the most beautiful days of sailing I can remember—crisp, cool days, with the wind steady from the southeast, the Kenyon (speedometer) never reading below eight knots, the moon at night framed by clouds, providing us with a kind of private, silvery superhighway, New York—Bermuda, Non-Stop, Reserved for *The Panic*—we hit a most awful storm. It came on us suddenly. It had been building doggedly but moving slowly, and now it began to run. We had an anemometer on board, and at midnight it clocked winds of seventy knots; anything over sixty-five is hurricane speed. Late in the afternoon, when it was blowing about fifty knots, I decided to heave to. I had never done it before, but this clearly was the time to see what the maneuver would do for us, so I gave Firpo the tiller and, with Peter, went forward, took down the No. 3 jib, and replaced it with the storm jib, which we led back through a snatch block to the windward genoa winch. We had already prepared the storm trysail on the track to the side of the mast, like a spare train, ready, when we pulled the switch, to run up the mainmast. Now we pulled down the reefed mainsail and ran up the storm trysail. The storm trysail is what they call "loose footed," which is to say that the foot (i.e., the bottom side of the triangle), like the forward sails, is not fastened to any boom, and air can spill out between the sail and the main boom, to which only its clew (i.e., the corner farthest aft) is fastened. We pulled the mainsheet as tight as possible, flattening the sail. Then I took the tiller and shoved it over as far as I could to leeward. The boat edged up into the wind, without the strength to come about but with enough to cause the jib, even though it was led aback, to luff: there was too much pressure aft. I could move the rudder back a little from its extreme hard-left position or I could slightly ease the mainsheet. I tried the tiller, and now the effect was eerie. The boat came to virtually a dead stop, both sails hard. I looked about me in triumph. We could have played a game of checkers in the cockpit, except that the checkers would have blown away. I took a piece of line and made a becket, securing the tiller in place—about as complicated as tying a shoelace.

Here is what happens when you heave to. To begin with, you hoist enough canvas (made out of the toughest material) to dominate the boat's movement but not enough to challenge the storm's machismo. Less sail than the two storm sails there isn't. If the wind is too strong to allow you to keep even them up, then you do something most appropriately named. You "run." Downwind. Always in a bad storm your objective is to reduce your speed in the water. *Pace* Pat, the bobbing-cork idea. Bear in mind that the wind does not distinguish between an obstacle made of canvas and one made of steel or wood, so even if you run, without so much as a handkerchief hoisted, you are still—as far as the wind is concerned—an obstacle, which is the square measurement of everything that lies above the water and is exposed to the wind. Enough of an obstacle, in very strong wind, to generate dangerous forward speeds.

High speeds are dangerous because there is no practical means of synchronizing your movements and those of the waves, which are always irregular and sometimes very erratic; if you are running at, say, eight knots, you will soon find the bow of the boat submarining into the bosom of a huge wave, which causes great havoc. In such situations, some boats can even pitchpole—that is, do a vertical somersault, the mainmast, for a moment or two, pointing down like a surrealistic fin centerboard, and the keel pointing up, like the dorsal fin of a whale. People have survived pitchpoling, but no mast has done so. One must assume that there are people who have *not* survived pitchpoling—survival, by the way, is likelier in a centerboard boat than in a keelboat. (*The Panic* is a keelboat.) Short of pitchpoling, there is the dangerous yaw, the bow digging into the water, the stern bouncing off, leaving your beam for the wind and waves to work on.

How, then, if you are running, do you keep down the speed of the boat? By trailing lines (the easiest way); each line is an anchor of sorts, and you can keep tying them together so as to form a huge bight. By trailing a sea anchor, which is like a large canvas parachute designed to brake the boat's motion by dragging underwater (and is sheer hell to retrieve). By using reverse engine power. Moreover, you can let the boat travel backward, if your boat is the kind that does that more comfortably—that is, trail your lines forward and haul up into the wind. But beware the rudder. Sudden backward movements with the rudder off center can wrench and disable it. It is better, of course, for the great breakers to attack you from the bow of the boat than from the stern, because they will be partly dissipated by the cabin trunk before reaching you. You can, when things have come to such a pass, put a can of oil in a bag filled with rags, punch a couple of holes in the can with an ice pick, and trail it from a point on the boat as far forward as possible—in the case of a boat like *Cyrano*, off the twelve-foot-long bowsprit. The instant slick of the oil is said to prevent most waves from breaking under its umbrella, at the center of which is you. I have never had to run, or use oil.

When maneuvering to heave to, you are fine-tuning right-left oscillations in the heading of a boat to the point of rendering them nugatory. The wind catches the little trysail aft, and, because the tiller is held over to leeward, or away from the wind, the boat's bow swings up into the wind. But no sooner has it done that than it exposes the forward sail, the jib, to the wind. Because the jib has been led aback—that is, fastened not to leeward, where it belongs, but to windward—you reach out for the wind, catching it before you are headed directly into it. The wind's force is now trapped by the jib, propelling the bow back to leeward. But the moment it has moved a mere matter of inches, the aftersail has again caught the wind, reversing the swing. A well-balanced boat, perfectly tuned, will heave to in such a way as to make the oscillations imperceptible. The wind is quite simply stymied, and you have become like the cork. There *is* forward motion (otherwise your rudder would be inoperative); but we are talking about two knots or so.

It was eerie primarily because of the contrast. The noise of the wind tearing through the shrouds and the lifelines was a continual howl. The waves rose and fell a dozen feet above our heads, and we rose and fell, but the waves did not break over us. The canvas dodger over the companionway protected totally the faces of the two men who nestled at that end of the cockpit, and it occurred to me that there was no reason for three men to stay on watch. There was nothing to do except sit there and wait it out, so we ate something and went through the night. I rested with some apprehension, always alert to the sibilant wind and roaring seas, and wondered what could possibly go wrong, and what I would do in the chaos if something did.

Nothing did go wrong. But the next morning, at about eleven, I made a mistake. The wind had abated slightly. It was back to fifty knots, and I was growing restless. We were pointed southwest, and Bermuda lay southeast. I thought that we should try to resume course and get the boat moving again by sailing with the wind abeam under storm jib alone, making at least a little progress toward our destination. So I loosed the becket and took the tiller in hand, and ordered the storm trysail brought down. The windward jib sheet was eased inch by inch and the strain taken on the leeward sheet. It was in tight when I said, "Here we go," and brought the tiller up, to take the bow downwind. We suffered an instant knockdown. (A knockdown is when the boat suddenly goes from vertical to horizontal, or nearly horizontal.) Generally, they hit you when your boat is practically at a standstill. If you are moving along, a sudden gust of wind will cause you to heel over, but the forward movement of your boat absorbs the suddenness of the blast, distributing it among keel, sails, and rudder.

I did not believe that *The Panic* could be made to suffer a knockdown when it was flying only a storm jib. But it did—one so severe that we were on our side, and a huge wave from abeam bulldozed into us, wrenching the entire binnacle from its mount on the cockpit floor and heaving it over toward the sea. Peter lurched out and grabbed it a second before it fell into the ocean, his torso stretched over the lifeline. Firpo grabbed him by the belt of his slicker, and kept him, and the binnacle, from going over. I yelled to loose the jib sheet, but it was almost immediately unnecessary. We were righting on our own steam, the sixty thousand pounds of pressure on the keel asserting themselves, roly-poly-dollwise. The cockpit was half underwater when we loosed the jib sheet well out, and within minutes we were making five knots toward Bermuda.

What I especially remember about the next six hours is the size of the waves. The wind kept abating, but the waves, as if sullen at the wind's default, grew proportionately hilly, then mountainous. They rose thirty feet high. But *The Panic* was untroubled, and in due course we had up our reefed mainsail, and then our No. 3 jib. At noon, the sun was briefly out, and I snatched a latitude and established our position as on a line that ran seventy miles north of Bermuda. The trouble was, I did not have any close idea of our longitude, and the sun wasn't out in the afternoon to permit me a running fix. Our radio direction finder began picking up a commercial station in Bermuda, and the crew was lighthearted in anticipation of arriving perhaps a little bit after midnight. The off watch declined its privileges, preferring to stay up now to the end. At about 6 P.M., a Bermuda patrol boat cruised up to us in the ebbing light. I shouted out, "Give me a course to Gibb's Hill!" A sailor shouted back, "A hundred and twenty degrees!" I was putting the information on the chart (Bermuda has to be approached with extreme care; it is like a starfish of coral reefs) when Firpo told me to come up and look at the extraordinary horizon. It certainly was extraordinary. We were completely surrounded by low, low clouds, not much higher than a steamer, black as pitch. The wind was suddenly gone. The skies grew grayer as the light faded, and the black noose began to tighten, and I felt a sudden touch of air in my face, cold, undecided. I gave orders to bring down *all* sails. Something was going to hit us immediately from somewhere. In five minutes, the storm was back; and, laboriously, once again we hove to. The wind was not as heavy as before, but it rained now from time to time—hard, passionate rain—and the direction of the boat kept changing as the storm danced around us. No one slept.

The next day was gray and lumpy, and now the serious question was *Where were we?* Miraculously, the sun appeared at about noon for exactly as long as it takes to get a single sight, and I put us at forty miles north of Bermuda—but, once again, longitude uncertain. Around 7 P.M., I noticed that the crew was demoralized. No one would eat. The dishes were piled up from the last three meals. There was no conversation, no unnecessary motion. I had encountered such a scene once before, in the infantry, when a company of soldiers completing their basic training was ordered to storm a hill to seize imaginary enemy installations. It was noon, the temperature a hundred and ten degrees. At midnight the night before, the trainees had been made to crawl on their bellies under barbed wire and tracer ammunition, only to be awakened at 2 A.M., for a forced march. They started up the hill, and then, as if rehearsed, they all stopped and sat down. Nothing mutinous. They simply could not move on. Discipline was out of the question. Our shrewd battalion commander was called in by walkie-talkie. He looked at the men only briefly, then dispatched four trucks from the base, loaded the men into them, and took them to a lake, where they swam.

A crew member slightly more alert than the others came back from the emergency storeroom with two large tins of hardtack. I reached into the tangle beside the icebox and got out a bottle of port. Hardtack looks like dog biscuits, but tastes slightly better, I think. Port goes well with hardtack. Soon everyone had a glass of port and was munching a biscuit. And beginning to talk. I said there was no point in trying to make progress under sail that night. We could not approach Bermuda without a more specific idea of where Bermuda was, because of the shoals. Under the circumstances, we would set only a No. 3 jib for stability, and more or less hold our own on an easterly course. Two men would stay up, but only for two-hour watches. The others would sleep.

The next morning, the recovery was complete. It was a brilliant blue day, and we spotted a cruise ship, obviously headed toward Bermuda. In a few hours, I had a running fix, showing that the storms had taken us forty miles west of Bermuda. We began to slog against the easterly, tacking, tacking. At 4 P.M., a Coast Guard plane buzzed down and recorded our sail number. At seven, we saw Gibb's Hill Light. (The radio direction finder was forty degrees off calibration.) Still there were five hours of tacking left to do before, a few minutes past midnight, we rounded the shoal area, easing, exhausted, into St. George's Harbour—seven days out of New York.

The radiotelephone had not worked. My wife's anxiety had mounted, and telephone calls between her and her mother in Vancouver had grown in frequency. That very morning, her mother had acted. She had telephoned Pat and announced calmly, imperiously, "Tell the Coast Guard to go out and find them. And to send *me* the bill." The airplane, that afternoon, had done its duty.

One night on *Suzy*, with Pat aboard, I proposed to cross the St. John River's Reversing Falls, at St. John, New Brunswick. I resist as somehow extraneous the temptation to describe the river, which is surely the most beautiful in the world. The subject of this story is the Reversing Falls. What you have on the one hand is the Bay of Fundy, with its famous gargantuan tide fall—forty feet is typical in the upper reaches of the bay. Enough power rushing in and out twice a day that if it could be harnessed it would generate electricity to light the world, or so they say. And what you have on the other hand is a 400-mile-long river, flowing through Maine and New Brunswick, with a tide fall of a few inches, which debouches into the bay. When the tide is out, the St. John River is falling into the bay, and the transitional mile between the river and the bay looks something like the runway to Niagara Falls. No boat could survive in those rapids for a moment; indeed, they are so spectacularly scary that tourists come from all over just to sit and stare. When the tide is in, the bay is pouring into the river, and the transitional mile between the river and the bay looks exactly the same as usual—except that the rapids are running in the opposite direction. Do not ask why, but it happens that three hours and fifty minutes after low tide, and two hours and twenty-five minutes after high tide, the Bay of Fundy and the St. John River fight each other to an ironic standstill, and then the water is as smooth as a skating rink. For ten minutes. That is when you power across.

Pat begged us to wait until the morning to make the crossing, but we cooed her into a resigned silence, marked time with a lengthy gourmet dinner, and took off at two minutes after eleven. We were two minutes early. I do not know whether our watches were off or whether through some inexplicable miscalculation we had taken the time from the wrong table. Reggie, as had been arranged, was below, leaning over the navigation table atop the icebox, to feed me quick-fire navigational instructions. But the current scooped us up, and while Reggie was intoning calmly, "Keep at two hundred and ninety-five degrees for exactly four minutes, toward the fixed white light," I was headed at twenty degrees toward an Esso gas station, which I would smash into in about two minutes. When the current is taking you faster than your engine drives you, the rudder has little effect. Reggie, crouched over his magnifying glass, and intent on his assignment, was saying things like "On your right, you should be seeing a flashing green approximately abeam." Meanwhile, a mass of yellow-gray foam surged toward us, like sea lava about to overtake us. It proved to be the discharge of pulp deposits from a mill that lets it all go just as the tide begins to turn. We were within a hundred yards of the gas station when, gradually, like the feeling that creeps back into your hands after a frostbite, the rudder began to respond. The equilibrium was finally upon us, and the amphibious operation against Esso Petroleum was aborted. The lessons are too obvious to expatiate upon. I have, in fact, wondered why the city of St. John does not indulge itself in a navigational light that turns green from red when the precious ten minutes begin. Perhaps it has to provide an occasional wreck to maintain tourist interest.

* * *

These are highlights from experiences of my own and of boats I have sailed. I have read a lot, and listened a lot, and doubt whether many seasoned ocean sailors would disagree with the following propositions:

(1) The chances of a well-rigged, well-sailed, well-constructed boat's going down in the open sea (you are safer there than near land) by reason of ocean conditions are so small in the safer latitudes in the safer months that you should not become obsessed with the question of physical survival. On the other hand, you must make emergency arrangements.

(2) The gravest danger is man overboard.

(3) There is one other very grave danger, and that is fire.

Astonishingly, the race from Newport to Bermuda, which has been conducted every second year for more than fifty years, has brought death by drowning to only a single human being. Several boats have been destroyed on the rocks around Bermuda, but the crews have always been saved. The exception was a member of the crew of a large yacht in which a fire got out of control. The distress signal was caught by another craft, which powered in to render assistance. One by one, the refugees jumped aboard. One man slipped and fell into the sea in between the boats and drowned immediately. On *Cyrano,* we maintained two large and two small fire extinguishers, handily placed. A diesel engine is indispensable to one's peace of mind, since gasoline is so combustible. We also have automatic circuit breakers, which isolate short circuits. Needless to say, the gas cylinders for the stove are stowed on deck.

On our last long ocean cruise, Reggie agreed to serve as chairman, of sorts, of a safety committee. We pooled our knowledge, and decided to gear up for two kinds of emergencies. There is a third kind, but you needn't bother about it: a whale eats you, or a steamer runs you down in a storm. We defined as Emergency A any development that would result in *Cyrano*'s sinking within two minutes—the whale barges into you, let us say, or you hit an iceberg. Hanging on the davits was our unsinkable Boston whaler. It was packed with emergency food and water for ten people for ten days. It could be lowered into the water in about fifteen seconds. Sheathed knives, to be used to cut any lines that might foul, were strapped alongside. Forward of the cockpit-cabin area we kept a twelve-man life raft, neatly tucked into a smaller barrel, and packed with food, medicine, flares, and a radio that had the strength to emit for seventeen hours emergency signals to overpassing aircraft. Also, it was equipped with a kind of Arabian tent, to protect us against the sun's rays. The raft would be inflated immediately on hitting the water, and one hundred feet of light line would keep it attached to *Cyrano*. (I know personally of two shipwrecks in which a life raft was thrown overboard with no thought given to what would happen to it. What happened in both cases was that the raft drifted out to sea and was of no use to anyone. A raft should always be tied to the boat.) The right-hand locker next to *Cyrano*'s steering wheel was filled exclusively with life preservers. To each were attached a waterproof flashlight, a whistle, and a package of dye marker (a substance that, once you puncture its plastic container with your teeth, dissolves and colors the sea red).

We would work in pre-stipulated pairs, one senior partner, one junior. In Emergency A, only the whaler, the life preservers (tied loosely to one another, and jointly to the boat), and the twelve-man raft would be unloaded. Each crew member was then to jump overboard, swim to the life preservers and don one, and swim either to the whaler or to the life raft.

In Emergency B, we would know that the boat was going down but that we had five or more minutes. The life preservers would be donned first in this case. The captain would work until the last minute giving our position and a distress signal on the radio's emergency band. Two additional, eight-man rafts, tucked into cavities just beyond the pillows of the berths in the cockpit section, would be hauled out, inflated, and trailed alongside. We would fill them with as many supplies as we had time to gather together. In a raging sea, schematic arrangements of this sort are sheer fantasy, and you simply do what you can. But in a moderate sea, losing ground against, say, fire or an uncontrollable leak, you have time even to remember the corkscrew.

"Peter," I said late on a white summer afternoon about fifteen years ago to Peter Starr, "let's face it. Someday we'll have to sail across the Atlantic." We were walking about the mossy rocks that surround York Harbor, Maine, getting some exercise after a long day's sail from Gloucester, before returning to *The Panic* in the Hansel-and-Gretel harbor for dinner. Peter agreed. It wasn't until June of last year that I finally undertook the cruise across the Atlantic, on *Cyrano*, and Peter wasn't with me; he had to withdraw at the last moment, because of a business emergency. On board, in addition to a professional crew of three, were my son, Christopher; Christopher's friend Daniel Merritt; Evan Galbraith; Reggie; and my sister-in-law Kathleen Finucane, who is called Bill. We sailed from Miami to Bermuda to the Azores to Marbella, Spain.

You *never* set out on time for a cruise, even with fifteen months' notice, but Danny, with his invincible optimism, told me that the boat would be ready to sail forty-eight hours early. At the appointed hour, however, the loran (long-range navigation) was suddenly not working; the radar was not working; and the new automatic pilot was not finally installed.

One wonders just how much expertise an ocean sailor can genuinely rely on—"expertise" being a word that is precisely used by a total of about twenty people. I pause to define it as meaning a body of operative knowledge. It isn't synonymous with *expertness*. One cannot be an expert except in a field in which there is something to be expert in—i.e., in which there is expertise. A radar technician can be expert only insofar as there is room for expertness. Beyond that, he is extemporizing. It is, of course, one thing if a particular product is defective, or is defectively installed, and another if that product presumes to standards that it is not scientifically justified in presuming to. The gentleman who (eventually) installed our automatic pilot effected an installation that came apart during that day's midnight watch; Danny put it back together, using bolts rather than screws, and *his* installation held. But not the pilot, which suddenly stopped working when the professional crew started the return voyage. Six thousand miles without the automatic pilot. There are grounds for believing the installer sloppy, or inexpert, in installation, but the machine's breaking down after one month suggests defective design; or else there is a mystery. Mysteries abound at sea. I had an autopilot on *Suzy* that worked with exquisite precision for three years. One day, it stopped working, and I assumed the necessity of getting spare parts, or even of replacing whole units. In the course of four years, six technicians, three boatyards, and finally, the personal mechanic for the president of the manufacturing company tried to make it work again. (At this point, every component unit had been replaced.) It never did; never has. Come see.

The gentleman who looked at the radar in Miami succeeded in decocting from it only the faintest signal, eclipsed in less than a day at sea. A gentleman in Bermuda tried to fix it and couldn't. A gentleman in Marbella fixed it for $600—twenty-five percent of the original cost of the instrumet—and it lasted about a week. Now, this is a Japanese machine about which it is boasted that there are six completely discrete and replaceable components, so that the problem is supposed to be as simple as identifying the delinquent part, throwing it away, and inserting the new part. That turns out to be hogwash. One doesn't know whether it is intentional or inadvertent hogwash. Perhaps there is a man in Japan who, with his little tool kit, could have set the radar right in minutes. The question seriously arises whether that man's skills are thaumaturgic rather than mechanical. Or is he an artist? Artistic jury rigs are feats of individual achievement but one cannot deduce from them an expertise that sustains them.

Before we left Miami, a gentleman exhorted me there and then to buy a brand-new loran, with the latest gee-whizz digital scanners, which seek out the two relevant transmitting loran stations and their slave stations and track them automatically and continuously, giving you second-by-second fixes, which you then plot on your chart. I was persuaded, and bought. The new loran set stopped working about thirty minutes after we left Miami; was not revived even after a half hour's telephone conversation at sea between Reggie and an expert who gave minute instructions; and did not work even after a replacement unit was installed in Bermuda.

So it went; so it almost always goes. There are problems that beset what one might call middle-sized boats. The big boats have on board their engineer and electrician, who can fix or replace almost anything that goes wrong. The very small boats don't have radar or loran or automatic pilots. *Cyrano* is in the class between, and perhaps it is for that reason that there is an insufficient expertise to provide reliable electrical or electronic systems for her, though it must be observed that the little commercial fishing boats use the same kind of radar and loran that is offered to the sailboats—with, however, the significant difference that such boats are always operating under power, and their instruments no doubt adjust to, or are designed to adjust to, regular operation, rather than the episodic operation of the sailor anxious to conserve his electrical power.

ATLANTIC CRUISE JOURNAL, MAY 30TH: Peter's withdrawl left us short one qualified watch captain, so my idea of four hours on, eight hours off will have to yield a little on the side of rigor. Every other cycle the watch captains will get only four hours off between watches. I have made up watch rosters for years, and sometimes they're like the inside of a Swiss clock. Racing, a crew member is on duty half the day. I use the Scandinavian system, 4-4-4-6-6. The six-hour periods fall between eight and two and between two and eight, during the daylight hours. That gives everybody one longish sleep a day. Breaking up the day into five parts means that you repeat a watch only every forty-eight hours. Nothing is drearier than to come on board and learn that you are on duty every single night from midnight to four. I have tried on this cruise to devise a system that will keep mixing us up, so that every watch captain (Danny, Reggie, myself, and the professional captain, Philip Campagna) will alternate with the watch assistants, Christopher, Van, Aunty Bill. Campagna and Van are out there now, having relieved Bill and me.

The wind is steady from the southeast, getting lighter. We ended by powering a little and clutching in the automatic pilot. Lighter, ocean-racing sailboats now use, almost as a matter of course, autopilots that are governed by the wind. They are designed to maintain a boat's heading at a constant angle off the wind. The disadvantage is that they necessarily redirect the boat when the wind changes, and this may happen when you are asleep. If you instruct a wind-vaned autopilot to keep you headed ninety degrees off the wind (let us say), you could conceivably wake in the morning to find yourself going back home, if the wind changed direction by 180 degrees. The wind-powered autopilots were developed primarily for the single-handed ocean racer, and a gentleman who won the transatlantic race several years ago records that his own model was so marvelously successful that his hands were on the tiller for a total of only twenty minutes from Southampton to Newport—twenty-eight days.

Other boats, such as *Cyrano*, use autopilots operated by power. These have the obvious disadvantage of consuming power, offset by the advantage of maintaining a steady compass course irrespective of a) whether there is any wind at all and b) where the wind is coming from. They operate through a compass of their own, which, once set, sends out electrical impulses that keep the wheel turning in the proper direction to maintain the stipulated course. They require a little mothering, but are splendid mechanical achievements.

JUNE 2ND: The sun was bright, but we were without wind and had to power the whole day long. At noon, we stopped and swam. Christopher, the .222-magnum cocked, sat on the cabin deck, prepared to fire at any shark attracted to our flailings. Aunty Bill decorously stayed below, so that we could do without swimming trunks. If the Atlantic is polluted, it is polluted elsewhere than at Latitude 31, Longitude 79, where the water is a cobalt blue and accepts as confidently as trained dolphins accept their dollops of fish the traditional beer can you throw over the side, to marvel at its endless visibility as it sinks into ocean water unmurked by the detritus of civilization. There is a great fuss this season about the danger of sharks, thanks substantially to the best-selling scare story on the subject. There are, of course, sharks everywhere in the oceans, even as there are rats everywhere on land. Ten years ago, I took lessons off the Virgin Islands in the use of scuba gear, and during one underwater session my instructor, using a graphite pencil on a slate, wrote "Hammerhead shark" and pointed to an object floating about thirty feet away, apparently as contented as a cow, and more or less looking at us, but without any trace of greed that an amateur could detect. I followed my instructor along as he went on scribbling on his underwater palimpsest, describing the underwater population, which for the most part was harmless, but not entirely. There were several barracuda and one moray eel. On surfacing, he told me that the experience was altogether normal, though spotting a moray eel was "a bit lucky," and that the key to a serene relationship with sharks was simply this: Bear it in mind that they are so dumb you can neither anticipate nor outwit them. Accordingly, you play the statistics, which are vastly reassuring. Avoid swimming in tandem with outflowing garbage—which one would tend to avoid doing for reasons entirely independent of the fear of sharks. Don't swim if any part of your body is bleeding. If you swim at night, enter the water gradually rather than splashily. And look forward to a ripe old age, limbs intact. I respond joyfully to almost any permissive franchise, and have never since given a thought to the danger of sharks—a serenity I have not communicated to Christopher, who in guarding the ramparts visualizes the enemy and loses his appetite for disporting in enemy territory. The swim was very refreshing, and the lunch tasted better, and we were less depressed by the absence of wind.

JUNE 5TH: More properly, June 6th. Because we tied up at 2:50 A.M. at St. George's Harbour. Early this morning, the wind almost directly behind us, the gollywobbler up, we conducted a pool: At what time would we spot the light from Gibb's Hill? It is a powerful beacon, with a twenty-six-mile radius. Before the construction of the lighthouse, during the high days of Bermuda's role as a way station to Virginia and points south, hundreds of ships foundered on the treacherous rocks here, it is said. Even now, Reggie's schoolmate Teddy Tucker devotes himself full time to locating wrecks and salvaging 300-year-old cargo. He has found gold and silver and jewels, including a famous emerald crucifix, but mostly such stuff as lead and copper.

I picked 8:15 P.M. for the landfall, and bets were taken ranging from 6:30 P.M. to midnight. At noon, after the sun sight, I decreed that our watches should move forward by one hour. When the light at Gibb's Hill was spotted, at 8:10 P.M., just off the port bow, where it should have been, we were catapulted into a great legal controversy. Danny et absolutely al. v. WFB. Danny had "bought" 7:15 P.M., and insisted that since the bets were made this morning, before our watches were moved forward, he had clearly won the pool. I took the position that we were betting that morning on what would be the time on our wristwatches at the moment of the landfall.

Van, as a graduate of the Harvard Law School, was consulted by Danny, and I suspect that this appeal to his vanity suborned him to find, after appropriate deliberation, for the plaintiffs. The matter was economically moot at this point, since Christopher, Aunty Bill, Reggie, and Van had already paid over their dollar bills to Danny. I reluctantly gave my dollar to Danny, sniffing something about the dangers of ochlocracy. "What's that?" he asked. I told him it was the only kind of government that would find for *him* in a dispute with *me*. Reggie then proposed a loser's toast, to my navigation—a toast I acknowledged with a graceful speech minimizing the complexity of my achievement. We were all in high spirits.

There is an underappreciated phenomenon at sea in a small boat. This is the exasperating length of time it takes after spotting a major beacon to pull in to the wharf. The tendency on seeing the light is to think the trip over. It took us almost seven hours, even at eight knots, to get in (against a tide of about one and a half knots). These long hours are anticlimactic, and it is sensible to dampen the spirit of celebration. On making a landfall, the crew usually (except in a race) breaks out the bottle. If there is still six hours' sailing to do, that can make for a very wet landfall. Van, experienced in these matters, retired to his cabin to read a book. The boys eventually peeled off and went to sleep. Having given everyone advice, I failed to heed it myself—I cannot be wrenched from the wheel between a landfall and arrival. Coming into St. George's is a spooky experience: one flows in through a deep but very narrow cut that becomes visible only as you become convinced that you are headed right into a hill. The placid lights of seventeenth-century St. George's were suddenly before us, and for the first time in six days the ocean swells were suspended, and we crossed the harbor to the slip as if skating over ice.

JUNE 14TH: We've been gone fifteen days from Miami, and we have 1,100 miles to go before reaching Horta, the westernmost port in the Azores. It isn't hot, just warm. When we have a long stretch under straight power, I wonder about motors. I received from Pat osmotically a most preposterous superstition, which I have never quite been able to shake; namely, that motors should "rest." I have talked the matter over with

Reggie, who knows everything, and he once reminded me that the Perkins 150 we have on board is identical to the motor widely used by the little shrimp boats that go out for two or three weeks at a time without any sail whatever, except, perhaps, a little steadying sail to put up when the winds are very bad. Theoretically, you can use a motor forever if only you will keep it perfectly lubricated. That means (in our case) stopping and checking the oil every twenty-four hours, and changing it every hundred hours. The filters need to be changed more often. They collect the glop that would otherwise assault the cylinders. You are supposed to get almost perpetual use from a good, sturdy diesel, but you don't, of course—although, I am assured, if you don't get 7,000 hours out of the Perkins, you are neglecting your motor. That's 5,600 miles.

Early in the afternoon, a cargo vessel passed a mile or so behind us, heading northeast. Captain Campagna "spoke" her. To "speak" a ship means to establish communication with it at sea. The captain routinely asked her where she was headed (Amsterdam) and what her position was (she gave it). This intelligence was relayed to me, and I advised the plebes that the ship was in fact five or six miles south of the position she took herself to be at. This aroused great gales of parricidal laughter, in which Danny joined and, finally, Van, leaving me only Bill, who thought it an inescapable deduction that if someone was mistaken in calculating our joint position, it was the ship's navigator, and not her brother-in-law. I volunteered to rub the nose of any skeptic in the evidence of my sun sight and the dead reckoning of the mere hour and a half that had elapsed, but, I told them, since this would require that they exert themselves intellectually, I knew I was safe in making the challenge. Christopher and Danny *love* that sort of thing, and I happen to know that they are, with whoops of surreptitious laughter, planning revenge.

JUNE 15TH: We had our first big storm today, and hove to. I had never hove *Cyrano* to before. Captain Campagna favored running, but I elected not to, and as we struggled in the screech and wet to lead the two staysails aback, as tight as drums, I remembered prayerfully the representations of the sailmakers that these sails would stand up against the greatest stress. We would soon find out, because the wind was fifty knots, gusting well over that, and apparently building, like the seas. The spray came in off the starboard bow, and then one monstrous wave—though not of the size of one that hit us later, after we had resumed sailing—which caught me while I was forward with the sails. It is unsettling to meditate that one wave of that kind weighs many more tons than the thirty the boat weighs. After the storm trysail was up, I took the wheel from Danny to make the adjustments. *Cyrano,* not being a racing boat, responds less quickly than *The Panic* did, so I felt the necessity for a little rudder control. Otherwise, the oscillations that enable a boat to heave to successfully would probably have been a little too widely separated, making for distinct lurches first to leeward, then to windward. I gave the engine 800 rpm, which in a smooth surface would mean about four knots of speed. Then I began turning the wheel to starboard. (It requires nine turns to move the rudder hard over to the opposite position.) At about six turns, with that much engine, the vessel walked into the magical equilibrium that is the ecstasy of the boat successfully hove to. It was fine to look about at the drenched, wind-blasted, anxious faces of Christopher and Danny, Captain Campagna and Van, and, in the cockpit, Aunty Bill as, suddenly, *Cyrano* acted as if we had crossed the Reversing Falls into a lake. The wind and the noise, the howling and the waves seemed to mount in resentment of our insulation.

Three hours later, the worst was over—the wind, clearly abating, down now to about forty knots. So we eased off on the windward sheets; picked up the slack to leeward, first of the mainstaysail and then of the forestaysail; and—remembering the knockdown of fifteen years ago—let them luff as we turned decisively downwind until the air engaged them, and only then made an upwind adjustment toward the heading on which we had been sailing before the storm hit.

We ate dinner buffet-style—silent, mostly, but strangely exhilarated, and close to each other after an annealing experience. I halved the watches—two hours of duty seemed enough under the circumstances—and at 2 A.M. rose to take my own, with Van. By then, the genoa could come into service again. Christopher and Danny had experimented with it at my suggestion, then checked with me for the O.K. to douse it. No telling where we were, so I decided to put the boat on autopilot and, with Van prepared to take notes and clutching the chronometer, try to get a Polaris sight—for the stars had grumpily come out, giving us a horizon of abnormal clarity. I mounted to the top of the cockpit cabin with two safety belts, to make a sort of gimbal for me: one belt to keep me from lurching sidewise into the sea, the other to keep me from lurching off the roof. I positioned myself and, for a fleeting moment, got both Polaris and the horizon tentatively in the sextant mirror, when the mainstaysail boom banged against my head, and a spout of ocean water from a rogue wave balling the jack on my leeward topside drowned the sextant in salt. My job then became to clean the sextant quickly—salt water will corrode the mirrors in a few hours. Never mind the navigation: I'll figure out tomorrow where in hell the storm took us. After cleaning the sextant, and with the boat still under autopilot and making nine knots under sail, I sat for the balance of the hour forward with Van. From the area in front of the cabin you saw on the stampeding seas a kinetic fleck of red from the port running light, green to starboard, and a touch of white ahead, reflecting the forward light. The sails were snugged in and powerful, working in overdrive, leaving the boat almost erect as it tore through the ocean. The stars began to assert themselves, while a bottle of wine, secured by the boom vang between us, emptied slowly as we paid mute tribute to *Cyrano*, her builder, her designer, and the architect of the whole grand situation.

On the twenty-ninth, I decided, on impulse, to change course by twenty-five degrees, so that, at an expense of a mere ten to fifteen miles extra voyaging, we could lay eyes on the tip of Portugal that day, rather than head directly for Gibraltar. The crew approved, and at 1702 on the twenty-ninth we heard Christopher's excited voice from the crow's nest. "Land ho!"—Cape St. Vincent. Odd, but any other formulation than the traditional one would have seemed, somehow, affected, irreverent.

That night, sailing at hull speed in the Bay of Cádiz, anticipating Gibraltar late the following afternoon and Marbella before midnight, both Bill and Reggie approached me, separately, to inform me in whispers that the boys had, *sponte sua*, organized a Captain's Dinner. Bill, musing, added that she could not remember ever before, in all her life, "thirty days without tension." It was our last night, seated about the dining table: music; dumpy little low-gravity candles scattered about the chart table, shining through red, blue, green, and yellow glass; the gas lamp in mid-table; and the gourmet meal, beginning with a can of caviar, and champagne bought in Miami by Danny and Christopher. The meal was extensive and imaginative. "I decided to brighten up the dessert," Danny wrote in his journal, "with two huge sparklers I bought in Miami for just this occasion." The sparklers were explosively effective, and startling, and probably there had not been such elation in these waters since the Battle of Trafalgar.